"DON'T BE SO GAY!"

Law and Society Series
W. Wesley Pue, General Editor

The Law and Society Series explores law as a socially embedded phenomenon. It is premised on the understanding that the conventional division of law from society creates false dichotomies in thinking, scholarship, educational practice, and social life. Books in the series treat law and society as mutually constitutive and highlight scholarship emerging from the interdisciplinary engagement of law with fields such as politics, social theory, history, political economy, and gender studies.

A list of titles in the series appears at the end of the book.

"DON'T BE SO GAY!"

QUEERS, BULLYING, AND MAKING SCHOOLS SAFE

Donn Short

UBCPress · Vancouver · Toronto

21 20 19 18 17 16 15 14 13   5 4 3 2

Printed in Canada on FSC-certified ancient-forest-free paper
(100% post-consumer recycled) that is processed chlorine- and acid-free.

Library and Archives Canada Cataloguing in Publication

Short, Donn
   "Don't be so gay!" : queers, bullying, and making schools safe / Donn Short.

(Law & society, 1496-4953)
Includes bibliographical references and index.
Also issued in electronic format.
ISBN 978-0-7748-2326-5 (bound); ISBN 978-0-7748-2327-2 (pbk.)

   1. Bullying in schools – Ontario – Toronto – Case studies. 2. Homophobia in high schools – Ontario – Toronto – Case studies. 3. Gay high school students – Ontario – Toronto – Social conditions – Case studies. 4. Bullying in schools – Ontario – Toronto – Prevention – Case studies. 5. Bullying in schools – Government policy – Ontario. I. Title. II. Series: Law and society series (Vancouver, B.C.)

LB3013.34.C3S56 2013   373.15'8   C2012-906704-0

Canadä

UBC Press gratefully acknowledges the financial support for our publishing program of the Government of Canada (through the Canada Book Fund), the Canada Council for the Arts, and the British Columbia Arts Council.

This book has been published with the help of a grant from the Canadian Federation for the Humanities and Social Sciences, through the Awards to Scholarly Publications Program, using funds provided by the Social Sciences and Humanities Research Council of Canada.

UBC Press
The University of British Columbia
2029 West Mall
Vancouver, BC V6T 1Z2
www.ubcpress.ca

For Daryl
who makes all things possible, still

I was such an object of ridicule that they sent my
brother to talk to me. I guess that was a last resort.
And my brother, who was disgusted with me – his
loyalty was clearly to the other students, not to his
brother, not to his family – he asked me to stop acting
the way I was acting, whatever that was. I really wasn't
aware that I was acting in any way, but he said to me,
"Why do you have to be like that?" which is a very
cutting question and a very profound question for
a kid to hear and very upsetting because you're not
really sure that you're gay – you're not really aware.
I wasn't aware that I was being any "way." I was just
being me and, apparently, being me was not
acceptable to anybody else and they were letting
me know. I knew what my brother meant ... Yeah.

— GREG

Contents

Acknowledgments

I am very grateful to Bruce Ryder, my chief booster, for his enthusiasm, support, guidance, and telling appraisals. He gave me ideas and sometimes even words. This book would have been very different without him, and so I thank him for pointing out doors that otherwise I would not have tried.

Likewise, I want to thank Didi Khayatt for her suggestions and advice and for our many warm conversations that made all the difference.

I wish to express my appreciation for the support, helpful comments, and suggestions of Don Cochrane, Jennifer Jenson, Sonia Lawrence, Bruce MacDougall, Sean Rehaag, Liora Salter, Kate Sutherland, and Gerald Walton.

A round of thanks for the friendship, support, and encouragement provided by Arif Bulkan, Roy Cain, Ruthy Lazar, Ron Levy, Dorathy Moore, and Sean Robertson.

Thanks to Alan V. Miller at the Canadian Lesbian and Gay Archives in Toronto.

My very profound thanks to a pantheon of heroes: Azmi Jubran, Gabriel Picard, Ellen Chambers-Picard, Peter Corren, Murray Corren, Jeffrey White, and Tim McCaskell.

It is my great pleasure to thank the students and teachers who gave so generously of their time and shared their stories with me. Although they remain anonymous, this book would not have been possible without their commitment, courage, and candour.

Many roads led to this study, two winding through London. For the journey from Skelley Road to Earl's Court, my thanks to Simon James Green, Paul L. Martin, Keith Lodwick, Grant Orviss, and Paul Oliver.

I would like to thank my research assistant, Michael Jones. A very special thanks to Stephen Myher for research and editorial assistance beyond the call of duty.

Randy Schmidt at UBC Press believed in this book from the beginning. My thanks for the drink in Montreal and the unflagging support throughout, without which this book would not exist. My thanks also to Ann Macklem and Robert Lewis for caring so much.

Finally, I wish to acknowledge with gratitude the financial support of York University, Osgoode Hall Law School, the Law Foundation of British Columbia, and the Legal Research Institute in Manitoba.

Participants

Schools, Students, and Teachers

This book contains interviews with some people whose real names are used with their permission. Their work promoting equity and social justice in schools is a matter of public record. They are Murray Corren, Peter Corren, Jaime, Azmi Jubran, Tim McCaskell, Ellen Chambers Picard, Gabriel Picard, and Jeffrey White. I am grateful to each of them. Except for in the discussion of matters of public record, the names of the schools are fictitious, and the names of the students, teachers, and other allies below are pseudonyms. There would be no book without any of these generous people. I prefer not to describe them in detail here but to let their words speak for them; nonetheless, I hope this list will help readers to remember who is at which school. Of course, I spoke with more students and teachers than those who appear in this book. If I have not included them, it is mainly because their perspectives, stories, and ideas duplicated those I did include. However, my thanks go to everyone who permitted me to spend time with them.

Sylvia Avenue Collegiate and Vocational School
Sharon Dominick – teacher
Melanie Bhatia – teacher
Ian – teacher who walked into Sharon's classroom and was ridiculed behind his back
Barry – student who looked up to Jack McFarland on *Will and Grace*
Louise – student

Douglas Allington – student who wrote a letter of thanks to Sharon
Wayne – student who mocked Ian, a teacher, behind Ian's back

Burton School
Delores – teacher
Lazy Daisy – student who made art for me and created her own "alias"
Benjamin – student
Alex – student
Brent – student

Elizabeth Coyt Alternative School
Carla – student, girlfriend of Emma
Emma – student, girlfriend of Carla
Cal – best friend of Emma and Carla

Trimble Collegiate Institute
Lorna Gillespie – teacher who encouraged students to write on the walls
Len – student
Katie – student
Anna – student
Mike – student

Crestwood Collegiate and Vocational School
Diana Goundrey – guidance counsellor
Joey – student who wrote poem
Sian – student
Jerry – student who had graduated from Crestwood two years before I
    interviewed him
Larson – student
Kyle – student
Dalton – student who was very involved in queer politics in Toronto while
    in high school

Earl Grey Secondary School
Terrence – student
Sam – student
Greg – student
Mr. Taylor – teacher

Triangle
Ryan – student
James – student
Noel – student
Trista – student
Silver – student
Brian – student

High School Students
Jaime – male-to-female transgendered high school student, white, Grade 12
Michael – Grade 12 student I met at an anti-bullying conference

"DON'T BE SO GAY!"

I sat in classes for days wondering what there was to "observe" ... What should I write down in my empty notebook?

— GEORGE SPINDLER, *DOING THE ETHNOGRAPHY OF SCHOOLING*

1

Introduction

Navigating Safe and Equitable Schools

It's just, when you're walking down the hall, you hear, "Oh, that's so gay, dude" or "He's such a fag." My friend Robert is the only one in the school who's really out, and so if he walks by, you might hear some people say, "Oh yeah, that guy's such a fag." No one ever says anything to his face. No one says anything about him being gay to his face. You know – what you can get away with and what you can't. I mean, not officially, not what the school says, but you can. It's more complex than that. Yeah. It's a greater complexity, you know? You gotta change everything.

— KATIE

Successful strategies to resolve the problem of gay, lesbian, bisexual, and transgendered students being bullied in Canadian high schools remain elusive, and the bullying of sexual-minority youth remains routine behaviour in schools. In schools where no anti-bullying policies exist, scholars, activists, students, and their allies, who are committed to safe and equal access to education for queer students, ask that inclusive safe-school policies be written to include sexual-minority youth. They argue that policies intended to make schools safer for queer students must specifically mention this particular "at risk" group. However, notwithstanding that more and more schools are governed by anti-bullying or safe-school policies that, in some cases, specifically mention sexual-minority youth as an "at risk" group, bullying is familiar behaviour in schools.

The Toronto District School Board (TDSB) in Ontario has some of the best-written and most comprehensive safe-school, anti-harassment, and equity policies in North America, if not the world. The TDSB's *Equity Foundation Statement* specifically mentions sexual orientation and is thorough and specific.[1] In addition to the *Equity Foundation Statement*, a series of five supporting documents articulate in greater detail the general principles of equity set out in the *Equity Foundation Statement*. These documents call for more than "inclusion" or recognition of diversity. As a whole, on paper, they provide the means of recognizing, accommodating, and allowing safe and welcoming space for difference, in which safety and equity for students, particularly queer youth, can been achieved. One of the fundamental aims of this book is to interrogate to what extent this goal has been met. Evidence presented in this book suggests that it has not. The gap between policy, practice, and experience occurs for many reasons – some knowable, some not. With respect to creating safe and equitable schools, this book indicates that the gap between policy and practice often occurs because the policies fail to address the nature and causes of oppression, focusing instead on responses to victimization.

Since the early 1980s, there has been significant academic attention to bullying. In contemporary literature, bullying is no longer viewed as unassailable – an inevitable if unpleasant part of "growing up" with which all students must learn to "cope." This traditional view has let parents, educators, and policy makers "off the hook." Bullying is now commonly regarded as a damaging experience in the lives of students – with ongoing repercussions. To the extent that bullying was addressed in schools, students were often told to "stand up" for themselves because "bullies" were really just "cowards." One of the first and most significant scholars to investigate bullying was Dan Olweus, who has studied bullying for over thirty years. The impact of his work on academic conversations surrounding bullying cannot be overstated. Olweus's research has been largely responsible for focusing a worldwide spotlight on what scholars refer to as "bullying." According to Olweus, "a student is being bullied or victimized when he or she is exposed, repeatedly and over time, to negative actions on the part of one, or more, other students."[2] The model of bullying that Olweus has developed is one that takes the consequences of bullying seriously and seeks to critique and to eliminate bullying as a social practice; however, in the postmodern academic world that has unfolded alongside the increasing examination of bullying by the academy, bullying as a cultural experience has not been sufficiently contextualized. Instead, the Olweus model of bullying has been too readily accepted. Gerald Walton has described this conception of bullying as "generic," arguing that the Olweus understanding of bullying must be continuously interrogated.[3] Of course, he is right. The notion of bullying requires additional adjectives – homophobic bullying, racial bullying, classist bullying, gender-based bullying, and so on. Instead, the literature constructed around bullying has, with few exceptions, failed to regard sufficiently the numerous cultural bases of bullying.[4] These ideological aspects of bullying, in turn, have not been adequately considered when the issue of making schools safe has been addressed. Lacking this context, conceptions of school safety, not surprisingly, often have been primarily responsive rather than preventative.

For the most part, Canadian researchers, such as Debra Pepler and Wendy Craig, have endorsed the Olweus approach, investigating bullying at the psychological level and often linking it to the aggression and power imbalance between specific individuals. As Walton has noted, this approach presents bullying as "empirically measurable as specific acts" and, most critically, suggests "that solutions to bullying are found at the level of the individual – which is to say, by addressing issues of bullying and victimization to specific implicated students – even while it is perhaps also framed as a school problem."[5] No matter how severe and quick responses may be, incident-based policies – designed to come into force "after the fact" or to develop "empathy" prior to bullying "incidents" – are inadequate. As Walton puts it,

The dominant notion about bullying is an individualist one, that it is a problem of some children who often behave aggressively ... Power is acknowledged but limited to immediate interactions between or among particular students ... Anti-violence education renders invisible the power and privilege imbued within the social dynamics on the playground. Conceptualizing such interactions only as individual behaviour that potentially has effects upon other members of the school community leads to the application of anti-violence education as a rational response ... supposedly making the school community and society as a whole a safer place ...

When school-based violence is conceptualized as the result of the individualized pathology of only some students – the noxious weeds – it follows that educational administrators would treat it as such.[6]

Seeking protection from "the noxious weeds" leads to response-based approaches concerned with containing bullying but does not sufficiently address the "before the fact" cultural climate of schools that this book suggests better explains why homophobic bullying occurs. These cultural influences significantly impact the experiences of all students in schools and have specific meanings for sexual-minority youth, whose oppression can be better accounted for, and addressed by, policies and approaches that seek to intervene in order to transform the climate of schools. Obviously, such a safe-school strategy must first renovate current conceptions of bullying, as well as what it means to be "safe," to accommodate such a broad strategy.

Students as Experts

Scholars have paid enormous attention to the issue of bullying in schools in the last thirty to thirty-five years worldwide, particularly in the United Kingdom, Australia, Japan, the United States, and Canada. Most of the research in Canada has been carried out by researchers working in disciplines other than law. For example, educational scholars have contributed to research on bullying – most notably André Grace and Gerald Walton – and so have scholars in psychology, particularly Debra Pepler and Wendy Craig. Safe-school policies are coming under increasing critical scrutiny, but there is as yet very little published literature by socio-legal scholars on the topic. Some legal scholars in Canada, such as Eric Roher, have turned their attention to bullying primarily in dealing with school-liability issues and tort law.[7] Socio-legal scholars in Canada have largely been silent.

This book is intended to take up the challenge of responding to this silence by drawing on the voices of sexual-minority students themselves. The starting and ending point of my research – and what carries the research throughout – is the governing philosophy that we must value the knowledge of on-the-ground actors. Peter McLaren asks us to consider why some knowledge is valued more than other knowledge.[8] Why, he asks, is "high-status" knowledge – which includes the important traditional legal analysis that is usually presented by legal scholars – given such importance whereas the practical knowledge of ordinary people is often devalued?[9] This was a guiding concern as I conducted my study, considered the results, and contemplated the possibility of presenting the voices of ordinary people in a less traditional form. I would have missed the knowledge reproduced in this book if I had chosen any other method of investigation. In the end, content dictated form (again) and the substance of the voices, the "stuff" of what was said, shaped this book's ultimate structure. Therefore, this book has been undertaken with the conviction that sexual-minority students are the best experts on their own experiences and lives and that they and their allies are best situated to address the fundamental research aims of this book.

There are few law schools in Canada where education law or school law is studied or researched. None of these schools, as far as I am aware, has produced any empirical work with students or teachers. Hopefully, this book will be something of an introduction to such an undertaking for legal scholars in Canada.

Method and Participants

In June 2000 the Ontario Ministry of Education passed the *Safe Schools Act*,[10] which came into effect in September 2001. The *Safe Schools Act* did not define "safety." The particular focus of my research has been to examine the potential of safe-school legislation and equity policies to combat the bullying and oppression of sexual-minority students in high schools of the Toronto District School Board. I wondered how bullying and safety were understood and defined by queer students and asked to what extent their conceptions might differ from their reports on how safety was pursued at their schools. To explore the issue in ways seldom realized by doctrinal or theoretical approaches, I asked sexual-minority students in Toronto-area schools how they defined and understood "safety," particularly in the absence of legal guidance in the statute. I then inquired into how sexual-minority students reported that safety was pursued at their schools. Finally, I asked students, as well as teachers who identified as allies of queer students, to consider how these definitions and insights might be translated into law and policy reforms that reconceptualize current approaches to safety and bullying.

My research is based on information that was gathered over a period of three months and on interviews with twenty-five queer students, as well as fourteen of their advocates (e.g., teachers and guidance counsellors), from ten high schools in the Greater Toronto Area (GTA). The students I interviewed ranged in age from fifteen to eighteen and came from all grades, nine through twelve. Parental consent was obtained to interview students who were under the age of eighteen. With respect to the age of the student participants, I discovered over time that I was inclined to prefer students in the higher grades, simply because they had more experience in high school and tended to be more reflective, more articulate, and perhaps more open about discussing their sexuality and their school. There was also an enormous practical consideration: students in the upper years were very likely to be of age.

How did I find queer students? Teachers, committed to making a difference at particular schools, opened their doors to me, allowed me to sit in on classes day after day, and most important, encouraged students they knew to be queer to speak with me. How did I find the teachers? I began by attending conferences and workshops in the Toronto area – held at high schools and other venues around Toronto – to meet teachers and administrators who were already committed to addressing the issue of homophobic bullying in schools. I met Jeffrey White from Oasis Alternative Secondary School's Triangle program at a conference held at the Ontario Institute for Studies in Education. These teachers granted me access to their students and described their teaching experiences with me during recorded interviews, which were later transcribed. As I spent time in their classrooms, these conversations also included unstructured day-to-day conversations that unfolded over the days or weeks spent in their schools, which I digitally recorded. Interviews with students and administrators were also digitally recorded and later transcribed.

At each site, I relied upon teachers and guidance counsellors to introduce me to queer or questioning students. I also asked queer students to identify others. This technique is known as "chain sampling" or "snowballing."[11] The purpose was to obtain a sample of participants with first-hand knowledge of the experiences I was investigating. Snowballing in the educational context was the most useful and practical way to gain access because it had two crucial effects. First, snowballing at one site allowed me to access students who identified as gay, lesbian, bisexual, transgender, or queer, whom I would otherwise have had no way of identifying. Second, snowballing allowed me to access different sites, as I was introduced into different schools, usually through teachers at these sites who were informed about and involved with issues around homophobic and transphobic bullying or "queer issues" in general.

My interview with Tim McCaskell illustrates how snowballing was absolutely crucial to my investigations. As a former equity officer for the TDSB, formerly the Toronto Board of Education, McCaskell knew many of the teachers throughout the TDSB who were concerned about queer issues and queer students. Moreover, he was able to identify teachers who might be interested in talking with me and granting me access to their schools and students. McCaskell provided me with the names of three individuals – Sharon Dominick, Diana Goundrey, and Lorna Gillespie. Gillespie was no longer working as a teacher when I called her. Both Dominick and Goundrey invited me into their schools. Sharon, in turn, introduced me to Gillespie and several other teachers. Sharon's generosity to me was critical to the success of this study.

Accordingly, I interviewed approximately three to five "out" students at each school. Limiting my interviews to students who identified as queer meant that I had a small pool from which to draw. I discovered that it was difficult for me to locate five students at any school who were "out" and willing to go on the record to discuss harassment with me. Not surprisingly, only at Triangle, a high school program for gay, lesbian, bisexual, transgendered, and queer or questioning (GLBTQ) students, was it possible to find so many queer students willing to talk.

Student Interviews

I was particularly interested in student awareness of safety and equity legislation and policies, their assessment of the implementation of these policies, and the details of their day-to-day experiences at school. Some students, understandably, had more to say than others; as a result, the length of the interviews varied from one to two hours. I quickly learned that many queer students resist self-identifying through a simple male-female binary, choosing instead to place themselves somewhere along a male-female continuum. In addition, I interviewed several students who did not identify as queer but who were, nonetheless, subject to homophobic harassment by their peers. Such was the case of Azmi Jubran, a heterosexual male high school student, who was repeatedly assaulted verbally and physically throughout his five years at a high school in North Vancouver and who successfully prevailed in a human rights action against his school board.

There was an obvious trade-off between having a reliably representative sample (more likely with larger numbers of participants) and logistical limitations on the depth and quantity of interviews I could undertake. Nonetheless, I was interested in the richness of detail made possible by a smaller sampling. This book is concerned, primarily, with the standpoint of queer students and their allies at their high schools in the GTA. Their perceptions of homophobic and transphobic bullying, the presence of a heteronormative school culture and its impact on queer students, and the experiences of queer high school students provide a useful and reliable basis for a descriptive and critical-prescriptive analysis. Their observations can be confirmed as truthful renditions of experience in several ways. First, some of the stories related to me are remarkably similar to my own personal experiences in high school. For instance, the story told to me by Ryan, a gay fifteen-year-old student at Triangle, about the "gendered" distribution of textbooks in his Grade 9 English class was startlingly similar to an experience I had when I was in Grade 10. Other researchers have produced data that confirm the experiences of these participants.[12] In May 2011 Egale Canada[13] published its *Final Report*[14] on its safe-school survey of queer students across Canada. The survey was funded by Egale Canada, the University of Winnipeg, and SVR/CIHR[15] and included questions about sexual orientation, the language used by students in schools, bullying, the curriculum, and teacher advocacy for queer students.

One question I considered was whether to focus solely on a specific gender. However, it struck me as problematic to insist on focusing on subjects who were on either the male or the female side of an essentialized gender binary – the very binary queer students often seek to challenge (or fit within, or both). If I had focused solely, for example, on male students, presumably this would have meant interviewing only students who identified as male and leaving out students of various stripes, including Jaime. Jaime was male before he returned to his high school after Christmas break having decided to present as a female for the final six months of Grade 12.

I also interviewed Gabriel (Gabe) Picard, a high school student in Thunder Bay, Ontario, as well as Azmi Jubran, who had previously attended Handsworth Secondary School in North Vancouver and was twenty-five years old when I interviewed him in 2005. In addition to Gabriel Picard, I interviewed his mother, Ellen Chambers-Picard, a teacher at Gabe's high school, who was instrumental in preparing his human rights complaint and in negotiating the settlement in his case. Both Gabriel Picard and Azmi Jubran filed human rights complaints against their high schools for failing in their duty to deliver a safe educational environment as required under provincial human rights legislation. Picard is gay, whereas Jubran is not. My interviews with Azmi Jubran and Gabriel Picard were substantially longer than most of the interviews conducted in this book.

In June 2007 I conducted an interview, also in Vancouver, with Peter Corren and Murray Corren, who filed a human rights complaint against their son's school board in British Columbia. In addition, in December 2004 I interviewed Tim McCaskell, who was the student program worker for the Toronto Board of Education from 1983 to 2001. Except for Ellen Chambers-Picard, Murray Corren, Peter Corren, Azmi Jubran, Tim McCaskell, Gabriel Picard, and Jeffrey White, the names in this book of the students and teachers I interviewed are pseudonyms.

In the three-month period during which I conducted the interviews, I spent full days in the schools observing students, teachers, and administrators in classrooms, hallways, and other social spaces in and around the schools. I also engaged in informal conversations with, and observations of, many other students, teachers, and administrators at these sites, as well as at several conferences I attended before I began the interviews and once the interviews commenced. These conferences were held primarily in Toronto-area high schools and were in most cases organized by students for students. The conferences included informational as well as dramatic and other artistic presentations. I should note, however, that in addition to the three-month period of continuous time in schools, I spent time speaking with students and teachers (including Azmi Jubran, Gabriel Picard, Peter Corren and Murray Corren, Jeffrey White, and Tim McCaskell) over a period of approximately two years.

Overview of Results

I constructed three dominant themes from the data I collected through these interviews and my time in the field. The first theme deals with safety, focusing on conceptions of safety and bullying as they are understood by the participants but also as they have been socially constructed and pursued by schools as objects worthy of policy intervention. The second theme is barriers to implementation. The participants discuss what they perceive to be the barriers to implementing safety and equity policies intended to address problems arising from the heteronormativity that animates the cultural climate of schools. The third theme is barriers to the effectiveness of state-issued policies and legislation when these policies and legislation are implemented. This theme explores the socio-legal concept of legal pluralism and maps, according to the interviewees, the influences of other normative orders at work in youth culture in addition to formal law and policies.

Chapters 2 and 3 address the first theme, that of safety. My fieldwork indicated that schools approached safety in different ways. According to interviewees, the ways that schools pursued safety fell across a range of four possible conceptions – control, security, equity, and social justice. At the extreme ends of the range of possible conceptions of safety were, first, schools that viewed the task of keeping the students safe to be synonymous with controlling the students. This particular approach extended to controlling not only student behaviour but also student identity, and it had particular ramifications for black male students. On the other extreme end of the model were those schools (two in this book) that conceived and implemented safety not as a matter of control or even as a matter of keeping the school secure but as a matter of creating a climate of "social justice." The distinction between "social justice" and "equity" related to the degree that a school was proactive in pursuing equity.

Chapters 4 and 5 address the implementation of safe-school policies, with an emphasis on equity. Participants identified a series of factors or circumstances affecting implementation that can be expressed as follows:

1 Participants indicated that legislation and policies were not implemented or were less likely to be implemented as a result of the following barriers:

   i   insufficient or no funding;
   ii the political nature of the vice-principal's office (vice-principals were identified as among the most conservative of citizens occupying space in schools and as being a point of significant obstruction to policy implementation);
   iii teacher homophobia;
   iv teachers' failure to regard the pursuit of safety, equity, and social justice as part of the work they were hired to do (here, teachers viewed their task as disseminating information, not changing culture);
   v   teachers' fear of lack of support from other teachers.

2 Participants indicated that current legislation and policies were more likely to be implemented in circumstances where the following factors were present:

   i   teachers worked to support GLBTQ students despite administration indifference or opposition;
   ii Gay-Straight Alliances (GSAs) were present in school;
   iii policies suggested or mandated GLBTQ curriculum content;
   iv life experiences of queer students were reflected in school social spaces (e.g., posters promoting school dances);
   v   students held conferences at schools on the bullying of GLBTQ students and life experiences of queer students;
   vi queer realities were reflected in school culture (e.g., drama, art, music);
   vii heterosexual students were implicated in curriculum regarding the social construction of gender and sexuality.

3　Although participants focused primarily on barriers to implementation of law and policies, they also found it difficult not to address issues of effectiveness in situations where they were implemented. When legislation and policies were conceptualized and put forward as an attempt to transform school culture, the effectiveness of their implementation was greater, and the participants were more likely to believe in the possibility that the larger school culture could change. Issues here included:

　i　participants indicated that when law and policies were conceived narrowly, the policies had a limited reach and were likely not to be implemented at all as a result of a lack of belief in their ability to bring about change;

　ii　participants favoured a robust understanding of bullying and safety to inspire faith that the policies and legislation were "worth the effort" to implement;

　iii　even with well-defined and published policies intended to punish victimizers, participants indicated that the larger school culture was not likely to change when policies were conceptualized as incident-bound – responsive to isolated incidents – no matter how wholeheartedly punitive-based measures were brought to bear on victimizers.

Chapters 6 and 7 address the third theme, with a focus on how the reach and effectiveness of current legislation and formal policies are complicated by the influence of other normative orders at work in the educational context. It is not a sufficient answer to the problem of homophobic bullying for school boards to point to policies "on the books" no matter how well written. Policies must be implemented; however, the results of my research indicate that even when policies are followed, there is an additional factor that must be taken into account: law and policies must originate at the ministerial level to have significant opportunity for purchase on the ground. Other normative orders such as religious beliefs, family beliefs, and informal codes of behaviour among youth (what one informant referred to as "street code" or what was generally discussed as the "anti-snitch," "anti-rat," or "street" culture) come into play and interact with official law. Which code of behaviour do students follow – the official code of the school or more informal orders that also attempt to regularize responses, even educative ones? The possible outright impermeability of youth culture, in general, was identified in this thematic cluster. However, all culture is subject to change, and my optimism suggests there are answers. These are discussed more fully in Chapter 8, which concludes this book.

In sum, a series of factors affect and shape the implementation, reach, and effectiveness of written policies, and these policies may thus be fundamentally limited, at least presently at the current sites of study, in their ability to resolve the hostile reception and treatment of queer students and the threats to their safety in high schools. My research suggests that the rule of law currently may have only a tenuous foothold in the high school environment. Law and policies responding to specific incidents of violence – rather than educative practices aimed at transforming the larger heteronormative climate of schools – are insufficient no matter how vigorously they are pursued. Legal responses that specifically target the culture of schools may be more promising.

Finally, then, I present nine conclusions drawn from the data that capture the concerns of sexual-minority students and their allies regarding the inadequacies of current approaches to safe schools and homophobic bullying. Together, the following suggestions point the way to the transformative culture that so many of the interviewees cited as the only way to achieve safe schools. These suggestions must be met if sexual-minority youth are to receive safe and equal access to education:

1 Current conceptions of safety are insufficiently robust and must be reconceptualized so that safety comes to be viewed as incorporating a pursuit of equity and social justice.
2 Safe-school and equity policies must include an educative element and not be only punitive and responsive.
3 Endless calls for law and policies that are inclusive merely sustain oppression and threats to the safety of queer students, precluding an understanding of the day-to-day lives of queer students in schools. Inclusive policies do little to address systemic power imbalances and oppression.
4 The educative element of educative and safety law and policies must be widespread and mandatory and come from the ministerial level; otherwise, teachers will not implement transformative content in curriculum, nor will transformative possibilities in general be easily achievable.
5 The educative element must start early in the school curriculum and in the social spaces of schools (i.e., kindergarten or Grade 1).
6 The goal of making equitable and safe schools for sexual-minority youth is long-term.

7 Teachers must have the philosophical and financial support of the school board, the administration, and fellow teachers.
8 Queer realities must be reflected in course content and in school culture.
9 Heterosexual students must be implicated in schooling processes and the regimes of silence, invisibility, and oppression of the official and unofficial curricula and general school life. Curriculum content must not be merely a presentation of information about queer students received by hetero-sexual and nonqueer students in their normative positions. Inclusive education alone is inadequate. The general school life must include and celebrate queer youth and friendships between heterosexual and queer students.

Threats to the safety of queer students in an educational context were characterized by the students as "expected," "inevitable," and "encouraged" by a heteronormative school culture that promotes a hegemony of gender and sexuality in which students monitor their own behaviours and presenta-tion and those of each other for signs of "difference" and "otherness." In this way, the norms of both gender and sexuality are under surveillance, and transgressions may be enforced with looks, words, or physical force. A good deal of critical investigation has explored the social mechanisms through which difference and otherness are socially constructed. On a purely theor-etical level, inquiries into "difference" and "otherness" have yielded valu-able results, but in the absence of any sustained empirical research into what sexual-minority students – and particularly so-called straight students – are up to in their daily lives, these explorations remain flat instead of animated and careful as opposed to radical or rooted in transformative possibility. Policies that merely advocate inclusiveness in response to vio-lent incidents are inadequate in two ways: first, they add to the oppression of queer youth because they do little to lessen threats to students' personal safety or queer identities; second, they excuse those who call for policies of inclusiveness from investigating what is unfolding on the ground in the lives of students who experience the results of difference and "otherness" in a real way in schools as subjects of their own unreported investigations. Additionally, responses to the bullying of queer students (if there are any official responses) that promote acceptance of queer kids, labelling the bullying of queer kids as a problem associated only with "queer" sexuality, mischaracterize what needs to be done. This book demonstrates that what needs to be done is to introduce education in the schools about sexuality and gender that implicates the so-called straight kid and is nothing less than transformative of the entire school culture. Neither "queer content" in the curriculum nor effective "legal" responses to incidents of queer bullying and violence will change the overall hostile environment queer students encounter or reduce queer violence until social justice for queers is pursued, heterosexual students are implicated in education about otherness and difference, and the notion of what it means to go to school in Canada is transformed. Nothing less should be pursued.

This book is offered as a means of entering into the debate surrounding bullying in Canadian schools, a conversation that has been limited by narrow conceptions of safety and bullying. By focusing on the TDSB, where policies grounded in equity are already "on the books," I attempt to suggest that something else is needed beyond policies – no matter how well written. Solutions must include an understanding of the relationship between our education system and its purpose of fostering a normative order within a broader cultural landscape. We must begin by acknowledging that multiple, intersecting normative orders are, in fact, at play among youth culture in schools. By locating the book within this knotty cultural framework, I hope to present a better understanding of the complicated social order that gives rise to bullying and oppression and to bring greater intelligibility to the intersection between formal law and policy and the heteronormative day-to-day life of youth culture in schools. Intervention and transformative strategies must be mindful of the complexity of this site.

Gabriel Picard told me that he initiated a human rights action against his school "to change a culture."[16] His principal told him that changing a culture was "impossible." The need to transform a culture emerged as a consistent theme in my interviews. Katie, a Grade 12 student, told me that "transforming the culture is what it's all about. It's the fucking map, the compass, and the moon, all in one. It's everything queers need to find our way out of oppression and the only thing that will do it."

The voices of the students – and their allies – are presented in this book as voices that articulate new knowledge. The students respond to questions, initiate discussions, and animate and inform the book in articulate and poetic ways. In an attempt to contribute to an increased awareness of the realities of sexual-minority youth in schools, all of the participants addressed the need for the radical, shared goal of transforming schools, even as they acknowledged the difficulty of transformation and the likelihood that the kind of change envisioned by so many of them could take years to achieve. They spoke in support of nothing less than changing the entire cultural experience of "going to school."

Knowing Our World

Much of the challenge of critical inspection of culture lies in the questions historicism poses about "how we know what we know" about our world and in questions about what, therefore, constitutes data and explanation in a world that embraces multiple ways of knowing. As Kath M. Melia puts it, "At its simplest, postmodernism holds that there are no grand theories, overall explanations or generalized ways of explaining experience and that social life can be better understood as a series of discourses where none is privileged."[17] How did my choice of method assist in the analysis of data, the assembly of explanation, and perhaps, the ambition of producing new knowledge? First, I hoped to measure qualitatively the extent of the implementation of the current provincial legislation and TDSB policies on school conduct and their effectiveness in making schools safer places for queer students. Second, I aspired to build a critical analysis of the current policies and circumstances of their implementation. Finally, I have attempted to generate prescriptions for policy based upon these findings. I chose to undertake this work by speaking primarily to queer students themselves. They were asked to indicate their awareness of laws and policies, if any, that were intended to make schools safer. The responses included the *Charter*,[18] the Ontario *Human Rights Code*,[19] the *Safe Schools Act*, and specific policies of the TDSB, including the *Safe Schools Foundation Statement*[20] and, most notably, the *Equity Foundation Statement*. Respondents indicated that these laws and policies were well written and comprehensive. This book, therefore, was undertaken in a context in which laws and policies "on the books" were accepted as thorough, the product of many years of work by people like Tim McCaskell and others doing equity work in Toronto high schools. My focus was to interview GLBTQ students, and teachers who identified themselves as advocates of GLBTQ students, in order to measure the impact of formal law and policies in combating the bullying, discrimination, and harassment of this group. I should point out that teachers and guidance counsellors were very helpful in addressing how schools implemented the requirements of the *Safe Schools Act*, as well as in speaking about the extent to which a particular school tried to implement TDSB equity policies.

I employed a series of semistructured interviews – combined with observations in the field documenting and critically inquiring into the reach and effectiveness of these safety documents – to address a more focused pair of questions: How was safety conceptualized at a particular school? How did sexual-minority students conceptualize their position in schools? This led to a series of specific inquiries: What is oppression? What is bullying? What is violence? How effective was the *Safe Schools Act* in making a particular school safe? How effective were TDSB safety and equity policies on the ground? What are the obstacles to effective implementation given that schools are unique cultural sites? What barriers could be identified to account for the fact that the effectiveness of even well-written policies is sometimes limited? When laws and policies were successful, why were they successful? What solutions could be proposed to overcome the barriers to successful implementation of policies?

This book is by subject matter and approach interdisciplinary, engaging with multiple, distinct approaches to the issue of bullying. In the end, what I hope it contributes to the ongoing conversations about bullying and school safety is a socio-legal corrective to any overly positivistic assumptions about the reach and effectiveness of formal law, both legislation and policies, as well as a reconsideration of what theorists and researchers of these issues mean by "safety" and "bullying."

2

Safe Schools

The Struggle for Control and the Quest for Social Justice

At the beginning of the school year, we'd always run through
the school rules or whatever they were, and they'd always
mention the *Safe Schools Act*. But I would think to myself:
I'm gay. Am I safe here?

— GABRIEL PICARD

Sharon Dominick teaches English and media studies at Sylvia Avenue Collegiate and Vocational School, a large high school in downtown Toronto. There are approximately 1,000 students at Sylvia Avenue, including a large number of black students – although their numbers are decreasing – and a rapidly growing number of special-education students. One student described Sylvia Avenue as a school for "rejects" and said that anyone with academic ability – and the means – transfers out. Many teachers and students told me that the philosophy of the school, in most matters, is dictated by the powerful pool of technical and "machine shop" teachers.

Sharon's classroom looks unlike the other classrooms at the school. The walls are covered in images torn from magazines of all stripes – large-breasted women, men in cars, domestic images of women, men drinking beer – as part of Sharon's ongoing efforts to bring issues of gender and sexual stereotyping into her curriculum in media studies. According to Sharon, many of the "powerful" teachers in the school, as well as the administration, were not happy with her approach.

Sharon becomes exasperated each time she overhears a student in the classroom, or in the hallway, say, "That's so gay." And the students use the phrase frequently – notwithstanding that "Miss Dominick" will, in Sharon's own words, "get you if [she hears] anybody say those words." Sharon and I are walking to the school cafeteria between classes. If we were anywhere but in a high school, this would be characterized as running – here, it is the normal pace. Students, and two or three other teachers, are in the hallway flowing steadily, noisily, in the same direction. Students shout to each other without much self-censoring of thought or the particular words used to express them. The tumult and stir exhaust me, whereas Sharon barely notices. Her wits and senses are as alert and quick to respond as radar. As a vegetarian, my mind has been distracted by worry over what food we will find, or not find, in this school's cafeteria. Sharon, however, has stopped to consider a student to her left. As soon as his eyes catch Sharon frowning in his direction, "the jig was up," as Sharon told me later. "I'm sorry Miss Dominick," the student said immediately. He knew what the offence was and what the penalty was likely to be, but if Sharon had not explained to me afterward what had happened, I would have missed it.

Instead of letting offenders off – we were, after all, "walking" to get food, and time was short – Sharon never lets an incursion go by without saying something when she hears anybody, including teachers, say, "That's so gay." During a break between classes, Sharon expressed her frustration at what sometimes feel like futile attempts "to stem the tide of homophobia and heterosexism" that seems so "unstemmable" at her school:

> It's constant. It never stops. Sometimes, I feel like I'm making
> some difference, and then other times, it seems hopeless here.
> It's so difficult to make an impression. But it's a big part of what
> I do in the classroom. The students know it's not acceptable to say
> these things, but then you get in the halls, and I hear what they
> say. Not just to each other, to inflict hurt, but just casually, as if
> they don't realize that what they're saying could hurt or threaten
> somebody's safety.

Lorna Gillespie expressed the same frustrations to me. Lorna, a close friend of Sharon's, and an English teacher at Trimble Collegiate Institute, is vigilant about the language she overhears but admits that taking the "right" stance is sometimes "draining." The schools at which Sharon and Lorna teach are physically located at opposite ends of the city, but the work they try to achieve with their students is not as dissimilar as the neighbourhoods in which the schools are situated:

> I'm like Sharon. I nail them every time they do the "it's so gay" thing. The students say, "Oh sorry, Miss." So they know, they *know* it's not "right," but I don't think other teachers typically nail them, certainly not in the hall. Either the teachers don't think it matters, or they're homophobic themselves, or they would say, "The students don't really mean that." That's what the *kids* say, too – the word has changed now, right? That it doesn't mean "gay" the way most people mean it.

Two weeks after meeting Sharon, I sit at the back of Lorna's classroom during lunch to discuss the differences between generations of students. Students frequently come to Lorna's classroom to eat their lunch. Like Sharon's classroom, the walls are decorated with artwork, magazine clippings, and photographs. Obligingly, and right on cue, an offending student at the front of the class cries out to one of her friends, but also loudly enough for Lorna to hear, "That's so gay!" Lorna does not miss a beat. "I heard that!" Lorna turns to me and shakes her head:

> It does get exhausting. There are times when I let it go. Some kid I don't know right behind me in the hall says it in conversation, I'm not gonna go into a big stink about it. I go into a big stink about it in the class, where I can actually talk to them about it. It's not new.

Sharon and Lorna both expressed to me their shared belief that homophobia, heteronormativity, and heterosexism are at the root of the bullying of sexual-minority students. Both acknowledged the pervasiveness of homophobic language used by students in their daily course of school events and recalled the use of homophobic language in their own high school experiences. Neither recalled any teacher ever intervening or responding to the use of homophobic words by students. Both remembered teachers who used the words themselves. Sharon was the first to suggest to me that the threat to the safety of queer students is broader than mere physical violence:

It's not just the out-and-out homophobia of other students. It's
not just the threat of the punch. It's also the threat of the heteronormative culture all around these kids. It's stifling and threatening.
I try to explain to students who say "That's so gay" or, God, even
"fag" that they are threatening someone's safety. They don't see it
that way. The queer kids do. That's why there are so few of them
who are out. I don't know of any "out" students at this school.
It's not safe.

Theories of Bullying

The most widely cited definition of bullying by researchers and theorists in
all disciplines is the definition put forward by Dan Olweus, a professor of
psychology at the University of Bergen, Norway. Olweus is universally acknowledged to be the first important researcher to investigate bullying in
schools. Like Michel Foucault's work, whose initial scholarship was situated
in history and philosophy and is now influential across many disciplines,
Olweus's work was initially positioned within psychological literature but
is now cited and engaged with by scholars working in many disciplines.
Olweus's substantial contribution to bullying scholarship is based upon
lifelong research he began in 1973 in Sweden and continued in Norway.[1]
Olweus's initial studies concentrated on victims, whom he called "whipping
boys."[2] Subsequently, he investigated the role of bullies and then undertook
a consideration of bystanders and spectators. Olweus's definition of bullying
is much-quoted: "I define bullying or victimization in the following general
way. A student is being bullied or victimized when he is exposed repeatedly
and over time to negative actions on the part of one or more other students."[3]
Olweus goes on to explain that "negative actions" occur

> when someone intentionally inflicts, or attempts to inflict, injury or dis-
> comfort on another ... carried out by words ... by threatening, taunting,
> teasing and calling names. It is a negative action when somebody hits,
> pushes, kicks, pinches or restrains another – by physical contact. It is also
> possible to carry out negative actions without use of words or physical con-
> tact, such as by making faces or dirty gestures, intentionally excluding
> someone from a group or refusing to comply with another person's wishes
> ... The definition above emphasizes negative actions that are carried out
> "repeatedly and over time" ... In the context of school bullying, the target
> has usually been a single student.[4]

Olweus intended "negative actions" to encompass a wide scope of possibilities, including the negative actions of a larger culture, whether the harm is intentional or not. But in most discussions of bullying, negative actions are treated as though limited to physical or verbal actions between specific individuals that occur during specific and limited, if repeated, episodes. It is this conception of bullying that has been adopted by many other researchers. For example, in their 2000 report *Making a Difference in Bullying,* Canadian researchers Wendy Craig and Debra Pepler define bullying by stressing the roles of the victimizer and the victim,[5] inadequately calling into question ideology and culture. Pepler and Craig define bullying as "a form of aggression in which there is an imbalance of power between the bully and the victim."[6] Olweus and other scholars further classify "negative actions"[7] in terms of four discrete types of victimization that appear throughout the literature on bullying: physical, verbal, attitudinal or relational, and cyber-bullying.[8] In 1994 Olweus suggested that to qualify as bullying, negative actions should be characterized by three principal elements: (1) an intention to harm the victim, (2) repetition, and (3) an imbalance in power between the victim and the perpetrator(s).[9]

As recently as June 2007, "negative actions" were conceptualized by Olweus and his co-researchers as follows:

> We say a student is being bullied when another student, or several other students:
>
> 1   say mean and hurtful things or make fun of him or her or call him or her mean and hurtful names
> 2   completely ignore or exclude him or her from their group of friends or leave him or her out of things on purpose
> 3   hit, kick, push, shove around or threaten him or her
> 4   tell lies or spread false rumours about him or her or send mean notes and try to make other students dislike him or her
> 5   and other hurtful things like that.[10]

Although it is arguable that the fifth characteristic of bullying on this list may leave open the possibility of including cultural or ideological harm, the phrase more likely lacks the necessary focus and purpose to specifically do so. Where, then, does this conceptualization of bullying lead? Craig, Peters, and Roman Konarski report that bullying is associated with "externalizing problems": "children who bully ... display antisocial behaviours such as physical aggression [and] ... hyperactivity."[11]

Olweus's work is pioneering and still important forty years later. It would be difficult to overstate the value of his ongoing contribution to resolving the problem of bullying in schools. Similarly, the contributions to research on bullying made by Pepler, Craig, and others reflect an almost two-decade-long commitment. Yet there is still space in this research for a broader approach to bullying, one that not only indicts the victimizer but also makes cultural and ideological factors the subject of study, an approach in which bullying is not viewed as limited to discrete episodes among specifically implicated individuals. For sexual-minority students, there is a further concern: not only is it crucial to examine bullying (and to do so in cultural contexts), but it is also important to examine the oppression of sexual-minority students in school more generally. It has been left to such scholars as Eric Rofes, Kevin Kumashiro, and Debbie Epstein to take a broader approach to the oppression of sexual-minority youth in schools, although none of these scholars has researched the Canadian context.[12]

The emphasis has been largely on bullying's psychological and cognitive determinants and on the involvement of specific and limited numbers of students – the larger culture has not been implicated. Bullying is conceptualized and studied as a cognitive and behavioural "moment"[13] rather than as an expected outcome of cultural and ideological factors. To the extent that the cultural context of schools has been considered, the contributors to most of the literature in which bullying is a focus have been content to deal mainly with the presence of teachers in school space as a factor in curbing or containing the bully. The research on bullying has been driven by contributors who emphasize a psychological approach.[14] A review of contributors to this literature reveals that until the mid-1990s the study of bullying was much less common in Canada than in the United Kingdom – where the literature is extensive – and, to a lesser extent, Australia. Most of the research on school bullying has been conducted in Scandinavian countries by Olweus, in the United Kingdom by Michael Boulton and Kerry Underwood,[15] and in Japan by Yoshio Murakami.[16] More recent research has been conducted by other scholars[17] and through studies funded by the United Nations Educational, Scientific, and Cultural Organization (UNESCO).[18] In Norway, Olweus reported in 1994 that approximately 15 percent of Norwegian school students were bullies or victims of bullies,[19] and Boulton and Underwood reported in the early 1990s that approximately 23 percent of British children and adolescents experienced bullying.[20] A 2000 study by UNESCO and the Ministry of Japan confirmed that in the early 1990s the United Kingdom had approximately two times as much bullying as Norway. The United Kingdom has implemented many anti-bullying programs, including a blue-wristband anti-bullying campaign that involved celebrities such as soccer player David Beckham and U2's lead singer, Bono.[21]

Similar results with respect to levels of bullying have been found in the United States. One study reported that up to 29.9 percent of students were involved in bullying, either as victims, victimizers, or both.[22] Olweus has commented on the threat to school safety that bullying poses: "Every individual should have the right to be spared oppression and repeated, intentional humiliation, in schools as in society at large. No student should ... be afraid of going to school for fear of being harassed, or degraded, and no parent should need to worry about such things happening to his or her child."[23] In the United States much of the literature on bullying has unfolded alongside the literature on school violence and is often viewed in the context of school shootings such as those at Columbine High School. Gerald Walton has argued that the influence of this approach has proven "problematic" in a Canadian context, even though gun violence in schools does occur in Canada and is clearly a serious concern. As Walton notes, American concerns about extreme violence have significantly influenced discussions about school safety, such that factors like equity in schools are not emphasized. According to Walton, this approach has given rise to a "moral panic" about physical violence, particularly gun violence, and this emphasis on extreme violence – having been established as the primary focus of the discourse in Canada – has proven difficult to scale back.[24]

Theories that limit bullying to specific incidents of personal conflicts between individuals have policy implications for the creation of safe schools. This conception of violence in schools ignores many other aspects of school life that have profound and negative effects on school climate, particularly for sexual-minority students, whose needs are not addressed when the efforts to keep schools safe emphasize exerting control and are focused on extreme physical violence or gun violence.[25] Research has established that bullying occurs more frequently in Canada than in the United Kingdom and Norway:

> In Canada, the rates of bullying and victimization are considerably higher than in many ... countries. In the recent World Health Organization (WHO) Health Behaviours in School-Aged Children ... survey, Canada ranked a disappointing 26th and 27th out of 35 countries on measures of bullying and

victimization, respectively ... Among 13-year-olds, 17.8 percent of the boys
and 15.1 percent of the girls reported being frequently victimized.[26]

Pepler and Craig have made frequent contributions to the study of bullying
in a Canadian context, often focusing on Toronto-area schools. Utilizing
social-psychological factors, such as the family backgrounds of victimizers,
they have looked at the pathology of bullying to determine why bullies vic-
timize.[27] While importing and sustaining the Olweus approach, they have
emphasized policy intervention and the behavioural factors of implicated
individuals in a bullying "moment."[28] Although Pepler and Craig acknowledge that the "negative actions" of bullies, victimizers, and bystanders
occur within "the wider system of the school," they view this wider context
primarily as the site where a bully's "actions" play out, a place where teachers and administrators are condemned for failing to get involved. Scholars
such as Walton, André Grace, Kristopher Wells, and George Smith emphasize ideology and culture, regarding the school as a place where bullying
is a predictable by-product of school culture and climate. One of Pepler's
observations that has particular resonance for socio-legal scholars is that
bullying does not unfold in isolation but rather in a "peer context."[29] Rona
Atlas and Pepler make a key remark in a 1998 study, noting that intervention programs must be "aimed at all students": "Interventions to reduce
bullying problems should not be limited to children who are at high risk for
involvement in bullying problems, but should comprise a preventative
agenda *aimed at all students*."[30] However, I have some concerns about the
content of *what* is being aimed at students, about the policies proposed.
Atlas and Pepler make a two-pronged recommendation:

> A component of the intervention must be aimed at peers in several ways.
> First, schools must strive to increase children's sensitivity to victimized
> children and cultivate an ethos of peer support ... Early intervention aimed
> at developing student attitudes against bullying and against viewing the
> victim negatively may be an effective approach to the prevention of bully-
> ing in schools. Through classroom activities such as role play, storytelling,
> and drama, students may develop an awareness of the perspective of the
> victim. When students begin to experience the role of victim, they may
> begin to empathize [with] and support the victims.[31]

To be of any value, this approach would have to be undertaken with the
recognition that it is simply not enough and that this kind of intervention is

aimed at students *in their existing normative positions.* There is a need, therefore, for an approach that addresses the power differential between students based upon gender, class, race, or sexual orientation. Programs that fail to do so reflect the shortcomings that have long plagued anti-bullying strategies that aim to prevent normative and powerful students from acting against "different," less powerful peers merely by enrolling bystanders in responsive roles. This sort of limited approach is not inconsistent with – and would in fact be usefully augmented by – a strategy that identifies and contextualizes culturally based power differentials. Atlas and Pepler articulate the second component of what they are proposing as follows:

> The second approach for intervention with peers involves lessons on the definition of bullying, providing strategies, and a language or script for intervening. Providing children with a language to stop bullying empowers children to use their voices and to take action against bullying ... With an increased understanding of how peers are part of the problem of bullying, they may be likely to intervene.[32]

The second component tackles bullying *in medias res,* emphasizing intervention by bystanders rather than the play of cultural factors that could be addressed preventatively. It is a strategy that puts responsibility for resolving bullying on the shoulders of students – reminiscent of the outdated Elmer the Safety Elephant campaign discussed later in this chapter – by setting its sights on individuals, but it fails to adequately acknowledge the culture of schools and the need to target the heteronormative climate of schools. Walton critiques these obsolete approaches and programs: "They focus on behaviour but do not delineate forms of bullying, nor describe how they arise in the public sphere ... Bullies are taught to feel empathy for others. Such actions may benefit individual students, but institutional complicity at reinforcing negative associations with difference remains unchallenged."[33] These kinds of strategies have policy implications: they ignore how ideologies and socio-legal factors participate in and influence conceptions of what it means to be safe and how safety can be achieved in schools.

School-based efforts to combat bullying, harassment, and violence, then, are often limited to strategies that attempt to "understand" the bully and to "contain" his or her actions, whereas the needs of queer students, which this book suggests are different from those of nonqueer students, are ignored. By contrast, Walton criticizes the emphasis on individualization and behaviourism. Instead, he proposes a line of analysis in which the cultural, historical, and ideological dynamics of bullying predominate. Walton argues that the specific needs of queer students are ignored when bullying is approached at the psychological level — the result being partial knowledge about bullying as well as a limited impact on policy approaches to achieving safe schools:

> The dominant notion about bullying is an individualist one, that it is a problem of some children who often behave aggressively, misuse power against their peers, and have an intent to harm ... Power is acknowledged but limited to immediate interactions between or among particular students ... Anti-violence education renders invisible the power and privilege imbued within social dynamics on the playground. Conceptualizing such interactions only as individual behaviour that potentially has effects upon other members of the school community leads to the application of anti-violence education as a rational response. The justification for such educational initiatives is that individual students will get help for *their* problems, supposedly making the school community and society as a whole a safer place.[34]

Walton's concern about the outcomes of investigating bullying through a social-psychological line of reasoning is especially pertinent for sexual-minority students. The consequences of ideology, of what is transpiring in schools and schoolyards because of the larger culture in which schools operate, must be accounted for in making schools safe for sexual-minority youth.[35] For Walton, safe-school intervention strategies must be based upon a more expansive perspective that locates bullying in its ideological context.[36] Interventions for Walton must indict not the individual or a "few bad apples" but a larger cultural framework, one that discards the "weeding out" approach of the behaviourists, and stresses, instead, as Eric Rofes has also suggested, the need for dramatic and widespread cultural transformation.[37] Rofes, a queer educator who has written extensively on the need for queer content in the curriculum, has also noted that school-based efforts to confront the issue of homophobia and anti-queer harassment have been grounded in psychological approaches to homophobia that focus on the hatred of the individual victimizer. Rofes opposes this approach for two reasons. First, although he acknowledges that the bullying of queer students occurs "in a peer context," he argues that confronting such bullying requires not simply understanding the role of bystanders in bullying "moments" but also comprehending the sheer size of the solutions that will likely be needed to create safe learning environments for queer students:

> The limited ways in which we consider antigay behaviours in schools might contribute to our bafflement over the limited effectiveness of our efforts ... A lesson to be taken from programs to combat bullying ... in schools is that even ambitious interventions fail to alleviate the problem ... Perhaps more radical approaches are needed, with a more dramatic transformation in the organization and culture of schooling.[38]

Second, Rofes points to research indicating that bullying, in general, unfolds in elementary and middle schools and drops off significantly by high school. The harassment and bullying of queer and gender-nonconforming students, however, transpires primarily in high school.[39] Different approaches are required, such as those proposed by Walton, that de-emphasize the individual and emphasize the cultural reasons that may account for the apparent raised awareness of sexual and gender difference among "straight" students in high school. The "catch up" game, Rofes argues, is necessary and is well served by Walton's uneasiness over "research-based solutions [that are] in large part implicitly predicated on rooting out bullies, like pulling noxious weeds from an otherwise aesthetically-pleasing garden."[40] Walton complains that because we have comprehended bullying "through the lens of scientism, bullying has become defined, objectified, categorized and psychologized."[41] His re-envisioning of bullying to stress its "cultural antecedents" gives rise to a broader conception of what it might take to make schools safe for queer students:

> A re-reading of bullying would work to subvert social hierarchies that perpetuate negative associations with constructs of difference. Rather than maintain normative gender scripts, for example, schools could be locations where the proliferation of gender identities and possibilities is supported, and thus, the pervasiveness of homophobia in schools would be challenged. More generally, schools are valuable sites from which to dismantle the power and privilege of some at the expense of others.[42]

Objective definitions and approaches tend not to accommodate the complexity of the felt experiences and sources of oppression of queer students. School board safety policies and curriculum delivery are aspects of the

legally regulated environment of schools that carry a potentially transformative power. Expanding policy approaches and curriculum content may be
among the most effective ways for schools to address the kinds of oppression
and safety concerns that students and teachers in this book have identified.

Legislation governing schools, promoting safe schools, and promoting
policies formulated by individual school boards is not able to respond to the
particular needs of sexual-minority youth when bullying is narrowly conceptualized. Notions of who is protected and in what ways will be limited
to an emphasis on extreme physical violence or other safety concerns that
are not necessarily reflective of the safety concerns of queer youth. Human
rights law, with its purposive approach to remedying inequalities, may be
able to accommodate queer experiences but only to a limited extent and in
a reactive way that puts a burden on students to initiate a human rights
action when their rights are arguably infringed. Missing in the law and policy
governing schools is a proactive approach to changing the day-to-day experiences of queers in schools. Human rights law remains complaint-based
and places the onus for a legal response on the individual, signalling that the
state has no legal obligation to proactively intervene in securing equal access to education for queer students.[43]

The legal literature on bullying in Canadian schools suffers from a lack
of good empirical studies, particularly from a socio-legal perspective, that
document how schools deal with the safety of sexual-minority students.
There is a significant amount of writing that looks at school and laws from
a constitutional-law perspective or that assesses school liability in the context of tort law.[44] Eric Roher, a major scholar of school law in Canada, has
written about safe schools, citing Olweus, Pepler, and Craig. His wide-
ranging scholarship includes discussion of significant Canadian case law
and provincial legislation governing schools, as well as the impact of the
Charter[45] and concerns about negligence and human rights law. His work
is a vital entry point on school law, generally, and on an educator's duty of
care to provide for the safety of students. His work stresses civil and criminal liability for bullying in schools. Bruce MacDougall is another Canadian scholar who has created a significant body of work dealing with the
law and education, especially in examining how the judiciary balances
sexual-minority rights with religious interests.[46] His writings, overall, are a
valuable critical response to judicial decisions affecting school life, most especially with respect to school curriculum and judicial attitudes to schools.
MacDougall's most recent work surveys a number of Canadian decisions in

order to demonstrate the cloaking of queer students from judicial view. Although this work includes a denunciation of the physical and verbal harassment of queers, MacDougall is concerned principally with the judiciary and its unwillingness to "see the queer child."[47] As he puts it, "It is ... important for most courts to realize that ... gay and lesbian students ... need judicial recognition and support." He advocates "a judicial recognition of the devices and institutions that have been used to perpetuate queer student invisibility," noting that these students' "rights should not be dependent [on] or constrained by the prejudices and preconceptions of the adults in their world."[48] Overall, then, there is no qualitative study in Canadian legal literature dealing with school-safety policies in terms of whether they target the queer experience, and there are none dealing with bullying per se as viewed from a socio-legal perspective.

Canadian socio-legal scholars have not been heard from much.[49] Particularly lacking are studies in which the knowledge of on-the-ground actors is employed as one means of delineating how schools conceptualize safety and go about constructing safe schools. How schools choose to conceive of safety and to create safe learning environments – as they are required to do by legislation and policies governing them – needs to be examined by looking at the precise manifestations of these choices as they operate in particular schools. The literature would be well augmented by sound socio-legal empirical studies that document how schools deal with the safety of sexual-minority students.

In a Toronto context, the late George W. Smith conducted a very helpful study in the early 1990s in which he interviewed gay students in Toronto.[50] As his published research notes indicate, however, most of his participants had already left high school by the time he interviewed them – this approach can provide valuable material for analysis, but the study was composed primarily of students who reported on their experiences not contemporaneously but as they remembered them. Notably, Smith's study was carried out prior to the enactment of the *Safe Schools Act*[51] and the *Equity Foundation Statement*.[52]

To conclude, the study of bullying is characterized by a relatively static definition of bullying established within the social-psychology literature and imported, without adequate critical interrogation for the most part, into work in other disciplines investigating bullying. The Canadian context has largely reproduced this understanding of bullying, with the important qualification that the established reading of bullying has come under some scrutiny and critique in the educational literature in Canada, notably by Gerald Walton. The Olweus approach, introduced into Canadian research by Pepler and Craig, portrays bullying in a "generic" way,[53] emphasizing individual accountability. Studies, therefore, have not highlighted the ideological context in which bullying occurs, and the particular needs of sexual-minority students have been ignored in a conception of bullying that grapples with a bullying "moment" from the perspective of specifically implicated actors. This approach has policy consequences. How schools choose to conceive of safety and to create safe learning environments – especially for sexual-minority students – needs to be examined by looking at specific manifestations of these policy choices in particular schools as they are experienced and felt by sexual-minority students and by those teachers and others who work as allies on behalf of their safety. This examination must include, therefore, an understanding of how queer students conceptualize their safety needs and how their schools may or may not be pursuing safety in the same way.

Safe Schools and the *Safe Schools Act*

In 1993 a series of incidents in Scarborough, Ontario, spurred the Scarborough Board of Education to take action to deal with the already growing perception that the safety in its high schools was under threat. The popular press – newspapers, magazines, tabloids – was full of accounts of "extreme" violence occurring in schools. Three Scarborough teenagers were charged with sexually assaulting and extorting money from girls at Midland Collegiate in Scarborough.[54] A fifteen-year-old girl was attacked at knife point.[55] One Scarborough high school caught an adult drug dealer in one of the school's washrooms. At the time of his arrest, he was in possession of a gun as well as the drugs he was selling on school property. At Timothy Eaton Business and Technical Institute in Agincourt, Ontario, a student used a knife to rob a fourteen-year-old boy.[56] At another school, a seventeen-year-old student pointed a handgun at another student's head. Another violent incident occurred at a school dance where a student stabbed another in the back and neck numerous times.[57] At Agincourt Collegiate, a nineteen-year-old woman was arrested for aggravated assault, assault with a weapon, and threatening death after throwing a fourteen-year-old female student against a locker and slashing her with a switchblade.[58]

On 1 November 1993 the Scarborough Board of Education approved a policy on violence and weapons that came into effect on 1 December of that year – the first school board in Canada to introduce a so-called zero-tolerance policy with the goal of making schools safer.[59] Under the policy, principals were required to document all acts of violence at their schools and to report to the police all incidents in which weapons were used. Students who violated the policy were suspended or, in the case of assault, expelled. Conversations about safe schools had been going on for a number of years before the Scarborough Board was spurred to act. For example, the Scarborough Board had instituted a Safe School Committee, chaired by Stuart Auty, a high school principal, as early as 1989.[60] In a retrospective article written in 2007, Gerri Gershon, a Toronto District School Board (TDSB) trustee for Don Valley West, recalled the climate in the late 1980s when conversations were taking place about keeping schools safe:

> In 1987, I was one of several trustees involved in a confidential meeting with a group of secondary school principals.
>
> This was a couple of years before students were shot at L'École Polytechnique in Montréal and long before Littleton, Tabor, Dawson or Blacksburg. Our meeting was under wraps because it was about violence and it was not politically correct at that time to talk about the growing manifestation of aggression in student behaviour.
>
> At the Toronto District School Board, these conversations signalled a shift. It was the beginning of Codes of Behaviour, alternative programs to address students who were suspended or disengaged from the school system … It also led to increased security measures such as locking outside doors, installing cameras, hiring hall monitors, and employing security patrols.[61]

In 1990 growing concern about school safety prompted the Ontario Secondary School Teachers' Federation to set up a taskforce to address the issue.[62] A newspaper search reveals that, at this time, the discourse about school safety in the media concerned issues of school security, crime, and school violence. Setting the tone of the tenure of the taskforce, Auty conveyed to the news media the "sad reality" that Scarborough-area principals had believed for some time that security guards, electronic surveillance, and constantly visible student-identification tags were the kinds of security measures that were necessary to make schools safe.[63] Discussion of safety in schools throughout the 1990s was crisis-driven, underscored by talk of rapidly escalating school violence, and characterized by a moral panic about school safety.

In anticipation of the impending provincial election in 1999, the Progressive Conservative government of Mike Harris promised to implement a zero-tolerance policy toward violence committed by students in schools.[64] Once returned to office, Harris delivered on the party's promise, and in April 2000 the Ontario Ministry of Education delivered a *Code of Conduct*[65] for Ontario schools that, among other things, mandated suspensions and expulsions for certain behaviours and required police involvement for a variety of infractions: "Premier Mike Harris says students will face automatic suspensions if they swear at a teacher and immediate expulsion if caught providing drugs or alcohol to other students. While school boards have codes of conduct, Mr. Harris said, enforcement has been lax."[66] Within a month, the ministry introduced the *Safe Schools Act*, which amended and became part of the *Education Act,*[67] to give force to the *Code of Conduct*, granting principals and teachers more authority to suspend and expel students. The *Safe Schools Act* was passed in June 2000 and came into effect in September 2001. The TDSB responded to the various decrees of the Harris government and in April 2000 announced its own safe-school policy containing a comprehensive "Code of Conduct" applicable to all students. The "Consequences of Inappropriate Student Behaviour Charts," developed from the *Safe Schools Act* and the TDSB's own safe-school policy, indicate that the principal was expected to recommend expulsion for students who were in possession of or who committed an assault with any firearm; notwithstanding this stipulation, the policy purported to be governed by an underlying philosophy in favour of education and modification of behaviour. Gail Nyberg, chairperson of the TDSB, spoke about the policy to the media in April 2000:

> The goal is to have a consistent set of rules "with strong consequences for inappropriate behaviour," but not to kick students out for every misdemeanour ... Expulsion would be reserved for the most serious offences, such as assaults, drug trafficking or weapons possession – and only after a hearing.
>
> The proposed Toronto policy is tough, but not nearly as tough as the Ontario government's stated plan to impose a province-wide code of conduct that would give teachers the power to suspend students and principals the power to expel.
>
> The Toronto board is hoping the Ontario government will moderate its hard-line approach to discipline in schools before putting the final touches

on its promised legislation ... Any provincial law would take precedence, but we're hoping they'll use ours as a template ...

The school board is not in the punishment business – that's for the courts. It's in the modification-of-behaviour and education business.[68]

The preamble to the *Safe Schools Act* indicates that the legislation was enacted "to promote respect, responsibility and civility in Ontario schools" and was intended to ensure that "students and teachers are interacting in a safe and respectful learning environment."[69] As many commentators have noted, the *Safe Schools Act* drastically transformed how students were to be disciplined in Ontario's schools. Prior to the enactment of the *Safe Schools Act*, the suspension and expulsion of students were governed by section 23 of the *Education Act*. The power to suspend a student was restricted to principals, and the power to expel was restricted to school boards.[70] Both actions were discretionary. The basis upon which students could be suspended was limited, and a student could be expelled only where it could be shown that the student's conduct was so "refractory" that continued attendance at school would be "injurious" to fellow students or others.

The legislation required school boards across the province to turn their corporate minds to the issue of school safety – and to act. The *Safe Schools Act* required school boards to provide programs for suspended and expelled students – which did not often happen.[71]

School boards in Ontario began to pay attention to their safe-school programs and to amend policies even before the *Safe Schools Act* was enacted.[72] The TDSB, for instance, had already adopted a *Safe Schools Foundation Statement* with a zero-tolerance component, a *Police-School Board Protocol*, and a *Safe Arrival for Elementary Schools* document.[73]

Several provisions of the *Safe Schools Act* were characterized as requiring zero-tolerance responses to incidents of physical violence, and some called for police involvement. The provincial *Code of Conduct*, promulgated under section 301 of the *Education Act*, had already mandated the participation of the police for most breaches. Specifically, under the *Safe Schools Act*, the *Education Act* was amended to allow mandatory suspensions for the following infractions:

1   uttering a threat to inflict serious bodily harm on another person;
2   possessing alcohol or illegal drugs;
3   being under the influence of alcohol;

4 swearing at a teacher or at another person in a position of authority;
5 committing an act of vandalism that causes extensive damage to school
   property at the pupil's school or to property located on the premises of
   the pupil's school;
6 engaging in another activity that, under a policy of the board, is one for
   which a suspension is mandatory.[74]

Under subsection 2, the minimum duration of a mandatory suspension
was one school day, and the maximum duration was twenty school days.
Mandatory expulsions were to be imposed for these infractions if committed on school property or when a student was engaged in a school activity.
The significance of requiring discipline for students "engaged in a school
activity" under subsection 6 was that out-of-school conduct could also be
captured, such as:

1 possessing a weapon, including a firearm;
2 using a weapon to cause or to threaten bodily harm to another person;
3 committing physical assault on another person that causes bodily harm
   requiring treatment by a medical practitioner;
4 committing sexual assault;
5 trafficking in weapons or in illegal drugs;
6 committing robbery;
7 giving alcohol to a minor;
8 engaging in another activity that, under a policy of the board, is one for
   which expulsion is mandatory.[75]

Notwithstanding the touting of the *Safe Schools Act* as a zero-tolerance response to school violence and the widespread perception that the government delivered on its promise to bring zero tolerance to schools in Metro
Toronto, the *Safe Schools Act*, in fact, allowed for a consideration of a number of mitigating factors that on paper made the legislation less than a true
zero-tolerance approach. In practice, however, these mitigating factors were
often not taken into account.[76] Nonetheless, the regulations set out the following mitigating factors:

1 the pupil does not have the ability to control his or her behaviour;
2 the pupil does not have the ability to understand the foreseeable consequences of his or her behaviour;

3 the pupil's continuing presence in the school does not create an unacceptable risk to the safety of any person.[77]

In these instances, suspension and expulsion were not supposed to be
mandatory.

The Toronto District School Board

As required under the *Safe Schools Act*, the TDSB increased the list of infractions for which suspensions or expulsions were required in its own safe-
schools policy and developed a list of breaches that could be responded to
with discretionary suspension or expulsion. To make these lists easily com-
prehensible, the TDSB produced a document entitled "Consequences of
Inappropriate Student Behaviour Charts" or "Grid of Consequences" – or
just the "Grid," as many referred to it. The "Grid" listed the infractions for
which disciplinary action would be imposed as well as the minimum days
that would be imposed for suspensions and expulsions. The document was
laid out in the form of a table so that the vice-principal meting out punishment could immediately determine "time periods" of suspensions or expulsions and whether there was a requirement to call the police for a particular
breach of conduct.

Even though the mitigating factors set out in the *Safe Schools Act* and its
regulations were intended to rule out mandatory suspensions or expulsions,
principals still retained the right to impose discretionary suspensions or expulsions in any event. The *Safe Schools Act* set out factors that the principal
was to consider when deciding upon a suitable disciplinary answer – on top
of the number of days for the suspension or expulsion. When a student with
"exceptionalities" was implicated, the principal was required to take the
enumerated factors into account. Teachers were required to employ the
same philosophy with respect to their power to suspend. As a matter of
practice, however, the teachers' federations in Ontario advised their members to refrain from exercising this power and, instead, to refer all disciplinary decisions to the office of the principal.

True to the philosophy expounded by its chairperson, Gail Nyberg, the
TDSB, although not required to do so under the *Safe Schools Act*, instituted
four support programs for suspended students and one program for students enduring a limited expulsion. In conjunction with social services, the
TDSB also began two strict discipline programs. The concluding statement
of the TDSB's *Safe Schools Foundation Statement* indicated that the TDSB

would "offer support for victims of school-related violence, their families and school communities."[78]

Sexual-Minority Students

Public and media pressure gave rise to the *Safe Schools Act*. Notably, the legislation did not specifically mention bullying, sexual orientation, or verbal harassment. A review of the government debates regarding the legislation reveals that there was some discussion of the potential impact of the *Safe Schools Act* on disabled students but no mention of its impact on racial-minority students and no mention of how to make schools safe or safer for sexual-minority students.[79] The debates also failed to include any perspective that read bullying as a cultural practice that guarded categories of social advantage, and most detrimentally for queer students, gender and sexuality were not discussed as sources of such cultural privilege. These deficiencies, as well as the historicity of the legislation, provide a valuable background to some of the commentary throughout this book. Both students and teachers characterized their schools in terms of models of control or security, a tendency attributable, in the view of some, to the emphasis on these terms in conversations about safety throughout the 1990s. At the same time, the pursuit of equity was viewed by school administrators and safe-school committees as a separate goal, meaningful only for a few implicated students and not relevant to conversations about safety in general.

"The Race to Equity"

At the same time as conversations about making schools safe were unfolding in Ontario, what Tim McCaskell has referred to as the thirty-year "race to equity"[80] was also playing out in Toronto high schools. The pursuit of equity began in the early 1970s at the Toronto Board of Education and came to fruition (on paper) in 1998 at the newly amalgamated Toronto District School Board. Its aim was to bring anti-racist, anti-classist, anti-homophobic, and anti-sexist programs to Toronto's education system.

In 1997 the amalgamated City of Toronto was created by the *City of Toronto Act*, which replaced the *Municipality of Metropolitan Toronto Act*.[81] The legislation united the six Toronto-area municipalities (Metropolitan Toronto, Scarborough, York, North York, East York, and Etobicoke) into one "megacity" known as the City of Toronto. Around the same time, on 1 January 1998, the Mike Harris government enacted the *Fewer School Boards*

Act [82] to amalgamate the seven predecessor school boards (Scarborough, York, North York, East York, Etobicoke, City of Toronto, and Metropolitan Toronto) of these boroughs into one governing entity, the Toronto District School Board. Even though both proposals received pervasive public opposition in late 1996 when the Harris government first announced its intentions for the city and its schools, as of 1 January 1998 the Toronto District School Board was created as the sole governing entity.

According to Tim McCaskell, among all of the boards, the City of Toronto's Board of Education (TBE) exhibited the most profound commitment to equity. McCaskell began working with the TBE in 1979 as a contract worker and became a full-time employee in 1983. He described for me the nature of the work he undertook during those years:

> I did work with students focusing on getting them to identify and
> challenge first of all racism in their schools and then began to do
> anti-homophobia work as well. And as the board's policies grew
> and changed, I was a sexual-harassment resource person as well.
> So then I also helped students with sexual-harassment complaints.
> And I was still preparing curriculum documents on such topics as
> racism or disabilities or class bias.

When the provincial government proposed merging the seven school boards into one, McCaskell and other equity workers in Toronto were concerned that the gains made by the TBE's equity departments would be sacrificed. He recalled his anxieties when the new structure was first suggested:

> Those of us from Toronto tended to see the progress of the
> other boards as underdeveloped and narrower than what we had
> accomplished in terms of equity in Toronto. Nobody knew what
> position the new board would take on equity or what the new
> structure would look like. There was a widespread concern – well,
> a fear really – that the issues and the programs we cared about
> most and had spent so many years working towards might be
> gone or displaced.

In April 1997, after the passage of amalgamation legislation, to preserve the decades-long efforts of the Toronto equity employees, McCaskell drafted a document with input and support from others involved in the struggle for equity. He and other equity stakeholders in the TBE hoped this document could be used to represent and codify a commitment to equity by the newly formed superboard. The result was "Equity in Education: Basic Principles," approved by the board in 1997, which stated:

> Educational systems in Canada have not served individuals associated with certain groups. There is consequently a need for change to overcome institutional and individual racism, sexism, homophobia, class, bias, ableism and other forms of discrimination ...
>
> Equity in education requires pedagogy which encourages and equips students and staff to understand power relations and challenge unjust systems. It must be based on learners' experience and must be relevant to their lives. Teachers, students, families and communities are therefore partners in an exploration that encourages responsibility and critical thinking.
>
> Equity in education must help learners understand the connections, similarities and differences between different forms of oppression and discrimination. Only with such understanding is it possible to work together to build a more just society.[83]

Recognizing the individual and systemic bases of oppression, the document reflects a robust conception of schools, one whose concerns and proposals are pointedly different from those found in the discourse on safe schools. As conceived in the document, equity is not just an "add on"[84] but the substance behind creating safe and equitable schools. McCaskell told me,

> Having policies around harassment and bullying is certainly not
> enough to keep kids safe. You've got to have regular educational
> work to dismantle and constantly challenge the kinds of stereotypes
> the kids will be learning from the rest of their environment, and
> you've got to have all these systemic pieces in place, not only in
> terms of harassment and anti-bullying and anti-violence but in
> terms of equity being promoted. So, yes, you can do the "rules
> and consequences piece" around "no more bullying" and "anti-
> violence," but the other piece has got to deal with equity issues.

The document identified oppressed persons within the educational system as the "driving force" behind the hoped-for changes, endorsing their participation in devising and implementing proactive programs grounded in student realities.

Adoption of the "Equity in Education" document was not automatic. Powerful voices, primarily from the individuals previously employed at boards outside of the downtown Toronto area, bitterly opposed the document, preferring instead an equity policy limited to "race and culture" – meaning, at most, race and "faith." It was here, after the battle lines were drawn between those favouring the narrower approach to equity and those endorsing the broader approach embodied in the "Equity in Education" document, that the struggle gained public attention and widespread media coverage.

As the issue gained more prominence in the Toronto press, public support for the broader approach to equity took hold but only after a very dispiriting and drawn-out fight. Finally, in May 1999, a taskforce recommended that the board develop a basic equity "foundation statement" based on the "Equity in Education" document and recommended the development of corresponding documents with respect to gender, sexual orientation, and socio-economic class. The only deviation in language between the "Equity in Education" document and the final draft of the foundation statement was to move away from a recognition of oppressed communities as the "driving force" behind system-wide changes and toward a preference to "value and encourage"[85] the contributions of diverse community members. In June 1999 the board adopted the recommendation of the taskforce. The resulting *Equity Foundation Statement* is worth quoting at length:

> The Board recognizes ... that certain groups in our society are treated inequitably because of individual and systemic biases related to race, colour, culture, ethnicity, linguistic origin, disability, socio-economic class, age, ancestry, nationality, place of origin, religion, faith, sex, gender, sexual orientation, family status, and marital status. Similar biases have also impacted on Canada's aboriginal population. We also acknowledge that such biases exist within our school system.
>
> The Board further recognizes that such inequitable treatment leads to educational, social, and career outcomes that do not accurately reflect the abilities, experiences, and contributions of our students, our employees, and our parent and community partners. This inequitable treatment limits their future success and prevents them from making a full contribution to society.
>
> The Board is therefore committed to ensuring that fairness, equity, and inclusion are essential principles of our school system and are integrated into all our policies, programs, operations, and practices.

The Board will therefore ensure that:

1 The curriculum of our schools accurately reflects and uses the variety
   of knowledge of all peoples as the basis for instruction; that it actively
   provides opportunities for all students to understand the factors that
   cause inequity in society, and to understand the similarities, differences, and the connections between different forms of discrimination; and that it helps students to acquire the skills and knowledge
   that enable them to challenge unjust practices, and to build positive
   human relationships among their fellow students, and among all
   members of the society.

2 All our students are provided with equitable opportunities to be
   successful in our system; that institutional barriers to such success
   are identified and removed; and that all learners are provided with
   supports and rewards to develop their abilities and achieve their
   aspirations.[86]

The *Equity Foundation Statement* was augmented by five supporting documents asserting a commitment to achieving social justice based on class,
gender, race, religion, and sexual orientation. McCaskell explains that "getting something like that accomplished was huge," but he and other proponents of the broadly based approach to equity knew that simply having
positioned the policy "did not mean that 'things would automatically happen.'"[87] Tim McCaskell, Sharon Dominick, Lorna Gillespie, and many other
educators I met considered equity to be a crucial component of making
schools safe, particularly for sexual-minority students. However, in conversations and debates leading up to the introduction of the *Safe Schools Act*, it
was clear that equity did not form a part of these discussions but was a separate and distinct discourse within the TDSB and the province generally.

Bullying and the Law

Until recently, the term "bullying" was an artless word at law, possessing
little meaning in a legal context. "Bullying" had not been a term in any Canadian legislation. Criminal law recognizes "assault," "trespass," and so on,
and civil litigation permits legal actions founded on "assault," "battery," and
a failure to provide a sufficient standard of care where a duty of care is owed
to one's neighbour. The *Charter* and provincial human rights legislation af-
ford students, and others, protection from harassment and discrimination

in access to services, employment, and housing. There have been three human rights complaints founded in Canada based on what the media, public, and some academics would describe as "bullying," but none of these actions was grounded in "bullying" per se.

For five years, from 1993 through 1998, Azmi Jubran attended Handsworth Secondary School in North Vancouver, where he was repeatedly assaulted verbally and physically. He was subjected to homophobic epithets, spit and urinated on, and kicked and punched by male and female students. Before he graduated from high school, Jubran filed a human rights complaint with the Human Rights Tribunal in British Columbia alleging that he was discriminated against on the basis of sexual orientation, a prohibited ground. The basis of his complaint was that the Board of School Trustees was accountable for the discrimination because it failed to provide an educational environment free from discriminatory harassment by failing to respond effectively to the discriminatory conduct.[88] The Human Rights Tribunal found that Jubran's own sexual orientation – which he described to me as heterosexual – was irrelevant. The tribunal also found that the fact that Jubran's victimizers did not actually believe he was homosexual was not a basis to exclude protection under the province's human rights legislation. Jubran's high school was ordered to develop and put into place anti-bullying policies. The school board appealed the decision to the British Columbia Supreme Court, where the court decided that Jubran, because he was heterosexual, had not been discriminated against according to the language of section 8 of the British Columbia *Human Rights Code*.[89] The Court of Appeal reversed this decision, and the Supreme Court of Canada declined to hear an appeal. After over $30,000 in legal fees, twenty-four-year-old Azmi Jubran prevailed.

Also in British Columbia, Peter and Murray Corren, parents of a gay high school student, filed an action against the province's Ministry of Education alleging that the ministry discriminated against queer students, and their parents, contrary to section 8 of the code, with respect to an "accommodation, service, or facility customarily available to the public"[90] – namely, getting an education. The basis of the Correns' human rights complaint was that the British Columbia curriculum discriminated against gay, lesbian, bisexual, and transgendered students. Specifically, the Correns complained that the ministry failed to make the provincial curriculum inclusive of positive and accurate portrayals of gay, lesbian, bisexual, and transgendered students and same-sex families, or, as the Correns put it to me, "queer realities."

The Correns settled with the province in 2006 when the province agreed, among other things, to establish a Grade 12 social-justice course reflecting these "queer realities."

In Ontario, Gabriel (Gabe) Picard brought an action against the Lakehead District School Board, in Thunder Bay, alleging that the school board, in violation of sections 1 and 9 of the Ontario *Human Rights Code*,[91] had "discriminated" against him. Picard set out the basis of his complaint in his application:

> I am gay and I believe my right to equal treatment with respect to services, goods and facilities without discrimination because of my sexual orientation has been infringed by the respondents. I believe this is contrary to ... the *Human Rights Code* ... I believe this [because] ... since grade nine, I have been repeatedly harassed by numerous students because of my sexual orientation ... This has caused a poisoned and unsafe environment for me in the school.[92]

Gabe's complaint resulted in a settlement with the school board that called for a number of solutions. First, the board agreed to develop a series of programs intended to achieve what Gabe initially set out to do by filing the complaint – "change the culture" of the high school, which Gabe told me was the only way to ensure a safe site for queer students and teachers. The board committed to a review of its policies and agreed to make necessary changes. Most important, it agreed to promote curriculum resources and professional development in order to confront homophobia and the heterosexism at Gabe's school by establishing, among other things, a Gay-Straight Alliance and designated safe spaces in every high school in the school district. Under the agreement, a newly instituted Diversity Committee was charged with promoting additional programs and proposals in order to make district schools safer.[93]

After I completed the interviews upon which this book is based, the Ontario Legislature enacted Bill 212 in 2007.[94] Bill 212 came into effect on 1 February 2008 and made some changes to the safe-school provisions of the *Education Act*. One of the significant effects of Bill 212 is that the Ontario Legislature introduced the term "bullying" into the *Education Act*. As a result, "bullying" was now a prohibited action in schools, thereby making "bullying" an identifiable and meaningful term in Canadian legislation:

> A principal shall consider whether to suspend a pupil if he or she believes that the pupil has engaged in any of the following activities while at school,

at a school-related activity or in other circumstances where engaging in the activity will have an impact on the school climate:

1 Uttering a threat to inflict serious bodily harm on another person.
2 Possessing alcohol or illegal drugs.
3 Being under the influence of alcohol.
4 Swearing at a teacher or at another person in a position of authority.
5 Committing an act of vandalism that causes extensive damage to school property at the pupil's school or to property located on the premises of the pupil's school.
6 Bullying.
7 Any other activity that is an activity for which a principal may suspend a pupil under a policy of the board.[95]

Bullying was not defined in the *Education Act* but was defined in Policy/ Program Memorandum No. 144, which substantially followed the Olweus approach: "Bullying is typically a form of repeated, persistent, and aggressive behaviour directed at an individual or individuals that is intended to cause (or should be known to cause) fear and distress and/or harm to another person's body, feelings, self-esteem, or reputation. Bullying occurs in a context where there is a real or perceived power imbalance."[96] Bill 212 also removed the power of principals to expel and the power of teachers to suspend, and eliminated any reference to "zero tolerance" in the *Education Act*, the provincial *Code of Conduct*, or policy documents.

Notwithstanding that "bullying" now appears in the language of the *Education Act*, for several decades in Canada mainstream discourse has failed to move beyond "generic" conceptions of bullying. A more expansive approach is required to address the broad forms of oppression faced, for example, by sexual-minority students. Bill 212, now law, also raises questions about whether a progressive discipline framework that shifts the focus in the *Education Act*'s safe-school provisions from punitive discipline to supportive and corrective discipline – but continues to lack an emphasis on equity and social justice as significant parts of what makes schools safe – will play out differently in practice. Some teachers have told me that the students have "picked up on this" climate and take advantage of it. I do not know to what extent, if at all, this might be true, but I wonder at the irony: is it possible that easing back on disciplinary measures might lead some teachers – even those committed to equity – to move toward a disciplinary approach? I note these changes to the *Education Act* insofar as they are, at least, "on the books" and, like these initial teacher reports I have heard in some quarters, in need of future research.

Narrow conceptions of bullying and safety do not capture what Eric Rofes calls "the complicated nature of school and classroom cultures"[97] and reinforce "liberal understandings of complex matters such as identity, tolerance, safety, and equity."[98] The next task is to represent some of this complexity and to articulate both the threat that these "new narratives" present to the hegemony of privilege and the ways that the presence of non-heterosexual and gender-nonconforming students can and does prompt others to "draw a line in the sand."

3

How Schools Conceptualize Safety
Control, Security, Equity, Social Justice

> So as far as I'm concerned, kids would be afraid to come out.
> And so, if they're gay and lesbian in the school ... right now,
> because nobody respects anybody, they would just leave. I met
> a girl once that tried to come out. I think when they do, when
> they do try to come out and they get harassed and picked on,
> they leave.
>
> — MELANIE

Burton School: Equity

"It's here somewhere," Lazy Daisy says. I have spent lunch, a spare period, and now an art class with her. I am in no rush to say goodbye. Earlier in the day, we completed a more formal interview-conversation that lasted about ninety minutes. Lazy Daisy does not like being referred to as a woman. Sexually, she describes herself as "pansexual," typical of the varied vocabulary students in schools employ to describe these complicated sexual and gender identities they are creating for themselves and indicative, also, of the awareness most students generally possess of the significance and power of words. Lazy Daisy was not the first student I met who described herself as "pansexual." When I asked her to describe her gender, she said, "I'm a girl. I'm not a woman and I'm not a lesbian." However, I have noticed that when she is not consciously choosing her words, Lazy Daisy does refer to herself as "gay," a term I have noticed that female students use more frequently than I would have expected.

Lazy Daisy and I are in her art class. The teacher is nowhere to be seen, but Lazy Daisy assures me this is not unusual. "This school is cool," she tells me, still rummaging through an overstuffed backpack. Finally, she finds the crumpled sheet she's been looking for and hands it to me. "Here it is," she says. As I look it over, she says, "It's a piece of crap."

I read the caption out loud: "Be confident. Bullies don't like people who are not afraid." "Elmer the Safety Elephant," I say. "It looks like it's a hundred years old." She reaches for the sheet and takes it from me as though she has not seen it before, shakes her head, and tells me, for the second time, the story behind it. "I got this from my friend Jane. This is the kind of shit they're handing out at her school. It was in a booklet or something, so I tore it out." Lazy Daisy, like most students with whom I spend time, is well aware of the *Safe Schools Act*,[1] if not its specific provisions. Her anger, she tells me, has two bases. First, she is angry that the message of the image is that the burden of being bullied should ever be placed on students. Second, she feels that the image is infantile and misses out on the complexity of what "really goes on when somebody is being bullied, especially if they're queer for God's sake." I realize that I have already met and spoken with Lazy Daisy's friend Jane at another school, but I do not mention it.

As Lazy Daisy and I talk, she moves around the back of the art class, opening jars and mixing paints and carrying on side conversations with the other students, who show little curiosity about me and what I am doing. Now she is at some sort of printmaking machine that I do not recognize from any art class I ever took. "LD" – as she asks me to call her – assures me that the equipment at her school is superior, in fact, to that found at most high schools of the Toronto District School Board (TDSB). I do not ask her how she knows this, but it is obvious that she and other students I meet at Burton School regard their school as "special" and "not like other schools." As Lazy Daisy prepares to make a print, I ask her a question I ask everyone: Is she aware of any policies or laws that are in place in Ontario or in her school dealing with safety?

Most, if not all, of the queer students I have met or will meet have heard of the *Safe Schools Act* and are familiar with it, a larger group, happily for me, than I expected. In fact, in all of my experiences at schools, only two students prove hesitant to talk – but even this reluctance is not without meaning about conditions at a particular school. Most of the queer students

I interview or meet informally at conferences or in other circumstances agree that queer students – particularly "out" queer students – are probably more familiar with safe-school and equity policies than most other students. I certainly find this assumption to be true.

Among the students I meet, Lazy Daisy is one of the more knowledgeable and articulate about the *Safe Schools Act*. She has also heard of the TDSB's *Safe Schools Foundation Statement*,[2] although she is not familiar with the details of the policy. She is much more familiar with the TDSB's *Equity Foundation Statement*.[3] When I ask her to account for this difference, she explains that her school emphasizes "equity as safety," so her greater familiarity with the *Equity Foundation Statement* makes sense in this context. She tells me, "Oh, I'm very familiar with the *Equity Statement*." In addition to Daisy, every student I speak with at Burton tells me that this school pursues "safety" in terms of doing "equity." She tells me:

> There's no doubt about it that the equity policy is going to do a hell of a lot more for the safety of queer kids than the one on safety and certainly the *Safe Schools Act*.
>
> At this school, the school uses the equity stuff to "create a safe school environment." But I don't think you could get that going at every school. Everybody's too afraid of the gangsters and rejects at other schools. You could get some pockets of that happening if teachers or guidance would support it, but otherwise queer kids are pretty much on their own unless they're at a school like this, and there aren't a lot like this.

Lazy Daisy makes me two prints, both wet when she hands them to me. "You can't go yet," she says. "I can talk while they dry." After our formal interview that morning, Lazy Daisy showed me a print she had made that, in her view, more accurately addressed the kind of oppression that queer kids face in school, which, in her words, is not "just about bullying." When I asked her whether I could make a photocopy of the print, she offered to make me an original and asked me to meet her in her art class later that day. And here we are. I ask Lazy Daisy to explain to me how "equity" can possibly mean "safety" at her high school. She thinks for a bit, checks the condition of her print, and then tells me that "safety for queer kids is about changing things not protecting things. I mean, of course, you have to protect kids, but that's a given, isn't it? But it's not just about bullying, I mean, in a physical way. We're bullied by just the culture we're in."

The idea for Lazy Daisy's art came from her anger at the Elmer the Safety Elephant artwork. Her art is "anti-Elmer." She tells me that "it occurred to [her] in gay and lesbian studies class." I am a bit taken aback that her curriculum includes gay and lesbian content. She is taken aback by my surprise:

> Oh, yeah. I was in gay and lesbian studies, and I was just looking at the statistics of drug use and suicide among gay people as opposed to straight teens. And the results were actually like appalling because it's amazing how much more at risk I think queer teens are. Three times more at risk [of] suicide than straight teens growing up in high school because they have to face so much more in terms of the culture. So I made this really cool print that shows all that. It's anti-Elmer.

When I ask her to explain in greater detail what the print represents, she continues,

> It's a mirror, it's what you see when you're queer and you look in the mirror. It's the question we ask every day. And it has lines on it. And the lines are the rainbow flag. See, these are the colours. And it's got a little razor and it's got "Am I at Risk?" And there's a needle going into it, into the "A." And like the "R" is a joint. This is what the culture does, it threatens us in so many ways.

FIGURE 1 "Am I at Risk?" by Lazy Daisy, Burton School

As I watch Daisy make her print for me, she also moves with ease around the art class, yelling out to her classmates (and teacher) that she is making another "Am I at Risk?" print "for Donn – have you met Donn? Unless you're queer, he doesn't want to talk to you. We're talking revolution back here." Lazy Daisy and many of the students I have met represent a trend in anti-oppressive responses in schools – students making a difference. These students are out and making a difference in the culture of their schools. I ask Lazy Daisy about the question mark at the end of her "Am I at Risk?" artwork. She waits before answering but eventually admits that she is tired of the negative portrayals of queer youth as facing suicide and being troubled ("at risk") – as true as this predicament is for many and borne out by statistics.

Nonetheless, I cannot help but think of the work of many students who ground their negative experiences in a kind of activism in pursuit of measurable, cultural transformation. Gabriel (Gabe) Picard in Thunder Bay is this kind of student. When I interviewed Gabe, a few months earlier, he told me he had been bullied at school and did not feel safe. As a result of how Gabe felt at school, he filed a human rights complaint against his school. I asked him to tell me about what had happened that caused him to decide to take legal action. He described for me what life was like every day for him at his high school, but his frustration in doing so was apparent. Gabe and I had been talking about Azmi Jubran, whose experiences are discussed in the previous chapter, and the fact that Jubran had been physically assaulted and set on fire. Gabe tried to explain what it was like for him, but he could not really speak. He began to cry and for a moment could not say anything. Finally, after a long period of silence, Gabe told me that he filed his complaint not in response to any "extreme" violence but because he wanted to change the day-to-day culture of schools for queer students:

> I've been interviewed by other people before, and they always want me to go through the incidents, what happened. But I can't. I can't ever actually pull it out like that. You know this happened, and this and this happened, and everything got worse and worse. I feel like when I talk about it, it seems like it's less to people than it actually was. That's what I always think. I think that it's sounding like less than it actually was because nobody tried to set my shirt on fire like with Azmi Jubran or beat me up every day, but I'm trying to get across that it was big. The way it is. What people say. How they are. Because it was all the time – it was just there. It was the entire culture. People don't get that. It wasn't safe.

Gabe told me about what he saw as the inadequacies of viewing the threats to queer students solely as the outcomes of individual incidents, even if escalating. His depiction of the harassment that he described as "big" seemed to me a powerful condemnation of policy intervention based on a law and order response to individual incidents only when they exceed the limits of unacceptable conduct. Gabe underscored for me what other students would tell me – that how sexual-minority youth perceived safety and threats to safety often differed from what had been expressed in popular or even academic conversations:

> I got really, really fed up and I went into the principal's office, and I yelled at her and I told her, "Well, you're still letting this happen." And she's like, "Well, what do you want me to do about it, Gabe? We can't change the way it is." She told me that. Those were her exact words: "Gabe, we can't change the culture."
>
> That's what set me off, and then I told her that, if she couldn't change the culture, then she'd failed as an educator and that she was a failure as an educator.
>
> And I said, "What's the point in you becoming an educator, then, if you can't change the culture? That's the whole thing."
>
> That's what I told her. I told her, "That's the whole thing, that's what teaching is all about. Change." And then I told her that she failed as an educator if she believed she couldn't change it, and then I stormed out. So that's why I did it, filed the human rights complaint.

I asked Gabe to tell me how safety was conceptualized at his school. He laughed,

> You're kidding. At one point, they bought some door hangers to go on the door knobs – the school did – and it said "Safe Space" on it, but they didn't even *know* what that meant.
>
> They even brought those to the mediation for the case, and they're like, "Oh we bought some flags for the door knobs" – and then of course being super prepared like we were, with our bajillions of bags, I'm like, and I pull one out, I'm like, "These ones?"
>
> They're like, "Yeah, those are the ones, yeah." And I'm like, "But what does that mean?" I looked right at them and asked, "But what does that mean – 'Safe Space'?"

And they didn't even know what it meant. They didn't even
know what it meant. They had nothing to say. Safe schools, safe
space, they had nothing to say. Because it's so big what makes
school safe for us and they didn't get it.

Students like Gabe and Lazy Daisy are part of a new student-led activism
among sexual-minority youth. No longer merely "at risk," they speak up and
demand a presence in the culture of the school around them. Gabe sought
to change the culture; Lazy Daisy and other students I would meet – like
Katie – wanted to be acknowledged by it. This seemed like the right moment
to show Daisy a copy of the TDSB's *Safe Schools Foundation Statement* and
ask her to look it over. Did she think it represented her school and other
schools? This was the portion she pointed to:

The mission of the Toronto District School Board is to provide learning
environments that are safe, nurturing, positive and respectful.
    Such learning environments are peaceful and welcoming for all. They
must be free of negative factors such as abuse, bullying, discrimination,
intimidation, hateful words and deeds and physical violence in any form.[4]

Daisy did not want to talk very much about "environments" that were "free
of negative factors" as a solution to providing safe and equal education for
queers. "That's a given." For Daisy, it was about overcoming the obstacles:

I think for most schools, it's the second part, the second paragraph,
if they even care about that. Our school is more about the first part.
But it doesn't mention queers, does it? "Safe, nurturing, positive
and respectful" can go out the window when all of a sudden you're
talking about queers. And all the rest of this statement is talking
about violence on school property and things like trafficking drugs.
What does this have to do with queers? We're the ones experiencing
the violence in such different ways. And if queers do drugs, it's to
escape what's happening to them. I like my statement better.

I told her about Gabe, one of the few interviewees I had spent time with
whose experiences and statements are a matter of public record. She said,
"That's exactly it. You've got to change a culture – you've got to do more
than take away – what was it? Negative factors. You've got to put in some
positive factors. That's why for my school, it's more about equity." After a

few minutes of being quiet while she checked the status of the print, she had more to say:

> About that Thunder Bay guy, he's right. If you just punish people for homophobic attitudes and stuff like that, or incidents of out-right homophobia, like when there's discrimination and people attacking other people, it's not gonna help. Even with crime in general, I think it's about changing the attitude, the root of the problem, not just doing something about an isolated incident. That guy is right.

I showed her the TDSB's *Equity Foundation Statement* again and asked her whether this document represented the climate at her school. She said,

> Yeah, this is much more about how we do safety here than that other one. This part: "Students thrive in their learning when their environments are safe, nurturing, positive, and respectful. All students and staff in the Toronto District School Board have the right to learn and work in environments free of restricting biases."[5] Yeah, that part is true, like in the other statement, but here, in this one, look, this one mentions queer students. Yeah, it's got a whole page!

"Is it possible to change an entire culture? How do you do that?" I asked her. She responded,

> Well you start young, right? By implementing programs in school like anti-racism programs. There's Black History Month, there's all sort of things like that, but there's nothing for gay people. I mean, at my old school, they just started a Pride event, but it was a joke. They were just making the teachers do it. I feel there's not a lot of focus on it.

When art class was almost over, Daisy went to find something in which to store my print. "Yeah," she said. "Nurturing and positive. That's what we do here. For the most part. It's not as big maybe as [at] Coyt [Elizabeth Coyt Alternative School], but it's good. We contribute, you know?"

Benjamin attends the same school as Daisy. He attributes the climate of Burton School to its small size and to the fact that both the teachers and the students want the school to be a place that not only focuses on equity but is also "more socially active – like Coyt." Elizabeth Coyt Alternative School is immediately next door to Burton School. In fact, Burton and Coyt share the same city block with Sylvia Avenue Collegiate and Vocational School. Three schools, all distinct, each connected to the other. "Yeah," Benjamin says, "it's weird how all three schools are side by side." Both Daisy and Benjamin describe Sylvia Avenue to me as "threatening" and "not safe." I ask them whether this is true for all students or just sexual-minority students. They agree that Sylvia Avenue would not be as good a school for any student but add that for sexual-minority youth, it would be unbearable. Benjamin explains, "I don't think there are any out students at Sylvia Avenue. It's funny how the three schools are so close to each other and so different. Sylvia Avenue is all about being a prison. Coyt is like paradise, or that's what they think, and we're kind of more like Coyt, but not as much." When I ask Benjamin to describe his school to me, he says,

> It's like a little hippie commune. That's the way I like to think of
> it, anyway. It's pretty cool. Everyone here adheres to, even if they
> didn't like know it beforehand, a pretty open and accepting way
> about their day. There is no violence. There is no real homophobia,
> and the culture is cool for queers. Anything that's said and not
> liked is discussed versus just being dealt with authoritarian-style.

Burton School is composed only of Grades 11 and 12. Students come to Burton from middle school. Benjamin explains to me about getting in to Burton School:

> You have to venture there versus being assigned from your
> previous middle school. You make a point of finding it. Before
> coming here, I went to "Crappy Collegiate." I wasn't being academ-
> ically challenged, and socially there wasn't much there for me. You
> get immune to walking the halls and being called a faggot every
> day, but you also get bored of it. You'd like a different experience.

When I ask him to describe the rules in place at Burton School in terms of safety and behaviour, Benjamin insists, "There are none. You can do whatever you like so long as it's not offensive, and I've never seen anyone tread the line of offensiveness, personally. But you see, it's different here because they focus on equity. At Crappy Collegiate, I would say they had no policies and no rules, but I mean that in a different way." The TDSB has twenty schools within its district that are designated "alternative schools." Burton is one of them. The TDSB describes alternative schools this way:

> TDSB Alternative schools offer students and parents something different from mainstream schooling. Each alternative school, whether elementary or secondary[,] is unique, with a distinct identity and approach to curriculum delivery. They usually feature a small student population, a commitment to innovative and experimental programs, and volunteer commitment from parents/guardians and other community members.[6]

Benjamin corrects himself, telling me that there is, in fact, one very strict rule at his school: "We're not welcome in Sylvia Avenue. They're not allowed to come here, and we're not allowed to go there. Same with Coyt. But I think the rule is really in place to keep the students from Sylvia Avenue out of Burton and Coyt. That's really what it's for."

I will spend several weeks in all three schools. I agree with Benjamin's description of Sylvia Avenue. I found no out students in the school. The two students I met at Sylvia Avenue were not very forthcoming even in a confidential interview. Sharon Dominick had identified them to me as "questioning," and they had agreed to talk with me. Once in the interview, one of the students, Louise, denied that she was questioning. Both Louise and Barry admitted to being verbally abused by homosexual epithets, but only Barry acknowledged being queer. Sylvia Avenue very much conveys that it subscribes to an overall "lock down" approach to school safety. Sylvia Avenue and Burton are very different, albeit physically attached. Benjamin tells me that Burton uses Sylvia Avenue's gymnasium but is permitted to do so only at 7 a.m. on Monday mornings, the idea being that Burton School's students are expected to show up, use the gym and showers, and leave before students from Sylvia Avenue arrive. Benjamin, Lazy Daisy, and all of the students with whom I speak at Burton School take care to tell me that their school is "nothing like" Sylvia Avenue. In fact, the students at Sylvia Avenue agree with that assessment, making the same observation about their own school. Students at each of these schools possess a clear understanding of how their schools are governed and perceived and of how each stands apart from and in opposition to the others.

Benjamin explains to me that Burton School is trying to be more proactive about its equity policies: "Right now we're kind of pro-equity, but we're trying to be more socially active." Benjamin is more familiar with the TDSB's *Safe Schools Foundation Statement* than Daisy and, actually, asks me whether I have a copy of it when I ask him to tell me about the rules or policies on school safety at Burton School. He looks it over but does not seem very satisfied. He hands me one of the "Celebrate Diversity" stickers that he has been putting up all over his school. "For me, these stickers are more about the celebrate part than the diversity part. I'm tired of being 'tolerated' – I want to be celebrated." The sentiment is reminiscent of Bruce MacDougall's observation that the judiciary, and society at large, so far as gays and lesbians are concerned, has been willing to condone same-sex behaviour but that the celebration of same-sex lives is a remaining hurdle.[7] Same-sex marriage for many adults has been identified as this last hurdle in Canada. For the queer youth I meet, celebration seems less about any single identifiable cultural signpost, such as marriage, and more about living their lives safely, as they view safety, as well as about being embraced – rather than just being left alone.

I give Benjamin a copy of the *Equity Foundation Statement* and ask him how this compares with the *Safe Schools Foundation Statement* in terms of what goes on at his school. "Yeah, this is more like it. The Equity one has more to do with safety for us than the safety one." Benjamin believes his school could do a better job with social consciousness, which he perceives is achieved at Coyt to a higher degree than at his own school: "Our school is pretty damned good, but Coyt probably does more. Coyt probably doesn't even use this document much because they have their *own* – it's framed in their front door, you'll see it when you get there." Benjamin has drawn my attention to a portion of the *Equity Foundation Statement* that he tells me captures his school's overall philosophy with regard to school safety: "[Schools] must also clearly demonstrate respect for human rights and social justice and promote the values needed to develop responsible members of a democratic society."[8] When I ask Benjamin in what ways his school is trying to be more socially active, he impresses me with the breadth of what the students and teachers in his school are doing:

> We actually are a pretty socially active school right now. We do
> a lot of fundraising for charity. A fashion show just went by on
> Thursday – I basically spearheaded it, really – and we raised over
> five hundred bucks for AIDS charities. We have an active boycott
> against Coca Cola because of their union practices in South

America. Most recently, we don't like Wal-Mart. Christmastime
we do these huge bags for women's shelters. That's something I'm
big into. Even though every single person doesn't participate, the
fact that we do these things sets a tone for the culture here and
brings some sense of goals outside of academia, if you will. But
dress codes and lanyards and rules about how to behave? No, no,
no. Not ever.

Benjamin admits that the level of commitment of students toward these
kinds of endeavours "changes every semester," but he assures me that, as
far as he knows, "there's always something going on." He explains that "it
depends on the students and the teachers, but it's pretty cool. We have zero
violence because we have zero hate. It's really a culture that makes queers,
everybody, safe and sound, so we can think outside the school."

Delores is a teacher at Benjamin and Lazy Daisy's school. From her, I
obtain a copy of the course outline for gay and lesbian studies. The course is
not being taught the semester I am visiting, "but we do it every year," she
assures me. The course covers movies, literature, poetry, and media, and it
includes queer artists, perspectives, and history. I ask her who takes the
course. Her answer: "Anybody who wants to." I speak with Alex, a Grade 12
student, about his opinion of the benefits of the course:

> You know, it's a tough thing to say. To some extent, yes, it's good.
> A friend of mine is in TEACH, Teens Educating and Confronting
> Homophobia [a Planned Parenthood initiative that engages
> students to provide anti-oppression peer education combating
> transphobia and homophobia in Toronto-area high schools], and
> he goes into high schools to do anti-homophobia work. And he's
> working really hard. And one of the arguments that he uses in
> his work is that the level of homophobia in schools is completely
> unacceptable. It's on a level that would be unacceptable if we were
> talking about any other form of discrimination, including race. So
> to some extent, yeah, if students had better working knowledge of
> what queer discrimination looked like, then maybe there could be
> some strategies like this course to respond to it ... I remember at
> my other school, they had Black History Month, although there
> were very few black students in my school.
>   The only other example would have been students taking
> initiative themselves and actually doing independent studies, or

FIGURE 2
Gay and Lesbian Studies Course Outline, Burton School

Course Description: This course will focus on gay, lesbian, bisexual, trans-gendered and transsexual issues. These include position in society in the past and present, contributions to humanity historically and now, the fight for equity and contemporary issues of importance. We will investigate and discuss concepts of gender and gender identity, sexual preference and sexual expression in the context of patriarchy and its values, which permeate our culture. Health and body image issues will be explored as well as the lives of individual gay, lesbian, bisexual and transgendered people who have appeared in history.

Units

Unit 1   Introduction

Definitions	Gender	Socialization
Education	Media Portrayals	

Unit 2   Biography
GBLT people in history, politics, science, the arts and literature.

Unit 3   Political History
Homophile Movement, Gay Liberation, Queen Nation
The Law and Sexual Orientation

Unit 4   Health

Body Image	Health	Sexuality
Spirituality		

Unit 5   Contemporary Issues

Gay Pride Parade	Homophobia	AIDS

Unit 6   Literature, Arts and Entertainment

Methods	Lectures	Films
Speakers	Seminars	Group Work
Film, short stories and novels by GBLT		

Student Requirements: Each student will be required to write an evaluation once a week which records intellectual and emotional awareness with respect to the previous week's course content.

Assignments	Tests	Exam
Presentation of a biography	Independent Study – Essay and Seminar	

Evaluation:

Group Work, Class participation, Attendance, Presentations	30
Tests and Assignments	15
Journal	15
Independent Study (Essay and Seminar)	20
Exam	20

70 percent of the evaluation is based on course work and 30 percent is cumulative (Exam and 50 percent of ISU)

whatnot, which happened several times. So a whole course sounds great. I love it. But I just wish it was at the school I came from, because they need it more.

The course outline for gay and lesbian studies indicates that one of the goals of the course is to emphasize "the fight for equity" by queers and the contributions of queers to history. I find out later from one of the teachers of the course that one of the course's ideas is to include content that will be beneficial to all students by introducing the concept that gender and sexuality are culturally influenced and constructed. Lazy Daisy takes her time looking over the outline before speaking about the course. She explains that the outline reflects content and themes that are similar to what she experienced when she took the course:

> Yeah, this is all really cool. I was talking to my brother about whether he thought gay and lesbian studies should be in schools. And I was like, "Honestly, I think that the people who take the course aren't the people who need it, and it should be in the curriculum." And he's like, "Oh, well, why do I need to learn about that, you know? I'm not gay." And I'm like, "That's not the point." There just has to be general acceptance, like lessons taught early on to students, to just learn to treat everybody equally, and we need to have this kind of course for later on. I don't know, it should be taught really early on. It makes a difference to how people feel in general about queers, I think.
>
> [Coyt] has a much larger population than us and a different kind of environment, and they have a bigger budget than we do, basically. But we have our own things. We don't have the large events they do, but we have our own things. [Burton School] is the best school I've ever been to. It's very accepting. Even with gay guys like Alex and Benjamin, the straight guys will joke around with them. We even have an out teacher who has a partner. I think courses like this make that possible. It just sends a message, you know. Oh, I just love my school.

Since the early 1980s, research grounded in life stories, biographies, narratives, oral histories, subjectivity, and the telling of tales has become widespread within the social sciences, particularly among historians, feminists, and studies of youth in school. To achieve the best possible stories and narratives, it is helpful to understand that individuals grasp their lives in a narrative way and that narrative is "the fundamental scheme for linking individual human actions and events into interrelated aspects of an understandable composite."[9] This seems particularly true of the shared way students in high school (as well as graduates) look upon and shape stories about their years in high school from their particular position within the school. Dorothy Smith and Patricia Hill Collins have theorized about the slant of personal narratives in their explanations of standpoint theory, or "situated knowledge." A standpoint is a view of a particular segment of a culture that corresponds to an individual's unique perception of it.[10] The theoretical foundation of standpoint theory is to understand a culture from an individual's unique perspective within a social site.[11] A standpoint is a perspective from which the world is viewed by members of a particular group. Knowledge produced from such a standpoint represents a moment in time.

Depending on the cultural context, high school divides naturally into chapters, Grades 9, 10, 11, and 12. Although there may be little agreement as to what narrative structures from these various standpoints should look like, narrative structures of any shape or description allow individuals to converse about their experience.[12] Thus a core concern of a book like this one is to find and develop modes of representing lives and data, such as interviews and guided conversations, that allow for an exploration of ideas outside of conventional legal analysis. The purpose of pursuing a new mode of telling is to find a more creative method of delivering these voices, not to verify or to validate the stories or voices heard in this book. In this way, it is hoped that the presentation of the narratives will be enriched by the detail of these lives and, collaterally, underscore the historicity of the moment in time in which the stories are told and the experiences lived. Intrinsic to this method has been recognizing the unique place that documents of life occupy in these narratives. Accordingly, one of the most treasured documents of life I collected in my time in classrooms was the print given to me by Daisy (see Figure 1 on p. 48).

"Your print is still wet," Daisy tells me. "So you can't put it in this envelope yet. Actually, I made you two in case you fuck one of them up." I thank Daisy for the print, and the spare, and point out that artists usually sign their work. "But you can't use your real name," I add. She brightens: "Can I choose my own phoney name?" She writes "Lazy Daisy" on both prints. "And can you call me that in your paper?" I assure her – as though she needs reassurance – that she is in charge of naming her identity on all counts. "Elmer the Safety Elephant is whack," she announces. Lazy Daisy laughs and is already engaged in conversation with another student as she leaves the room. Without looking up, I understand that she has said "goodbye." I am out of her life. Like so many of the students I have met, I wish I could stay in touch with her, but I leave Burton School realizing, again, that this is not part of the deal.

Sylvia Avenue Collegiate and Vocational School: Control

At the end of my first day at Sylvia Avenue, Sharon Dominick walks me to the front door. "This is certainly out of your way, Sharon, you really don't have to do that." Sharon assures me that she wants to make sure I know the way out of the school and do not get lost: "I don't want the students to think you don't know where you're going. I just want to make sure you get on your way, okay." I thank her, tell her I will see her again tomorrow, and walk out of the front entrance of Sylvia Avenue. I walk slowly around the building to take some photographs. I take photos at every school I visit. I prefer to take pictures when students are not around, but sometimes this is not possible. I take a few shots and head down the tree-lined streets that are a direct route to the subway. Thirty yards out the front door of the school, I pass a group of male students I have not seen but who have, evidently, seen me. I judge that they are talking about me, pointing toward me. Certainly, they are all looking my way. One of them yells out, "Hey, white boy, you a fag?"

The schooling experience at Sylvia Avenue is very different from that at Burton School. The first thing you notice is the sheer size of Sylvia Avenue – almost 1,000 students. Only a few hundred students attend Burton School. There are other differences. At Burton School, the walls are still covered with posters announcing last week's fashion show in support of Fashion Cares, an AIDS charity. Pamphlets lying around the hallways, on book-shelves in the main office, and in classrooms deal with safer sex, the Rainbow coalition, and career choices. I find a few flyers announcing a dance. At Sylvia Avenue, a twenty yard walk away from Daisy's art class, an entirely different set of handbooks is available in the guidance office.

Sharon Dominick was responsible for my admission not only to Sylvia Avenue but also to Burton School and Coyt. My admiration for her is un-limited. Long after my interviews had ended, I thought about her and the kind of work she is doing every day. She is the gold you hope to find in preparing this kind of book. On my first day at Sylvia Avenue, I met Sharon in the classroom where she teaches media and English. The walls of Sharon's classroom are almost entirely covered in images from the media – most of which address some form of sexism, homophobia, racism, or class oppression. Sharon is always trying to get her students to think about the interconnected issues of oppression by deconstructing the images, or "culture jamming" – the phrase Sharon uses to describe the process and illustrate the pervasiveness of what she is talking about.

On this day, Sharon has introduced her English class to the concept of a white-nonwhite binary opposition of race. She has divided the class into two groups, one composed of white students and the other of nonwhite students, and has asked them to consider a list of questions on the book they have just read, Harper Lee's *To Kill a Mockingbird* (1960), but also on broader themes of race. Later, they will come together as one group and compare answers, but for now she wants them to feel they are two distinct groups, one "white" and the other "nonwhite." As they are working loudly on the assignment – during which several arguments break out – Sharon returns to the side of the class where I am watching and sits next to me. "What are those tags they're all wearing?" I ask her.

"Lanyards. ID tags. A lot of the students miss classes because of those lanyards. If they forget to wear them or don't have them with them, they're not allowed in the building."

"Even if you know who they are and they're in your class?" I ask her.

"That's right. You should talk with Melanie, one of the teachers here. She's even more opinionated than I am about the lanyards."

"I can't help notice your walls. Are most of the classrooms like this?"

"Check out the rest of the school," Sharon advises me.

Sharon told me about a former student of hers named Jason. Two years ago, one of Sharon's students called Jason a "fucking faggot" in class. The student who shouted these words at him was a Muslim girl. In Sharon's words, Jason "stood up to her" and called her a "bitch." Sharon told me, "So obviously, he wanted her to feel the sting of words. And what was the response of the administration here? They encouraged Jason to switch schools. They were both suspended, and basically, the administration forced him to go to another school eventually." Sharon was angry telling me the story even though it had occurred some time ago. She wrote a letter of protest to the administration. As Sharon explained to me, "That girl's statement was unmotivated hate speech. What Jason said, he said defending himself. You don't have the same expectations when people react because they are being attacked."

The administration responded by instituting a Gay-Straight Alliance (GSA) – but for teachers only. I was sure I had misheard. "For teachers? Only?" Sharon nodded.

It was for teacher training, but it was painful and I couldn't take it
for very long. I think it was a liability thing or they wouldn't have
done it. The attitude was: "We're providing training, what more
can we do?" Teachers went to it, but nobody cared. Nobody wanted
to be there. I heard homophobic comments the entire time I was
there. One of the teachers there said about Jason, "I don't have any
problems with those kinds of people, but what does he expect
when he's flaunting it?" Mercifully, the whole group died.

Following the demise of the teacher-only GSA, Sharon and Melanie Bhatia,
a teacher I would soon meet, decided to start a Student League for Social
Justice. Sharon explained, "That's the sort of thing they do at Burton School
or Coyt all the time, and I thought we should do it here, where it could
really do some good. But it didn't last long. The administration didn't like
it." Looking around at the photos, music lyrics, and images on her wall, I
said to her: "Well, your classroom is the kind of room the students will remember years from now." Sharon smiled at this, thinking for a moment. "At
this school, safety is framed as an issue of control, not equity. Security
guards, surveillance cameras, always talking about crime and the dress
code. There's a toxic environment at this school. It's not safe for students." I
asked her what this school was like for queer students. Sharon's answer was
immediate:

> It's not a safe school because teachers don't challenge homophobia.
> The whole 'it's so gay' thing. The use of the word 'fag' by students
> – by teachers! I tell the students that using those words threatens
> the security of gay kids, makes them and me feel threatened. They
> don't get it because that's not part of the message of what it means
> to be secure or safe around here.

There are two security guards at Sylvia Avenue. When I met Melanie later
in the week, she told me that she thought the security guards were abusive
to the students. Melanie is originally from "the Islands." Entering teaching
in 1981, she taught in High Prairie "with the Native kids" for less than a year
before returning to school to study theology. When Melanie spoke, she was
focused and almost never used contractions. Her sentences had a formal
construction, although she was relaxed, friendly, and informal. She seemed
to understand the interviewer's need for full sentences. She spoke easily in
highly quotable sentences when I asked her to describe the school. In 1988

she had joined the Toronto Board of Education. Before coming to Sylvia Avenue, Melanie taught at Bloor Collegiate. When Melanie first came to Sylvia Avenue, she regarded the school as a "safety net," a "safe place" for visible-minority students and students from low-income families who had been tossed out by other schools. No longer holding this view of her school, Melanie now viewed Sylvia Avenue and other schools with significant visible-minority populations as places that were decidedly unsafe. She blamed the changes made under the government of Ontario premier Mike Harris, particularly the introduction of the *Safe Schools Act:*

> I have noticed that this school uses the *Safe Schools Act* to sort
> of weed out certain groups of students. So now the school has a
> larger number of gifted kids, academic kids. There is still a large
> number of "special ed." kids, but quite a few of them are Anglo or
> sort of white kids who do not necessarily come from family
> housing, from low income. So they are the kids who maybe were
> not allowed to go to one of the more desirable schools, so they
> come here for the "special ed." program. But make no mistake: we
> still have a large number of visible minorities who live in metro
> housing projects.

Melanie told me that she had given a number of interviews about her school. She had strong opinions about how safety was pursued at this school. I did not have to ask many questions, but I did ask her how safety was expressed in daily practices. She said,

> In my opinion, with the dress code, lanyard, security guards, and
> surveillance cameras, the school is a prison. If this makes schools
> safe, then why isn't it implemented in all the schools in Toronto?
> But it is not. These rules only operate in certain schools, our
> school, with large minority populations. The message is clear.
> These schools have dangerous kids.

This message was articulated all around the school, even as you entered the building. An enormous stone sign on the garbage-strewn lawn at the main entrance announced the name of the school, which was difficult to read because of all the graffiti. No one removed the predominantly red painted graffiti that covered the sign during the time I spent there. In the guidance office and in the main office, where students guilty of "offensive behaviours" waited

to meet with the administration, there were piles of pamphlets quite different from what I saw at Burton School or what I would subsequently find at
Coyt. At these two schools, posters and pamphlets were geared toward university, study abroad, issues of equity, and even social justice – like Benjamin's
fashion show or Daisy's self-made "Queer Safety" art. Sylvia Avenue was
littered with posters and handouts that seemed grounded in fear, not in
achievement or in equity and social justice.

Fear infused the school for another reason. Six months before I arrived,
a shooting in downtown Toronto commanded intense media attention
throughout the city and across Canada. Jane Creba, a fifteen-year-old student, was killed near the intersection of Yonge and Dundas on the day after
Christmas. "The Boxing Day Shooting" – or alternatively the "Jane Creba
Shooting," as the incident came to be referred to in the media – involved
several black youths and adult males who were subsequently charged in the
shootings, one of whom, a minor, was a student at Sylvia Avenue. Unidenti-
fied in the media because of his age, he was one of Melanie's students. A
month before this shooting, another incident involving guns had grabbed
the headlines of Toronto's newspapers when three brothers were shot on
15 November 2005, one fatally. Melanie informed me that one of the
brothers was also one of her students:

> I know one of the boys and he was a very kind and nice, good kid.
> However, what is happening, the kids I think are keeping their
> anger inside at how they're being treated, having their identities
> taken away, while they're at school. And slowly the school itself
> is turning them into criminals.
>
> The students lose respect and confidence in the adults and in
> the teachers and in the administration. And often, when they're
> always being targeted, even their parents start to feel that they're
> bad kids.

Melanie and I talked a long time about what she described as "the socially
constructed dangers at Sylvia Avenue." Part of our conversations dealt with
issues of "self-fulfilling prophecies" associated with visible-minority students. Melanie's frustration derived in large part from how the self-fulfilling
prophecy played out with respect to black male students. Treated as innate-
ly dangerous and low-achieving, "even though they are not," these students
"internalize this school's treatment until they break." For Melanie, the actors
who "formulate and implement safety protocols within this school create a

narrative that practically guarantees that result." Melanie explained how she viewed the cultural trajectory of these students:

> These kids are always being targeted from the minute they enter the school, and then they have to look for new families. This is the way they decide to get their power through gangs or guns. If they cannot get [acceptance] and feel empowered in the school itself, then they just give up and they go for anything that represents power to them.
>
> And unfortunately, today, it's violence and gangs and guns. And I really feel that our school has contributed in turning a lot of our students, black males, into violent young men.

I asked Melanie whether Sylvia Avenue was a violent school – whether there had been any recent incidents of violence inside the school – and the question seemed to pain her. After a moment, she took a deep breath and explained,

> The truth is it's ongoing. A lot of things cause the kids to lose their temper. If they're just walking along the hallway, the security guard might just stop and say, "Show me your lanyard. Where's your ID?" And the fact that the kids have to take it out to show it or put it around their neck, and even the tone of voice that the guards use to ask them to produce their ID, I think a lot of the kids feel disrespected, and some of them lose their temper and ... so, it's ongoing. And then, of course, the school responds to these incidents by removing the student rather than examining its own role in creating this incident or, in fact, the general climate of unsafety when the school is supposed to be doing just the opposite and making the school a safe place.
>
> Unfortunately, a simple thing like the security guard pulling a kid out of the lunch line can aggravate the situation. These kids, at that time, could look or appear to be violent and aggressive, and from there it could turn into a worse situation. So the first thing the kids see is these security guards that represent this police-like power of the state. So I think it starts from that, and it goes on in a more, how would you say, a civilized way, once the administration gets involved. But by then, it's inevitable what the result is going to be.

But I think the way it starts is not a civilized way. It starts with
these rules forcing this and forcing that, and this one person has
power, and the school is controlling the kids. And I think that is
what happens in a lot of the tech schools. The visible-minority
students and teachers often feel powerless. Violence in the school,
it's ongoing.

Sharon introduced me to two of her English students, Barry and Louise.
She told me that Barry had written a personal piece for English class identifying his "ideal partner" and had indicated that his ideal partner would be a
male. Louise, the student who had been identified to me as "questioning,"
was far more guarded in her answers to any questions I asked her. Sharon
had given me some background information about Louise, but when I spoke
with Louise, she gave me different information. Both Barry and Louise had
heard of the *Equity Foundation Statement* in Sharon's English class. There
had been no mention of equity, as far as they are aware, from the administration in any context. "Just lanyards," Barry responded with a grin. "They
talk a lot about lanyards."

"I have something to show you." Sharon was the first person to show me
the "Grid." She was the only teacher I met who had all of the TDSB safety
and equity documents, which she kept in a binder. No one had given her
these documents; she had hunted for them. The "Grid" is properly called the
"Consequences of Inappropriate Student Behaviour Charts." Sharon told
me this was "probably the only document of the bunch in this binder that is
in every vice-principal's office." Everyone I spoke with was familiar with the
"Grid" – the TDSB document listing the specific measures principals were
required to implement in response to unbecoming student conduct. Sharon
showed me all of her equity documents. "This school doesn't emphasize
equity as much as they do the 'Grid.' It's handy, huh? The VPs can tape it
right on their desks for reference." Sharon offered her view on "this school's"
refusal to conceptualize safety in terms of doing equity:

> There's an intelligence and creative freedom at other schools, but
> here it's a police mentality focusing on getting rid of the so-called
> dangerous students. Academically, the focus is on content, but I
> treat them all like they're going to university.
>
> As teachers, we should come to the table prepared for equity. If
> the students here go into Burton School or Coyt, they're suspended.

The students in Burton School and Coyt are scared of our students.
They don't come here.

It is clear that Sharon conducted herself and her classroom in opposition
to the general pattern of enforcement around her. Sharon Dominick was
viewed by the students as a person of some leadership in the school –
because she is white. Sharon and Melanie, however, believed the real power
in the school was held by the male physical-education and "tech"-department
teachers, who together formed Sylvia Avenue's Safe School Committee and
Dress Code Committee. In their view, the power was used to control students, not to make school space safer. Melanie attributed the undisguised
and widespread use of controlling power to the *Safe Schools Act:*

> It all comes back to the *Safe Schools Act,* which has allowed the
> school to make rules and regulations that would "make the school
> safer." The legislation means they do not even have to hide or be
> subtle about it. And this included allowing the principals and
> teachers to be able to suspend and expel students. Now, this is a
> very heavy thing, to get rid of students, but they do it under this
> whole umbrella of making the school safe for students. And that's
> how it started this acquisition of power.
>
> Each school is able to have a Safe School Committee and a Dress
> Code Committee. Yes, because the board allows them to have these
> suspension and expulsion policies. These are very powerful groups
> because they really do make the rules. Nobody really wants to go
> against their rules. Once the committee votes on these regulations,
> it passes. I call them the "power committees."

Melanie understood who occupied leadership positions in the school and
who did not. She offered a calm assessment of her own role in the school,
describing herself as "a colonized person." She was well aware of the difference that race made in being listened to and sought out in the first place by
students looking for support, particularly if the student was a minority
student:

> I know for myself, the students see that I am one of the unimportant
> visible-minority teachers in the school. They know that if they
> need help, they have to look to the white teachers who are either

in the tech department or who are closer to the administration.
And that's the only way they can get help.

I, as a visible-minority teacher, know this as well. So when my
students come for help, I have to look around for a white teacher
to tell them the problem the student has in order for them to get
help. So the kids know that there's a difference of power. And when
you're white, you're empowered; when you are of colour, you have
no power.

I was aware that, until two years ago, Sylvia Avenue had had a white principal. The principal is now a black male. I wondered whether this made any
difference in the school. Melanie told me that when the new principal arrived, he "opened up" the "power committees" and that, at this time, she
indicated her interest in contributing to both the Safe School Committee
and the Dress Code Committee. She joined both but felt her input was ignored. Melanie recognized that the two "power committees" were trying to
"shape the identity of our students." The rules developed to foster a safe
school environment seemed aimed solely at black students and "most of
what the school was concerned with was controlling who they were – and
the 'Grid.'" One of the first things the school did was to implement a "hat
policy." Melanie told me that "students were not allowed to cover their
heads – no hats or head coverings of any kind." Sharon, Melanie, and the
two students with whom I spoke, Barry and Louise, understood this rule to
be directed at keeping students' faces visible for the two security guards
who patrolled the school's corridors and cafeteria, as well as for the cameras. No hoods, no "do rags," no hats. Girls were told they could not use
scarves or barrettes to manage their hair. Melanie talked about the policy:

> When I went there to the Safe School Committee – this is when
> I first discovered what they really do – that they make motions
> and rules that would control the kids, who they are, and govern
> them. I brought up the point that black students, black people
> have [a] different texture of hair. Their hair is very wiry, very curly,
> and it stands up. It's not easy to be just laid out flat like maybe
> [the hair of] the Asian or white kids. And maybe the students tie
> their hair in scarves or do it, or whatever they do, to hold their
> hair back. If they don't do this, they either have to straighten it,
> they have to tie it up, part it up. They have to spend money to fix
> their hair if it's not shaved off or cut off short.

At that time, the staff, the committee said in a staff meeting,
"Well that might teach the black kids to wash their hair before
they come to school, and maybe then it would lie down." But I
don't think they realize that their hair is very different from ours,
right, when they crack down on it.

In Melanie's view, the "crackdown" on hair – and the implementation of
other security measures in the name of school safety – was really a crackdown on the identities of visible-minority students, particularly black students, primarily black male students. The *Safe Schools Act* was being used to
materially and symbolically reconfigure the composition of students at
Sylvia Avenue and at other schools. The rules restructured the school in one
of two ways, either by eliminating black students from the school's population or by reconstructing the pupils who remained as "white." In this sense,
the dress code, for example, could be read as a cultural device reinforcing
dominant social relations and restricting the cultural identities produced.

Targeting visible-minority students has had a corresponding and inevitable chilling effect on the environment of the school for sexual-minority
students. Both Sharon and Melanie told me that sexual-minority students
do not come out at Sylvia Avenue. "Sexual-minority students are not on the
administration's radar, and they know it," Melanie told me.

I am aware of one girl that tried to come out. I think when they
do want to come out, they get bullied and picked on. They transfer
to Coyt as soon as they are in Grade 11. So as far as I'm concerned,
kids would be afraid to come out here if they're gay and lesbian
because nobody respects anybody here. It's a whole cycle of
control of some, neglect of others.

What Melanie and Sharon objected to was the general climate of "safety as
control," which actually led to the very problems the Safe School Committee
had intended to target and eliminate. In particular, they underscored the
summary way that students, who were the targeted victims of this control,
rebelled against it and then were removed from the school for doing so.
They complained about the complete refusal of the school to conceptualize
safety in terms of doing equity, an approach they believed was the only way
to create safe schools for sexual-minority students as well as for visible-
minority students and others. When, in response, Sharon and Melanie

formed the Student League for Social Justice, they were shut down. Melanie recalled the way that the safe-school legislation was first used to initiate this cycle.

The first stage in Sylvia Avenue's dress code was to include coats among the list of items students could not wear once they entered the school. The proposal originated with the tech department on the grounds that students could be hiding drugs and knives in their coats. As a result, students were compelled to remove coats when they entered the school and were not permitted to wear them in classrooms. Later on, the committee decided to include backpacks, banning them from being worn or carried into classrooms. "So now they have to keep all their things in their locker, which is hard to do," Melanie explained. Having decided to articulate a hat policy, a coat policy, and a backpack policy, the Safe School Committee then decided that, if students were going to house their belongings in lockers, the committee should have access to the lockers, so it imposed an additional rule that required students to purchase locks from the school. Melanie told me, "If they did not buy it from the school, they would cut the kids' locks. I think the school had the numbers of every lock. So they could open it at random and search the lockers of their kids." Failing to comply with any of these rules resulted in suspension from the school "or some other form of punishment." The most recent addition to the dress code – up for discussion at Sylvia Avenue when I was there – was whether to introduce a school uniform consisting of a white shirt and dark, tight pants for boys and dark pants or a skirt for girls. Melanie gave me her view of this proposed policy:

> They were literally wiping away all the black kids' cultural influences
> that made them who they were. It was removing their identity. It
> was like they weren't allowing the kids to be black. They had to try
> to be white, by dressing and straightening their hair and doing
> things that looked more like the white culture. And if you had a
> gay kid, who might want to shake things up a bit in terms of what
> they wore, that would not be allowed here either. Of course, in this
> school, I think most gay kids would be afraid to transgress.

The school banned the boys' practice of leaving underwear visible above the waistband of jeans. Melanie told me, "So now the boys have to wear tight pants. I think they were trying to remove the fact that the kids are different – they did not want the black kids to look like the hip hop culture."

The regulation with which Melanie took greatest offence was, undoubt-edly, that respecting the lanyard. She felt that lanyards were like "dog tags" and interfered with the ability of students to acquire an education. For her, lanyards were the most effective control mechanism used by the adminis-tration: "A lot of kids, they have gaps in their education because they're skip-ping school. And why do they skip? Because they don't have the lanyard and they can't come in." I had heard from several students and teachers at Sylvia Avenue that students constantly lost their lanyards. If they were caught by the security guards without a lanyard, they were suspended. "Sometimes it's a day; sometimes they just can't come back unless they buy a lanyard. So strictly speaking, without these ID cards, they can do nothing in the school. No classes. No sports. It's policing; it's not a safety issue."

Melanie told me that the administration policed classrooms, at random, actually bringing classes to a halt in order to ask teachers for their own lan-yards or to ask the students, randomly, to produce them. "If they're not wearing ID, the teachers are told off, and they have to get one. And threat-ened for their job. And the students again are removed from their classes, so it stops the classroom teaching right there, the ability to educate our students."

If the lanyard was intended to distinguish strangers from members of the school, how was such "policing" justified? Melanie told me she won-dered the same thing and had asked the administration this question, to no avail. "In the classroom, the kids often say the teacher knows who they are. The students are sitting in the classroom. Why are they coming into the classroom to check if we're strangers when we're sitting in the classroom listening to our teacher? The administration has a larger agenda." In Sharon and Melanie's view, the students who are targeted for such "policing" are often visible-minority students, usually black. Summing up, Melanie con-cluded, "So I think the whole idea of safety and controlling who the stu-dents are, they sort of blurred that whole thing. And gay kids, not part of that agenda."

Barry is one of Sharon's favourite students. He is a small, always smiling, fifteen-year-old Asian boy. Only when he moves across the classroom do you have any sense of the exaggerated movements of the television character on whom Barry has obviously patterned his physical gestures: Jack McFarland from *Will and Grace*. Sharon has tipped me off in advance. Sharon smiles every time Barry is in her classroom – it is obvious he is a favourite. Barry talks quietly about being verbally abused at his school. He cannot bring himself to use words like "fag" or "queer," so I write the words down on a piece of paper, and he looks at me and nods, "Yes, those were the words. Especially that one," he says, pointing to "fag."

Barry told me that Sylvia Avenue was "a school of rejects. It's where everybody goes when they don't really know where to go or don't really like the other schools," he said.

"Why do you come here?" I asked him. "Do you have a choice?"

"Yes. I could go to another school, but my friends are here. I come here to be with my friends." I asked whether this was a safe school for queer students. "No. Gay students are kind of ignored. They don't have the cameras for gay students." I could see Barry was thinking about his answer, then he added, "Well, the administration ignores gay students, the students don't. You feel like you've got to stay in line. If you don't, well, who can you count on to look after you then? You only really feel safe in Miss Dominick's class. It's a different world in there."

Sharon and I have returned from the cafeteria. Lots of students come to Sharon's class during lunch because she will let them use the computer. Sharon explains to me that the students feel safer in her classroom than in the cafeteria or in the area outside the school. When class starts, without warning, Sharon introduces me to the class: "Everybody, I want you to meet Donn." I did not expect Sharon to introduce me to the class, although it makes sense and has happened before, so I am not sure why I am surprised. "Donn is interested in safe schools." I notice that Sharon does not mention sexual-minority students. "Donn is a student at Osgoode Hall, which is a law school. Some of you want to go to law school. Does anybody have any questions for Donn? Use your hands."

Several hands go up. "What do schools have to do with the law?" I am prepared for this question, as I have been asked this question before. I explain that schools were created by the law. I mention the *Education Act* and the *Safe Schools Act*. I talk about school boards, and I talk about policies and how the laws and policies set up the schools and now regulate them. I am surprised to find myself talking about informal laws, the ways that students regulate themselves almost as though they "had their own laws." The students are very interested in this angle, and we talk about it for a few minutes before I sit down.

Sharon says to the class, "Okay, let's discuss school safety. What are we told will keep us safe? You don't have to use hands." One student shouts, "Lanyards." Sharon writes "lanyard" on the board. Other answers produce a list that Sharon writes – effectively I think – vertically on the board:

* lanyard
* security guards
* police
* cameras
* rules

"What safe-school policies do we have?" Sharon asks. One student looks directly at me and yells out, "The law." There is general laughter, comments such as "you would know," and more laughter. Another student says, "The *Safe Schools Act.*"

Sharon moves to a different blackboard. "Okay, let's make another list. What are we told about equity?" There is absolute silence in the classroom. Sharon repeats the question. One student ventures, "Muslim prayer on Friday." Sharon writes down the one response on the board. She asks, "Anything else? Okay, then, what equity policies do we have?" A tall black male student, named Wayne, whom I notice never takes off his coat, says, "There is no equity. It's garbage." This gets the ball rolling, and several answers are shouted at once: "Dress code." "No hats." "No nothin'." "Black students are stopped more." If there are gay students in the classroom, they are silent. Certainly, none of the heterosexual students mention the needs of gay students. Sharon listens until there are no further suggestions for the list, and then she asks, "And is that equity?" Wayne answers again: "Here it is. Equity is shit."

Ian, another English teacher at Sylvia Avenue, came into the classroom later in the day when the students were working. Sharon introduced me to him. Ian stayed only a few minutes to talk with Sharon and then left. Sharon told me that Ian is gay and has had a partner for twenty-five years. I asked whether Ian was "out" to the students or to other teachers and whether there were any "out" teachers here. The answer was "no." "He tells his students he is married and that's all. He's so afraid of the students and the administration finding out." As Ian left the classroom, I saw that several of the students, including Wayne, mocked Ian with exaggerated "limp wrist" gestures and unrestrained grins and whispers.

One day when I was at Sylvia Avenue, I talked with Melanie in her classroom during a spare period. Students gathered in the room in the same way they did in Sharon's classroom. When I asked her whether the students were required to wear the lanyard in gym class, she yelled over to one of the students, "Do you have to wear the lanyard in 'phys ed.'?" No, they did not. "And in tech, I think. They wear an apron in tech." We sat at the back of the classroom. The walls of her classroom were bare. "I've stopped having the battles that Sharon's having with the administration. I prefer to operate under the radar." I showed her some pamphlets I had found around the school.

She flipped through them as she spoke. "'Your Record Doesn't End When You Turn 18.' I won't have this stuff in here. Such threats, eh? Stay in line now or you'll pay for it later." She sighed looking at the documents. "In a practical way, if there are no models for the kids to show them how important it is to respect differences, then they don't learn that. What does this tell them about who they are – and about who anybody is?" Melanie feared that the negativity instilled in some students as a result of how the school treated them could lead to intolerance of other students, particularly gay students. Melanie looked at every one of the flyers, posters, and pamphlets I had collected before speaking:

> In the English curriculum, if you look at it, it calls for all of these
> things, right? To teach the children the differences. But there's one
> thing you teach someone out of a book from words. And then
> practically, you show them a different example. So in one way, yes,
> the kids did programs on same-sex marriage and debates on it and
> so on – but the kids still, in practice, will go against it, with homo-
> sexuality, because politically, in their own lives, they know it's not
> the accepted thing. The same thing with equity. We study all kinds
> of things on equity in every curriculum and in every subject. But
> there's no equity in the school or in the classroom.

Tapping her finger on the booklet "Your Record Doesn't End When You Turn 18," she said, "So I think what we teach and what we practise are two different things."

Sylvia Avenue has a Dress Code Committee and a Safe School Committee, but it does not have an Equity Committee. Melanie explained:

> When I asked for one, it was a big deal. I asked in a staff meeting,
> I asked why not, and they said because the last principal did not
> have one, and the curriculum leaders did not think equity was an
> important enough issue on which to have a committee. And I
> called them on it because I said, "You have a paper committee in
> the school that deals with what to do with paper, but you don't
> have equity?" And many schools in Toronto do look at equity as

an important issue. Look at Coyt. Coyt is right there, I told them, as if they needed to be told. Why is it that our school, with so many different cultures, including gay kids, does not think equity is important?

As a result of the meeting, Sharon and Melanie attempted to form an Equity Committee, but none of the other teachers at Sylvia Avenue showed any willingness to join. Melanie said, "Nobody wanted to have any part or discussion about equity. So it was just left because I think teachers did not want to be harassed by other teachers, so they just stayed away from this whole idea of equity."

The emphasis on the organization and management of safety in terms of equity is absent at Sylvia Avenue. Notwithstanding that equity is taken very seriously at a number of TDSB schools and, in fact, is supposed to be taken seriously according to the *Equity Foundation Statement*, Sylvia Avenue has had a history of shying away from equity since the *Safe Schools Act* was enacted. Melanie noted,

> The board, as far as I know, for a long time stressed that schools should have equity programs, and they claim that their schools do; however, I don't find that at this school. We haven't had equity programs or an Equity Committee for awhile. I think when the Harris government came into power, equity became almost a bad word, an embarrassing word. The teachers and the administration came to understand equity was not politically correct, not under Harris. So they did not talk about equity. I think the *Safe Schools Act* itself threw the whole topic of equity out the window.

Trimble Collegiate Institute: Security

Lorna Gillespie and Sharon Dominick used to work together at Trimble Collegiate before Sharon voluntarily transferred to Sylvia Avenue. Lorna reflected on Sharon's decision to transfer: "I think she wanted to cut down on the amount of time she was commuting every day." Lorna also considered the result of Sharon's transfer: "Sylvia Avenue is an awful place. I wish Sharon would come back here. Sylvia Avenue is all about controlling the students. We're not that bad here, but we do focus on security more than equity." Trimble Collegiate is, in the words of each student I met, "a very multicultural" school, with high percentages of students of black, Asian, Muslim, and Russian descent.

Lorna told me that the high composition of multiracial students made it impossible for the administration to try to control identity "like they do at Sylvia Avenue," but at the same time, because of the racial composition of the school, "safety definitely means·security here." Trimble Collegiate is equipped with cameras in each hallway. Insofar as there is a dress code, the policy is not as strict as at some schools, certainly not as strict as Sylvia Avenue, but "hats are out." Each of the students I met with told me that there was one reason for the "no hats" policy: "So the cameras can see your face." Len is a seventeen-year-old gay student in Grade 12. He told me that there are "forty-four cameras watching the school, inside and out." When I asked him how he knew how many cameras there were, he laughed, "We all know."

The first day I met Len, he was wearing a pink lacrosse shirt and sunglasses. His hair, looking shiny and wet, was swept up to a severe point over the middle of his forehead. As he approached me in the hallway, which is where I first met him, he said "hello" and immediately commented on his appearance. "I dress like this – with the shades, the hair, and the expensive shoes – because I'm in Grade 12, because I'm old enough to get away with it. You can't in Grade 9 or even 11." Once we settled into a classroom to talk, I asked him about equity programs in the school, and he was quick to answer: "There is no equity here." Len conceded that the school celebrated Black History Month and Asian Awareness Month "but only because the board makes us, and then you never hear of it again the rest of the year." There is not, in his opinion, much other "critical race work" being done.

In addition to Len, I conducted formal interviews with four other gay or lesbian students. All were familiar with the *Equity Foundation Statement,* and all believed they were more aware of equity than "nonqueer" kids and even than visible-minority students. Len told me why:

> I think queer kids, particularly, understand the power of equity
> and what it can do, but that's the history of gays and lesbians in
> Ontario, isn't it? We've studied the history of the [Ontario] *Human
> Rights Code*[13] and getting sexual orientation included. Look at how
> that changed space. It allowed queers to fill up public space in a
> way they hadn't before. Same with the *Charter*[14] and same-sex
> marriage. So I think there's an awareness there.

They all articulated, in their own words, the same problematic of emphasizing security over equity. Schools that do so remain places where, for queer kids struggling with their identity, self-actualization is not encouraged or possible. For these students, and many others, this may be why safety is conceptualized in terms of equity or impediments to self-actualization. They perceived lack of self-actualization as the most constant threat to the integrity of their "queerness."

When I asked whether there was queer content in any of the courses at Trimble Collegiate, particularly sexual education, Len told me that only in Lorna's class was there any significant attempt to incorporate queer content. "'Sex ed.' is just reproduction and that's it." According to Len, he and another student attempted to establish the school's first Gay-Straight Alliance, but "the administration put the kibosh on it. It doesn't fit with their idea of safety for gays, the idea that lesbians and gay students need to find each other and themselves. Safety in numbers, safety in knowing who you are, so you can protect that. Safety is more than just making sure you don't get a kick in the nuts."

These students felt that the reluctance on the part of many schools to emphasize equity discouraged discussion of the cultural privilege that keeps alive the segregation and loneliness of queer teens in schools. It was in the context of discussions around this reluctance that the concept of resistance first emerged from the participants. The concept of resistance is used by critical-education theorists to explore opposition to categories of social privilege. The ways that sexual-minority students draw from their own set of experiences to develop an oppositional stance at a site where safety is read as security or control, but not equity, was notable at Trimble Collegiate. Resistance came from Lorna and the students, whereas at Sylvia Avenue the charge to influence the culture of the school was led by Sharon, not the students. At Trimble Collegiate, Lorna and a number of students repudiated silence, choosing to be heard in the face of forces that commanded silence. Discrimination and oppression by silence and invisibility – the general failure even to be contemplated – has a long history among sexual-minority persons. Lorna was continually "getting into hot water" with the administration over her attempts to push the borders of her school's conception of safety: "The question of how to make a school safe is not a matter of security alone. The question is one of support for queer kids and then celebrating queerness, but at the same time asking straight kids to ask questions, too. And the most important question is 'why do you think what you think?'" Lorna told me that every year, she plans a fieldtrip for her homeroom class. If possible, she prefers that these trips be connected in some way to equity. During the time I visited with her, she took students to an anti-homophobia conference in downtown Toronto at the St. Lawrence Market. Lorna wanted

FIGURE 3 (above and facing page)   Student-identity walls at Trimble Collegiate

to take the students on this trip "because they discussed gender identity and sexual orientation, so I thought okay, we've got to go. This would be good for the gay kids and the straight kids." The moderator conducted the panel in a very informal way. The panel included a gay man who was Tamil, a lesbian from Kenya, and a sixteen-year-old transgendered student whom Lorna thought "was incredibly brave and articulate. I thought it was amazing." In Lorna's view, this is the sort of exposure that all students need, but she was disappointed that a large number of heterosexual students who received parental approval for the trip failed to show.

On a day-to-day basis, Lorna battled the "confines of the administrative approach to safety" by means that often resulted in tussles with the administration – some of which caused the administration to take disciplinary action against her and required the intervention of the teachers' union. The walls of Lorna's classroom were awash with "graffiti," but unlike the urban scrawl outside the school that many high schools struggle to avoid, Lorna encouraged students to "take ownership of the school" by expressing themselves directly on her walls. "The problem is just that students do not have pride of ownership, pride of place. They find themselves in a space dominated by security measures. So I decided a few years ago to open things up." Lorna's approach brought her into direct conflict with the school's principal. Lorna saw a distinct difference between her school and Sharon's school, "where safety means controlling the students' identities." Acknowledging that the administration at Trimble Collegiate was "all about security and nothing about equity," Lorna wanted to ensure that student identities

remained uninhibited by the school's security concerns – hence the "student-identity walls." Lorna encouraged all students to "take ownership" but admitted she particularly encouraged sexual-minority students to "stake a claim" to the walls. "It's a way of resisting what's going on in other parts of the school," Len agreed.

When word of the "student-identity walls" and the "direct application" methods employed by the students to mark the walls (i.e., writing on the walls) spread to the principal's office, the principal ordered Lorna to stop giving the students permission to "deface" the school. The principal ordered that the "graffiti" be painted over with yellow paint. Lorna responded by filing a grievance against the principal, and for three years, while the grievance was being processed, the principal was not permitted to speak with Lorna. As a solution, the principal agreed to have the walls covered with a removable clear plastic sheet so that no actual painting occurred on the classroom walls. Lorna chuckled recounting the story to me:

> So now the room is covered in artwork that is actually on clear
> plastic that's affixed to the wall, which could be removed, but after
> a while, even that she objected to. Her complaint was that this kind
> of artwork encouraged graffiti on the rest of the school. So back we
> went at it. So the deal I finally struck with her was that the plastic
> could stay, but if I saw anyone who was marking up the walls
> inappropriately in other parts of the school, then I would agree
> to report them to the office. But I would have done that anyway.

FIGURE 4 "Katie," by Katie, Trimble Collegiate

Lorna introduced me to Katie, one of her Grade 12 students. Katie had flair, a love of art, and a singular way of making her queer presence known. I was struck by the method she had fashioned not just to declare herself in Lorna's classroom but also to assert her identity more publicly. Katie had put her artwork up in school art displays at the front entrance of the school.

Employing a simple but understated technique, Katie's artistic scheme articulates a solitary, resistant voice among what she called the "heterosexist shouts of the crowd around me." Katie's artwork consists of her name, executed in the colours of the freedom rainbow, repeated over and over. "'I'm here and I'm queer,' as the saying goes," Katie said when she explained the purpose behind her eponymous art. "My name is Katie. And it's right next to the football trophies."

Elizabeth Coyt Alternative School: Social Justice

Visiting Coyt, you cannot help but come away wishing this had been your high school. It is difficult to imagine anyone not feeling this way. Despite its name, Coyt is not an alternative school, but it is different, born out of the vision of the founder for whom the school is named, Elizabeth Coyt. Unlike Burton School, Coyt offers a full range of high school grades, 9 through 12, for its 500 students. Like Burton School, Coyt physically borders Sylvia Avenue, and students from each of the schools are prohibited from trespassing on the other's property. Lazy Daisy speculated that this "no trespass" rule is really aimed at the students from Sylvia Avenue, and each of the students with whom I spoke at Coyt agreed. Carla explained, "We are technically not allowed in Sylvia Avenue, but it's more about Sylvia Avenue coming into our school – or going into Burton School. The idea is to keep the students from Sylvia Avenue out of Burton and Coyt."

There are numerous ways that equity can be put to work to promote safety in schools. Burton School and Coyt are models for these approaches. In a most striking way, Coyt conceives of safety not only in terms of equity but also, more proactively, in terms of safety as social justice. "Yeah, social justice," Carla fairly beams at me. She is proud of Coyt and happy to be here. I have just asked her how her school conceptualizes safety:

> We're all about being proactive here, and we think in terms of
> social justice, not just equity, which I think our school feels is
> more about acknowledging or appreciating diversity. It's an open-
> catchment school, so anyone across the city can go, but we all
> wear uniforms. We want to avoid all that stuff with brand labels
> – and it just takes that whole level of pressure out for being in a
> high school, so it is a high school that focuses on promoting equity
> and social justice, and it's a totally cool, comfortable environment.
> We refer to all our teachers by their first names, so it's a really
> friendly, really open environment.

Carla is a terrific informant. She is articulate, energetic, and happy to talk about her school. She seems to be happy generally and to be a very friendly, caring individual. Her blond hair is long and thick, and she strikes me more as a university student than a high school senior. Carla seems too old for high school, but she is not. About to graduate, Carla has attended Coyt throughout her four years of high school education. She is very familiar with the TDSB's *Safe Schools Foundation Statement* and *Equity Foundation Statement:* "Equity aims for the achievement of social justice: social justice is equity achieved. I think it's become so ingrained in the culture of the school, you almost take it for granted. It's just the way it is – probably in the way that at most schools, it's exactly the way it isn't."

Carla was in Grade 9 shortly after the introduction of the *Safe Schools Act,* of which she is very aware and wary: "We just do things differently here. It's a great school. Here, there's more emphasis on establishing a culture rather than [on] responding to what students do, but not doing anything else the rest of the time." Carla continually punctuates her conversation by telling me that Coyt is a "great" school. When I ask Carla what her favourite subject is, I am given some insight into why the school is special and why her conception of school safety looks to social justice:

> My favourite subject is probably the course I took last year, which
> was film and video expression. Basically, throughout the year we
> were given a video camera and told to go film different assignments,
> so it was really fun and creative – especially because I want to go
> into film. It's kind of what spurred me into it. So it was a different
> kind of course. A lot of them are, though. I decided to go around
> the city and video all the hetero stuff I could find to show how
> hetero-dominant our culture is, sort of to intervene and say, to
> anybody who would see my video, wait a minute here. You were
> talking about what makes schools safer for queer kids before –
> I think seeing that kind of video does.

The push to safety in many other schools in Ontario has been driven more by law and order interventions, epitomized in many Toronto schools by the reliance on the TDSB's "Grid." At the same time, defining bullying and responding to bullying as a violent incident perpetrated by a particular individual or group of individuals rids bullying of its cultural significance. Accordingly, many schools respond to the diverse sexualities of queer students, if at all, in reactive ways. The needs of queer students are considered only when a violent incident demands consideration of their needs, limiting this consideration to an appropriate "response." Of course, what the queer students (in this book) consistently argued was that there is no such thing as a homophobic moment of harassment but only inevitable consequences of being queer in a culture that makes no space for it. Coyt, however, actively intervenes in combating homophobia and celebrating and making space for different sexualities on many fronts.

The difference between what could be accomplished by an acknowledgment, even an appreciation, of diversity and what could be accomplished by a more expansive social-justice approach is a theme I heard expressed many times throughout my interviews, most notably from the people involved with human rights initiatives: Gabe Picard, Ellen Chambers-Picard, and Peter and Murray Corren. When I spoke with Peter and Murray Corren, they made the same distinction between diversity and social justice. In the Correns' settlement with the Ministry of Education in British Columbia, it was agreed that the ministry would produce a "very practical document" to provide teachers with lesson plans that included content dealing with equity across the curriculum. For example, the document would let teachers know how they could incorporate Aboriginal content into their curriculum. For this document, the Correns proposed the title "Making Space, Giving Voice: Integrating Social Justice across the Curriculum." Murray Corren explained to me, "We didn't want this word 'diversity' or 'equity' used. We want[ed] the words 'social justice' used. Appreciation and valuing diversity is not social justice – equity is a frame of mind that you need to have in order to do social justice."

"Doing social justice" is a theme that confronts you no matter where you are within the walls of Coyt. Coming through the front door of the school, you cannot help but notice the difference between the cultural artefacts on these walls and the bleak posters greeting you as you enter Sylvia Avenue. Inside the front door of Coyt, a plaque proclaims the founder's philosophy for the school:

> First of all, I hope that the school
> will be an exciting place of learning,
> where students will discover the
> joys and challenges of gaining
> knowledge and understanding.
> Then, I hope that the school
> will become a place for building

lasting friendships among
students, parents and teachers.
    And, finally I hope that the endeavours
being made in the school to build
knowledge and understanding will
extend out into the broader community
and that the community, in turn, will
enrich and support the goals and
dreams of the school.

The walls of the main floor are covered in a large mural depicting musical notes on sheet music that disappear into the distance. The mural is so long that I could not fit the length of it into the viewfinder of my camera. I wondered why it was there, what composition the notes were from, if any, and what they meant. No one I asked was able to tell me what the notes meant, but when I was leaving the school several weeks later, with a better appreciation of Coyt, an older teacher came to stand beside me and we looked at the mural together.

FIGURE 5 Wall at Elizabeth Coyt Alternative School

Next to the plaque enshrining the founding philosophy of the school is an Over the Rainbow–sponsored student-made poster for the Stephen Lewis Foundation for AIDS Education and Research. Each year Coyt hosts Unite, a multischool event organized by Over the Rainbow. Over the Rainbow is the driving force in the school. Even its name distinguishes this group from other Gay-Straight Alliances (GSAs). Carla told me,

> We have Over the Rainbow, which is a big, big group at our school, which basically says, "We're past 'Are you homophobic?' We're just getting on to 'Okay, we've accepted it. Now we'll deal with the issues and try and promote queerness within our school and, of course, the community.'"

Carla's girlfriend, Emma, is also in Grade 12 at Coyt. When I met them, they had been dating for over a year. Carla and Emma held hands whenever I met them at the school and sometimes kissed in the hallways. Neither would do so, however, outside the school or when they were near Sylvia Avenue. "Not safe to do that near Sylvia Avenue," Emma told me. "A guy and a girl threw a can of pop at us when we walked by there once, so we've never done it again." Emma agreed that Over the Rainbow was more than a "regular" GSA:

> We have Over the Rainbow but that's kind of a different sort of thing. Not that all GSAs are the same, but Over the Rainbow is not like any GSA I've ever heard of. For one thing, it's not about combating homophobia. That's just not there at this school. In fact, you definitely get a little marginalized if you are homophobic, so you learn very quickly to keep it to yourself. I really don't know of anyone who would say anything homophobic. And besides, Over the Rainbow is more like an entire student council or government. It really runs things here.

Emma told me that Over the Rainbow posters were put up all over the school for its events but that they would never be defaced. Her favourite Over the Rainbow poster read, "I'm straight but it might be a phase." "Another really good one," she told me, was "Why in this society are we more comfortable with two men holding guns than holding hands?" But all the students with whom I spoke agreed that Over the Rainbow's best-known achievement was Unite, an annual multimedia conference celebrating sexuality:

We do Unite every year, almost every year, which is a conference
that usually involves sexuality and art of many forms like film or
photography. And lots of schools come, but it's not open to the
public. Over the Rainbow really affects all parts of school life. We
didn't get to do it this year because two teachers who really do a
lot for it were away this year, but last year, we did. It was a TDSB-
wide thing. There were at least 500 people here. Unite is celebrating
sexuality in art. It's a fairly broad topic. There is queer content, but
it speaks to everybody. It is really cool and it was a lot of fun to
organize.

The notion of promoting equity as social justice – the difference between
equity and diversity, on the one hand, and social justice, on the other – was
an important theme that each informant at Coyt underscored without
prompting from me. Carla told me that "Over the Rainbow is about what
the school is about." Emma agreed: "Over the Rainbow is about sexuality
and gender issues and just letting people blossom. We're so past just acknowledging and tolerating differences." When I pressed Emma for details,
she said,

> We do tons of stuff. We have a policy of sexual harassment that's in
> there – this cannot be done, that cannot be done. We spent a little
> too long talking to the equity department at TDSB, talking about
> changing the "Mother and Father" on forms, just lots of stuff like
> that. Reshaping on paper how families have changed now, for
> instance. And, of course, we do tons of stuff for AIDS all the time.

Emma and Carla took me around the school to look at one of a number of
displays dealing with AIDS awareness and education.

When I asked whether there were "Positive Space" posters around the
school, Carla assured me there were but added, "That's the smallest thing we
do." I was reminded of Gabe in Thunder Bay and the administration's view
that its own proposal to settle his human rights complaint with a single
"Positive Space" sign was an enormous undertaking. I told Emma and Carla
about Gabe's story. Carla responded, "You can see how far schools have to
go, the range of responses that are possible to making safe space for queers.
In that case, it's just making excuses. If you compare that with what we do,
you can see what's really required."

When I asked Carla whether she had ever heard of any bullying or verbal harassment of queer students at Coyt, her answer was decisive: "Nope. I've had I think maybe two passing comments in the first years of high school, but that was outside the school, and there was one from students of another school nearby just in passing. Okay, it was Sylvia Avenue." I wondered whether the incoming students who arrived at Coyt to start Grade 9 were respectful of sexual diversity. Emma told me,

> Now that's a little bit different, especially the Grade 9 and 10 boys. Yes, I should mention that. They do call each other "fag" when they get here, but the seniors do smack them over the head, quite literally sometimes. Boys saying, "This project is so gay." The phrase "That's so gay" is also in there a lot with boys. Generally, if a student says that, someone turns on their heel and lectures them for about an hour.

At every school I visited, the students and teachers, males and females, acknowledged a difference between how gay boys and gay girls were regarded. Even with the apparent accomplishments of day-to-day life at Coyt, I wondered whether this disparity survived even there. Emma agreed that the more overt demands were directed at boys:

> I think boys and girls are both definitely being monitored by other students, but it's much more out there for boys. There was one incident where another school was here for an "improv" competition. We have a big improv team, so we held the improv semifinals at our school. We had one school verbally harass my friend Cal for being gay. He came into the room as he usually does and went, "Ta da!" and they kind of coughed under their breath and yelled out, "Hey look, it's a fag!" And everyone from our school just kind of went, "Excuse me?" So we all got up and, boy, were those students ever not happy because we turned around on them, and it was not a good thing.

I wondered how Coyt would respond to an incident of verbal or physical harassment. Emma explained, "It would probably be mediation, and the principal would probably talk to both parties separately and try to figure out what happened, and there would be some punishment. I believe physical harassment is a serious suspension at least, as far as I know on the 'Grid.' But really, I can't imagine that ever happening here."

Benjamin from Burton School had told me that as progressive as Burton School tried to be, there were no gay books in the library. At Coyt there were many. Carla told me that a group of students from Over the Rainbow had gone up and down the shelves in the library placing rainbow stickers on the spines of any books with queer content, by queer authors, or dealing with "queer theory" – a component of several courses on Coyt's curriculum. Carla told me, "We also have stickers for African studies, we have stickers for French studies, feminist studies, we've got a huge range, so we decided to do it for queer content, too." Emma remembered that "in the span of two months, I did queer theory in English, queer film in videography, and an essay on queer theory in English again."

Several months earlier, I had interviewed two transgendered students at two different TDSB high schools. When I asked Emma whether the climate of Coyt would be likely to accommodate a transgendered student, she said, "It would probably be noticed, especially since we're a small school and you see almost everyone in the halls, but I don't think it would be noticed negatively, necessarily, because we're generally very supportive of each other. The important thing is that we have a culture here that can make room for somebody like that." Emma reminded me of Over the Rainbow's influence: "Our kind of motto is 'It's assumed that we're over being homophobic. Let's move on to something bigger.'"

I asked to meet Cal, the student who was called a "fag" at the improv competition. Months later, as I listened to the digital recording of my first interview with him, I remembered the speed of his speech, his sense of humour, and his confidence. Emma and Carla adored Cal and were instrumental in setting up my interview with him. The students at Coyt struck me as carrying with them a secure sense of self, and Cal gave off the same energy. The first thing Cal wanted me to know was that his school was "great." The first thing I wanted to hear about was the incident at the improv semifinals, but I decided to let the subject come up on its own. I began by asking Cal to tell me why Coyt was "great," what made it special and different from other schools, particularly Burton School. He explained,

> It's really open. We are very liberal, and we try to include all
> different types of religion and cultures and sexualities. The
> teachers are really great. If you just need to talk or something,
> they're really willing to make some time in their schedule. They

just listen to whatever you need to say. And students are like that, too. It's the whole environment here. The upper-year students really notice the lower-year students, and I think if you're in Grade 9 or 10, you value that. That's a pretty important part of the school in my opinion.

There's about 500 or 600 students here, and we're in the same building as Burton School and Sylvia Avenue. And it's interesting because those are very different schools. I mean Burton School is more like us, but it's still quite different. So we don't usually do a lot of stuff together because we are so different.

I pressed for details, and the first subject Cal raised was Over the Rainbow:

We have a group called Over the Rainbow, which is not a GSA – it's a group that is very open in teaching about sexuality, but all over the school. You have to know about Over the Rainbow to understand our school.

And two years now, we've held Unite. We reach out to different schools in the TDSB, and we invite a couple students from each high school to come here. And we have a bunch of different queer artists and musicians, and also different speakers during the year who just come in and talk to students about different things. It doesn't have to be about actual sexuality but just doing art and making music and stuff. We didn't get to do Unite this year because one of our teachers who is key to it is out of the country.

When I asked Cal what would happen to a student at the school who had no interest in Over the Rainbow, he told me that there was no way to get away from Over the Rainbow, but he could not imagine that anyone would want to do that. Cal confirmed what Emma, Carla, and others had told me about Over the Rainbow's influence extending to the entire school. He spoke extensively about the school's "social activism":

We've got a Guatemala project, which is where we're working on helping out people in Guatemala. So they're selling coffee beans, and all the money goes to help people who are losing land because of deforestation. They're losing businesses and stuff. And we just have so many different groups. It's hard to just name all of them. We have an animal rights group. A group that works for AIDS

awareness and support for PWAs [people with AIDS]. We've got
a couple of those, in fact. We're quite into being aware of globalization and HIV/AIDS work.

In contrast to Sylvia Avenue, Coyt is not geared to intervening in problems after they occur or to controlling students' identities. Cal described
Coyt as a safe school for students in general and for sexual-minority students in particular:

> The school is about social justice on all fronts. Not just queer stuff,
> but there's certainly an emphasis on queer content – not just
> fighting homophobia but doing more than that, making spaces
> safe for queer kids when they show up in Grade 9 or transfer in. So
> I would say safety at this school is about being active and making
> this a space where problems just don't happen in the first place.

There is a school uniform at Coyt, and the students I met there did not seem
to mind wearing it. I had a difficult time discerning the requirements of the
dress policy. I did not see any American Eagle or Hollister or A&F T-shirts
in evidence, but the range of acceptable "dress" seemed broad. Cal gave me
the specifics:

> It just has to be any of the school colours, really, so white, hunter
> green, maroon, or navy blue. A button-up shirt or a rugby shirt is
> fine. Really any kind of shirt, so long as it's those colours and no
> brand names. And we just have to wear blue pants or a blue kilt or
> a skirt. Any kind of socks and any kind of shoes really. So that's
> probably why you're not seeing a school uniform per se.

I wondered whether Cal or any of the students felt that a school uniform or
dress code was an attempt to control student identity and whether there had
ever been a rebellion. If there could ever be a successful student rebellion
against a dress code, Coyt might be the place. Cal responded,

> Oh, no, because there's no sense that's the overall scheme of things
> here. Our dress policy is about doing something for equality, part
> of a social-justice approach, so when it's given to you that way, you
> don't feel you're being controlled. We're trying to eradicate social
> status with it.

> I know that in different schools you go to, it's very ... you have
> to have name-brand clothing to be cool. You have to have this and
> you have to have that. And our uniforms just kind of cut away
> from all that because you can't really wear that stuff. So it's just
> everyone is equal because everyone's wearing the same stuff. It's
> part of being equal.

I asked whether the administration, or anyone else, had ever suggested that there were security reasons for having a dress policy in place. Cal mused, "I guess there ... could be. I mean the teachers can figure out more easily if someone's not supposed to be in the school, if that person doesn't have a uniform. But it's not the primary thing. It's more equality."

I also asked Cal whether all students in all years embraced the school's underlying philosophies, and like Emma, he immediately mentioned the Grade 9 boys and the issue of dealing with masculinity. Just as Emma had told me about the seniors' takeover of sex ed. as a partial response to the needs of the younger students, Cal told me about another school project that had developed out of the same concerns. Cal's videography class was very instrumental in producing a school movie. A school movie, Cal explained, was like a school play "except that it's a movie." This year the movie, which was written, directed, and starred in by students in all years of the school, was called "Boys Beware." Cal told me, "It's a gay-themed piece dealing with masculinity and dealing with the issue of the incoming boys."

This was a theme that was raised at every school. Without exception, every student and teacher with whom I spoke told me – sometimes reluctantly, not wishing to contribute to a hierarchy of oppression – that gay boys have it toughest in schools because of straight boys. Carla had already brought up this subject and provided me with her assessment of the difference:

> Just because this society is so masculinist, it's a lot harder for boys
> to come out because they're worried about what their guy friends
> will think. Masculinity rules. Meanwhile, for girls, it's like, "Okay,
> good." Because girls are allowed to be sensitive and touchy. And
> for a lot of guys, they're interested in two girls being together, but
> not two boys together.

Cal's take on the distinction was similar:

I think straight men prefer seeing two women – they're okay with that because it's hot or whatever – two women having sex. Whereas two guys having sex is totally gross and disgusting in this culture. I know one or two people who are in Grade 9 who are just like, "It would be okay for lesbians, but it's not okay for gay boys." I'm like, "Why? What's the difference?" Obviously, that kind of cultural bias expresses itself in expected ways.

"Hegemonic masculinity" was an issue that the senior students of Coyt had clearly identified as a crucial element of addressing the safety of all queer students in schools.

When I asked Cal whether there were any spaces in the school where he felt safer or less safe than other spaces, he returned to the subject of Burton School and Sylvia Avenue:

I feel safe pretty much all over the school. Going into Sylvia Avenue is kind of a creepy thing. And our auditorium is half Sylvia Avenue, half ours. So going into that area, there's Sylvia Avenue students allowed to be there, of course. So it's kind of weird going there. We can use their gym in the morning, but I think it's kind of scary going into Sylvia Avenue, especially for gay guys.

We don't do a lot with Burton School. I don't actually know a lot about Burton, either, but it's not scary. When I said I was going to come here, my mum was worried about Sylvia Avenue. Burton we didn't really question.

I've never had a problem with anyone from Sylvia Avenue. They've never harassed me or anything, but I've heard stories. I don't want to judge.

Throughout these interviews, I was impressed with the degree to which the students tried not to generalize or to judge others.

Cal made me laugh when we discussed school policies and governing legislation. "Policies? I don't know if we have any. We're very significant with our own way," he joked. I showed him the TDSB's *Equity Foundation Statement* and *Safe Schools Foundation Statement*, but he chose not to look at either one: "We work very differently than other schools. So it might be we're more different from other schools than, [say,] the TDSB head honchos. We choose to be separate from the TDSB because we do more." After finally looking at the documents I had handed to him, he said,

In this school, you're safe no matter what you are or who you are here. If anything were to happen, the entire teacher-student body would just be on that person *like that*. It's just so open, and if anyone had an issue or something, they'd just be in the office. But I can't really even imagine it.

I mean we help organize Pride Prom, which is kind of like a prom for students from other schools who are too afraid to take their partner or whatever to their actual dance. It's held at Buddies in Bad Times Theatre. We help decorate and we help come up with a theme.

And every year we walk in the Pride Parade. It says TDSB, but it's usually mainly us. We work very differently than other schools and things. We just finished doing a literary project on queer theory. Me and a couple of my friends, we did one. And we did a project on homosexuality in the media.

In fact, some months later, I looked for students from Coyt at the Pride Parade, and sure enough, they walked in the parade carrying banners promoting equity and rode on their "Pride and Equity" float. Their anti-bullying

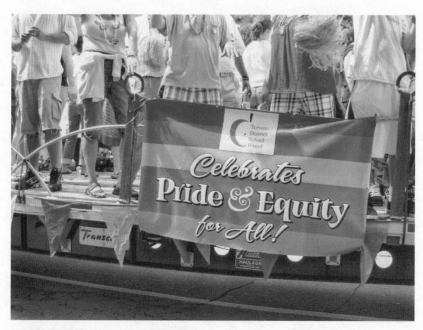

FIGURE 6 TDSB "Pride and Equity" float

posters and pro-equity signs elicited enthusiastic applause from the crowds as they moved along the streets of Toronto.

I was still thinking of the improv incident, so I asked Cal what would happen if someone in the school called him a fag. Do we not need rules to know how to respond to incidents like that? He explained,

> Half the student body would go up to them. There's just so many people that would respond to that on their own. It's just like I know one time we actually had an improv competition, and we had a couple of other students from other schools here. Well, they called me a fag. And my entire improv team ... that other team was just totally blacklisted – that entire team. We all ended up beating them. It was good.
>
> They were still allowed to compete, and we were debating telling the coach. We were debating telling the people actually running the improv games. But it really upset some of my teammates because they knew that if I had been black and they called me the "n" word – I don't really want to say it – that the team would've been off. But because of the society we live in right now, it's not really as punishable, I guess. People think they can do it.
>
> Sometimes the Grade 9s here will do that, say things, just because they're not used to it around here. But then, by Grade 10, they're completely open to it. So it just shows you, you can change it.

I had earlier asked Emma whether there was any way that Coyt could be improved upon for sexual-minority students. She told me, "Not really. I mean I came out in Grade 10 and the response was, 'Didn't you tell us that already?' Oh, I thought, okay. In some ways, I wish there was sort of more reaction." I asked Cal how the high school experience could be improved for queer students at other schools since he shared Emma's high opinion of their school. He replied,

> I think just making it more safe, and really cutting down on the harassment and stuff by having a place where it doesn't happen in the first place. Making sure that the students aren't getting beaten up, or verbally harassed, or cyber-bullied or whatever. You have to start with that because that's what's going on in schools now.
>
> Making it safer for them and just trying to get the teachers involved and making it part of the whole school. Because there's

even some teachers that can be homophobic. But mostly, more
education on the subject. Really trying to get it into people's heads
that this is an okay thing. Really being a social activist because just
getting involved after something happens doesn't deal with what
gays need to be safer.

Cal's vision of schools supported what I heard from Emma and Carla: merely
intervening when sexual-minority students are harassed or threatened does
not address queer conceptions of feeling safe. The complex assessment at
work behind this simple statement of approach is impressive. These students, however, are experts on their own experiences, living – and reflecting
on – life in school as sexual-minority youth. When I asked Cal to speculate
about what it must be like for queer students at other schools who do not
have this kind of environment, he said, "I think it's probably a lot harder. I
think that there would be a fear all the time and a sense that it wasn't safe.
There would likely be more bullying, more harassment. There probably is. I
know we have none here." The experience of Gabe Picard and the solitary
"Positive Space" door knocker seems far removed from how safety is constituted at Coyt. Both schools are in Ontario, and both are governed by the
same safe-school legislation, but each reflects a polar extreme on a scale of
differing conceptions of safety.

Model of Students' Conceptions of Safety

Ontario high schools are governed by the same safe-school legislation and
regulations. In the TDSB, each school looks to the *Safe Schools Foundation
Statement* and the *Equity Foundation Statement* to fulfil notions of safety
and equity. According to participants, however, there is a range of conceptions of safety at schools. This range corresponds to the degree to which the
safety concerns and needs of sexual-minority students are variously considered. For a few schools, this conception is a marvel for sexual-minority
students. At others, sexual-minority youth are ignored or incidentally considered when administrations are compelled to do so. This range can be
represented as follows:

| Control | Security | Equity | Social justice |

At one end of the spectrum, schools read safety as an extreme in which
control of identity of the students is paramount. In this arrangement, the

students (often black) are read as dangerous, and the particular group to be controlled is male. The process of "othering" or "social distancing" that results from this perception pushes black students, or some of them, away from the "normal" centre as the policy actors at the school define it. "Othering" marginalizes this population in such a way as to produce inequities, resulting in alienation. Because of the power of the policy actors and the possibility that black students internalize the labels, diminution of their social standing within the school is believed to give rise to self-fulfilling prophecy – that is, the label comes to be accepted even by the students, and the students, in fact, come to behave in ways the labels suggest they should. The minority fulfils the prophecy of the social construction despite the efforts of the controlling group of policy actors to ensure the opposite, namely, the "whiteness" of the black students.

At other schools, security is the primary focus of ensuring a safe school environment. The emphasis in the school is on physical safety. Measures include surveillance cameras, dress policies, security guards, and an emphasis on containing or, if unsuccessful, responding to violent behaviours. Equity policies are secondary to concerns about violence and the presence of gangs in the school. Schools in this category, as well as schools that might be classified as controlling identity, perceive their own students as the threat to certifying the safety of the school. Many, if not most, schools may fall into this category.

Further along are schools that promote equity as a means of achieving a safe and secure environment for students, teachers, and staff. At these sites, actors emphasize equality and focus less on monitoring their own students. Such schools may be uncommon, but the results of these efforts are effective in the estimation of students and teachers at the schools where equity as safety is stressed, notably for sexual-minority students.

At the other extreme on the safety spectrum are schools that not only promote equity but also actively pursue goals of social justice. The chief ingredient of this classification is a proactive approach in which justice is looked for in the school environment and sought in the larger community as well. This conception of safety was proposed by participants at Coyt as an ideal model for all schools, notwithstanding an acknowledgment that transformation would be only long-term.

Regardless of the category or categories in which these four schools might be classified along this model, their conceptions of safety are not absolutes. For example, a school that might be classified as conceiving of safety in terms of creating a climate of equity might also be concerned with social justice or even security. A school such as Burton School, which emphasizes a commitment to safety as equity, also tips toward social justice in some ways.

Is the representation in the figure on p. 95, which moves from control to social justice, a continuum? Does the pursuit of equity and social justice constitute a form of social control? Do the interviewees and critical educators merely replace one form of hegemony with another? Dan W. Butin has suggested that educators who insist that students gain knowledge and acceptance of anti-oppressive pedagogies are being just as oppressive as those who favour the practices that deliver oppressive, hegemonic perspectives. Butin has critiqued the anti-oppressive pedagogies as "limited" on the grounds that they "[remain] beholden to a notion of anti-oppression education as itself somehow outside of the potential for oppression."[15] Citing Michel Foucault, Butin critiques Kevin Kumashiro in particular and equity or anti-oppressive education in general:

> There is no ... possibility that anti-oppressive education may itself be a pedagogy of silencing which is resisted by those in disagreement. Foucault has shown that we should be skeptical of any discourse that purports to be outside of relations of power. In turn we must acknowledge that anti-oppressive education imposes itself upon students, from the texts to be read to the intellectual positions defended and attacked.[16]

What Butin appears to miss in his critique, however, is the emphasis on critical pedagogy in developing neither an ethos nor a mindset in the students but a freedom to question and to interrogate. Kumashiro responds to Butin's critique in this way:

> A pedagogy informed by "posts" perspectives[17] does not hope that students embrace or come closer to "the" anti-oppressive practice or perspective, nor does such a pedagogy need to resign itself to the fact that students might instead embrace oppressive ones. Rather, it hopes that students question the effects of a variety of practices and perspectives, including the ones their teachers say are anti-oppressive. In particular, it teaches students to *look beyond* a variety of practices and perspectives, not to reject what they are taught, but to examine and experience ways that any practice or perspective can *produce* different knowledge, identities, relations and so forth, sometimes oppressive ones, sometimes anti-oppressive ones, and sometimes both ... "Posts" perspectives on anti-oppressive education problematize the assumptions of educators that they can know with certainty

what is oppressive or anti-oppressive and that their students do not need to be examining the multiple and often contradictory effects of what it is that they are learning.[18]

In fact, Coyt exemplifies this same approach. Emma told me about an interesting situation at her school regarding her school's sex ed. curriculum:

> This year the seniors are planning to kind of take over Grade 9 sex ed. because they have decided that it's really no good. The school encourages us to take these kinds of roles, to look around and to critique what we see. And, in general, the sex ed. course in Grade 9, well ... because it's TDSB-written curriculum, there's no queer content. Or if there is, it's kind of mumbled somewhere in there. So we've decided to go in and teach the class. Even though the teachers thought they were doing something better than what's at most schools, we thought it wasn't enough.

The idea of senior students deciding among themselves to initiate curriculum change seemed extraordinary and difficult to believe. I was told that "the admin" had to approve it and that actually they had already done so for the next year. I asked whether any teachers would be involved in teaching this revised sexual-health curriculum. Emma explained, "No. I'll do portions of it and then different students will take other parts. There's still going to be the basic sex ed. and not just queer content, but we'll put that in, and then just focusing on just making sex not look like such a horrible thing."

I asked Lorna Gillespie at Trimble Collegiate whether teaching equity was merely replacing hegemony with hegemony. Here is her answer at length:

> I just did [William Golding's] *Lord of the Flies* [1954] with my class, which is all about societal control, as you probably know. Maybe if we need to look at control as setting limits for the good of everyone. Control of some sort is usually necessary in any institution, especially one full of often impulsive and foolish young people who sometimes can't see beyond the next five minutes or who come to school with a lot of negative baggage that they dump onto the school community. It's like the free-speech issue: free to a point, but we don't typically let racists or Nazi types bellow their crap in public.

In fact, your question is very timely, as the student population at my school is changing, and things are getting more and more out of control because of what I perceive as a lack of control being enforced by the admin. I think when students can yell "fuck," "fag," "bitch," etcetera down the hallway, when they can scream, roughhouse to the extreme, ignore or be openly rude to teachers, and simply refuse to do what a teacher says – teachers who are trying to keep the halls civilized, for example – we have a big problem.

You know that I'm an easy-going teacher, but I sure am not easy-going about people being mean, rude, disrespectful, "primitive," and obnoxious – not at all. In these types of cases, the equity stuff should form a foundation and be an ongoing campaign, but when it comes down to the behaviours I mention above, I don't shy away from certain "punitive" measures. However, what I would do is, for example, instead of suspending them and sending them home, have in-school suspensions or removal from classes, and in that context, put the student through a process that communicates – via their own reasoning, if possible – in no uncertain terms, why they may not behave in such a manner in the school, and why this is so.

Regarding reaching students through the students' own reasoning, first, I will say that whatever such a program might look like, I would make it very clear to the student right from the start that the behaviour in question will not be tolerated. I have no problem with the imposition of equity values. For example, one of the things I tell kids on the first day of classes is that if they are prejudiced, homophobic, or the like, they're not to express that in my room because I consider it completely unacceptable and ignorant. I just say that flat out. However, there are role-play exercises students can go through to get students thinking about the effect of their negative behaviour on other people. That might be one way to try to get the message across. Maybe peer guidance for some. And I think some reflecting and writing about whatever the issue is. Sometimes giving these kinds of students certain special roles or responsibilities is effective, putting them in charge of something, but that would depend on the situation. Another approach may be giving "problem students" some tasks to do in a restorative-justice style. Ideally, we would have social-service

back-up right in the school so that a kid could get ongoing help.
However, as you know, we don't get the funding for that and that's
unlikely to change.

Peter McLaren best articulates for me the kind of work I saw being done
at Burton School and Coyt and the kind of programs these students – and
teachers – wanted to see undertaken at other schools. They were less interested in the imposition of one hegemony to replace another than they were
in seeing schools as sites of critical inquiry:

> Schooling should be a process of understanding how subjectivities are pro-
> duced. It should be a process of examining how we have been constructed
> out of the prevailing ideas, values, and worldviews of the dominant culture.
> The point to remember is that if we have been made, then we can be "un-
> made" and "made over" ... Teachers need to encourage students to be self-
> reflexive about these questions and to provide students with a conceptual
> framework to begin to answer them ... Teaching should ... be a process of
> *constructing*, of building a social imagination that works within a language
> of hope.[19]

What I respond to in McLaren's work is the emphasis on hope. Invoking
Henry Giroux's summons to teach in the "language of possibility,"[20] McLaren
continues:

> Teachers can do no better than to create agendas of possibility in their
> classrooms. Not every student will take part, but many will ... Some teachers
> may simply be unwilling to function as critical educators. Critical pedagogy
> does not guarantee that resistance will not take place. But it does provide
> teachers with the foundations for understanding resistance, so that what-
> ever pedagogy is developed can be sensitive to sociocultural conditions.[21]

In sum, the horizontal scale from control to social justice does not necessarily represent unchallengeable truths[22] about these and other schools
but is, rather, a useful means by which to view the organization of safety in
education narratives on the ground. For many sexual-minority students I
interviewed, schools were not places of learning or even social development
but places where they were abused and terrorized and oppressed for being
different. What these conceptions establish is that this oppression takes

more forms than Gerald Walton's "generic" bullying.[23] Queer students perceived their safety to be threatened in ways that may have been different from the experience of heterosexual students. For example, to a high degree, heterosexual students failed to see their use of an expression like "it's so gay" as anything other than innocuous, whereas sexual-minority students and their allies saw the expression as a constant reminder that their security was under threat and their safety tenuous.

Reconceptualizing Safety: Law and Policy Reform

There are several key themes that emerged in discussions about safety with the participants, and they may be translated into calls for law and policy reform. A list of proposals were subsequently presented to the interviewees as possible reforms, and these were selected and supported by them on the basis that they highlighted the students' understandings and definitions of safety:

1 School boards and schools need to conceptualize bullying broadly in order to encompass not just physical violence but also verbal and attitudinal violence, including cyber-bullying – that is, bullying through computers and text messaging.
2 School boards and schools need to conceptualize safety broadly in order to give voice to equity and social justice as proactive components of the goal of constructing safe schools. Several students mentioned that it would be helpful if the *Safe Schools Act* had been called the *Safe and Equitable Schools Act* or if the TDSB's *Equity Foundation Statement* could be incorporated into the provincial *Education Act*.[24]
3 Mandated curriculum change is needed that reflects queer realities and queer lives, beginning in the early grades.
4 Mandated curriculum change is needed that also implicates the privilege and social rank of heterosexual students so that queer content in the curriculum is not merely "inclusive," thereby leaving privilege unchallenged. In this configuration, curriculum must examine the social construction of the sexuality and gender of all students in order to contest cultural hierarchies rather than sustaining a normative order of gender and sexuality (and other privileges).
5 Sufficient funding is needed to put equity into practice, including a well-staffed equity office at each school board.
6 Teacher training and workshops are needed that provide teachers with necessary information, as well as the support of colleagues.

In general, then, the interviewees agreed that it was necessary to begin a transformative process intended to dismantle the normative powers exerted in schools in a variety of privileged categories. Students recognized that transformation on this scale would be time-consuming but that this was not a reason to begin the process at any other time than immediately.

Conclusion: It Is Bad to Use the Term "Fag"

As I sat with Sharon Dominick on a Friday afternoon, she showed me a paper from a student who had offered it to her without a word:

> It is bad to use the term "fag" because it is not only wrong to stereotype but also to claim a group as wrong or bad. Even tho my wording was misunderstood, it should not have been used in the context of verbally bringing someone down. It is also unfair to the gay community to use a word that they pride, to use in my benefit as a negative. No matter if it is used in a sense of homosexual negativity or not. My words were used without contemplating the safely of others so my apologies for being me and taking away your sense of security.

I asked Sharon, "Does it give you hope? Or ...?" She smiled at me: "Or is it a flower in the desert? I'll tell you the truth, Donn. I don't have a lot of hope for this school. I'm tired of it. It exhausts me. I'd still like to transfer. I want to go somewhere else. Nothing I do makes any difference here because I don't have enough support."

Sharon retrieved a folder. "Have a look. This is not a new battle. I've been fighting it for years." What I found were a pile of notes and letters. Here are three:

> I don't really see how calling a rude women a cunt is bad. But it seems that it refers to women as just being some sort of object. I'm not sorry for my choice of words, but I should have released in a more dumb down way of expressing it. I realize women are not all bad and inconsiderate but it's those one or two on an off day that helped me get to the point of saying something derogatory towards women.

> This expression, I feel, is Okay. I think it is OK because it is used so commonly. I suppose the matter of context it is used in is also of importance. Teenagers and pre-teens use it on a daily basis. I would not describe someone as "gay" but to describe something as a movie or place is justified. Describing

someone as "gay" may be going over the limit. Thus, I feel it is OK to say "gay" depending on the context. Just because it is already commonly used.

I think that using the phrase "that's so gay" is okay to use as long as you are not offending anyone when you are saying it. In most cases someone would seriously be offended. Therefore it should not be said, and only thought of in the very least because the term is used incorrectly and offends people.

There is little doubt that the work being undertaken by students and teachers like Sharon is complicated, political, and long-term. The work, also, may seem more incremental some days than others. These documents of life contain experiences and stories – the stories not just of her students but of Sharon as well, a diary of sorts of accomplishments and resistance on the ground.

"The school fights everything I want to do. It doesn't fit with their idea of what makes a safe school," Sharon observed. "These notes," she said, "yeah, I might be reaching them, but you can see in them, also, a resistance to being reached. To a large extent, they are telling me what I want to hear and still they're justifying their attitudes."

Some schools, however, showed that a conception of safety that includes and proactively pursues equity and social justice is not only a worthy idea but also a reality. For these schools, pursuing safety as equity meant addressing the heteronormativity in schools, which many students viewed as being more immediately threatening to their personal identities and safety than bullying and physical or verbal harassment or violence. These students acknowledged, however, that for students in other Toronto schools, in smaller cities, and in rural settings, concerns about physical and verbal violence were significant and immediate. A common consequence of heteronormativity suggested by the students was that there was a high degree of what one student called "taken for grantedness" at schools – that all students were heterosexual and comfortable with the gender norms and ordering expected of them.

Although there may be unique challenges in implementing reform that acknowledges and protects sexual-minority students in new ways, and although the students and their allies were very much aware that nothing less than what might be a decades-long transformational process will bring about these changes, they also believed these are not excuses for inaction.

To this end, my purpose has been to listen to the conceptions of safety from the point of view of sexual-minority students and their advocates, to attempt to understand how these participants perceive what most threatens their personal identities, as well as their physical safety, to appreciate the unique knowledge of these on-the-ground actors, and to take seriously the legitimacy of their voices as an authority on their own situation in these spaces.

The perspectives of social psychologists have held sway over policy considerations about how best to deal with the issue of safety in schools when schools are perceived to be under siege. Policy approaches that emphasize the management and governance of conduct fail to engage with the multiple ways in which bullying props up normative cultural values and with the hegemony of privilege at the root of conduct unbecoming in schools. These interviews support a policy approach that does so.

4

Not Keeping a Straight Face
―――――
Heteronormativity and the Hidden Curriculum

Things are so great at Triangle. Not having to pretend.
The way we all had to be straight at my old school. What will
they do when they read this? What would the ramifications
for school policy be if they listened to students?

— RYAN

The house is restless. Diana Goundrey paces backstage, waiting for the "show stopper" she knows is coming. Diana is the guidance counsellor at Crestwood Collegiate and Vocational School and the person most closely allied with sexual-minority youth at this downtown Toronto school. Joey, a black Grade 11 student at Crestwood, is about to come out to his entire high school. Crestwood would fall along the spectrum of students' conceptions of safety as a predominantly security-oriented school. The guidance office is filled with the same booklets I found at Sylvia Avenue about what happens if you have a student record and about the *Youth Criminal Justice Act*.[1] There is a significant population of gangs, strippers, and self-called "deviants," many of whom are sitting in the audience.

I have been to a number of student-run assemblies and conferences in the three years that I have been researching bullying and safe schools. Each one feels like an "opening night." There is a sense of expectation in the air, a constant buzz of conversation, and a rush of bodies making the last-minute

preparations that usually precede a big event. It is exhilarating and inspiring to see students organizing these events, participating in them, putting
their own "faces" in front of their peers, and identifying themselves as sexual-
minority youth. At the first student-run conference I attended, when I
walked in the front door of the school, I had no idea where to go. Before
the first morning bell, the hallways were already crowded with students. I
scanned the walls for a poster that might point the way but could not find
any help. Finally, I asked a passing student if he could please tell me where
the auditorium was. Without much reaction, he said, "Oh, for the gay safety
conference? It's just down the hall to the left. You can't miss it." I was struck
not by the friendliness or lack of it in his voice but by the casualness of our
exchange. To be sure, my visits would confirm the profound homophobia
("Hey, white boy, you gay?") and risk to student safety that still exists in high
schools, but a "gay safety conference"? This was new and, at least for some,
not a cause of worry.

Joey's school was not as friendly, and this time I knew where I was going.
Joey was quiet and thoughtful, deliberate in his conduct and measured in
his choice to come out to the entire school. What is doubly interesting and
striking about Joey's announcement is that it came not at an event organized
or in support of sexual-minority youth but at a Black History Month event.
Whatever his thoughts, they were his own and he did not want to share
them with me afterward. But on that day, standing before several hundred of
his peers, Joey delivered a confident performance that will, I am sure, be remembered by some for years. Facing the crowded auditorium, Joey changed
his life – and, he hoped, the lives of others – when he spoke. He chose to
read a poem, preferring to follow a script in his declaration to his school.

Afterward, I asked if I could have a copy of the poem, and he gave it to
me. Even a brief excerpt captures how a bare stage was made majestic by
Joey's presence and the force of simple words, his own:

> Life ain't all
> That peaches and cream
> For I am determined
> To fight for my dreams ...
>
> People don't understand
> The pain that I feel
> They mock and they tease
> But I have to deal ...

I am strong, bold, courageous
For I am proud to be black
But people are unkind
They all say I'm whack

I tried to hide
I tried to run
But who I was pretending to be
Just wasn't any fun ...

I have come to realize ...

I can't change the colour of my skin
I can't change my hair, height or eyes
And I can't change the fact that I am gay
And ... Why would I ...?

Schooling the Practices of Heteronormative Knowledge

Policy development for effective intervention in resolving bullying in Canadian schools is an approach that has been restricted largely to issues of legal liability and tort law by legal scholars and to individualism and developmental issues by behavioural psychologists and most other theorists, namely, those who subscribe to the Olweus paradigm.[2] Programs designed to address the bullying of sexual-minority students in schools must include an understanding of the ways that our education system would be served by an approach to safety that conceptualizes safety in terms of doing equity. For the sexual-minority students I interviewed, pursuing safety as equity meant addressing the heteronormativity of schools. Terry Wotherspoon has described as well as anyone the ways that schools operate within a larger cultural process:

> Education, in its various guises, conveys important insights about particular kinds of societies and the people within them. The analysis of educational structures, practices, and outcomes can help us to understand, for example, what kinds of values, beliefs, and ideologies prevail in a given society [and] how people come to learn about and become organized within their social structures.[3]

The normative aspects of schooling include how most schools (Elizabeth Coyt Alternative School, described in the previous chapter, is a rare exception) convey dominant gender roles and heterosexist norms. In considering the implicated literature, I attempted to supplement it by asking students and their allies to contemplate obstacles to implementing equity policies. Too often the current approach to intervention is based upon a discourse in which bullying is considered a discrete, researchable, well-defined phenomenon.[4] This approach results in calls for policies in which anti-bullying strategies are primarily articulated as safety policies – where safety has been conceived in terms of security measures and control of students and only occasionally in terms of equity and social justice as helpful components of what it means to construct a safe school. When safety is conceptualized in this way, bullying is positioned in a context that already lacks sufficient consideration or investigation of the fullness of the ideological implications of what it means to be threatened in schools and that particularly lacks the perspectives of those who may feel threatened.

Sexual-minority students spoke to me about the problem of articulating a queer identity in high schools characterized by a hierarchy in which the higher status of heterosexual students was consistently vouched for and in which queer voices were consistently discouraged and stifled. Therefore, adhering to a conception of safety as security and control and restricting discussions of bullying to conversations about how to contain the bully's threat of physical violence have led policy makers to ignore or undervalue the ways that heteronormative gender scripts are privileged in the process of schooling. All of this occurs, of course, to the detriment of sexual-minority youth, who are not only devalued but also threatened in ways that are not being considered under current policy approaches. Investigating the ideological context of what it means to be safe and what it means to be bullied extensively broadens the definitions of both. As Gerald Walton has argued, by objectifying bullying as a "problem of individuals," we have allowed bullying to be viewed as a problem that can be resolved through anti-violence strategies. As he points out, in such a conception, the cultural and historical "antecedents" of bullying are ignored:

> Homophobic bullying needs to be discussed and addressed as a product of
> complex social, political and ideological conditioning before specific policies can be shaped to address it. Only then will school administrators and
> teachers feel more secure about taking action. Even heterosexual students,
> who are often the victims of homophobic bullying, will be better protected
> because of a better acknowledgment of diversity.[5]

Some theorists, including Walton, have begun to advocate for an approach to bullying in which the historical and cultural aspects of bullying are not only noticed but also emphasized. For Walton, "definitions of bullying are not mere objective realities."[6] Theories of bullying that derive their conceptions from the Olweus definition, propounded by researchers such as Debra Pepler and Wendy Craig,[7] are "embedded in discursive practice that arises from a network or system of institutional, historical, social and political relations."[8] Nonetheless, it bears mentioning that, in the past fifteen years, there have in fact been other researchers and theorists who have employed a broader approach to conceptions of bullying.[9] As well, more researchers are calling for programs that dispatch positive and preventative practices, not just punitive responses to a more narrow conception of bullying.[10] Walton's work, more than any other researcher, in my view, has been important in broadening how bullying is conceived.

However, some gaps in the research exist. Walton insufficiently acknowledges that the policies he often calls for are already in place at the Toronto District School Board (TDSB) in the form of its *Equity Foundation Statement*.[11] It is an extremely well-written policy statement that acknowledges in remarkable clarity the ideological and cultural influences governing schools and that points, in particular, to the teaching and schooling processes that have traditionally asserted and reaffirmed cultural norms of gender and sexuality. Yet even calling for this sort of intervention alone does not account for the implications inherent in an approach that appreciates a legally pluralist perspective. In other words, legal pluralism tells us that policies and law alone, although an important determinant of students' experiences, may be insufficient without also taking into account other normative orders operating within youth culture. Additionally, I think there is space within Walton's own exemplary work for descriptive and analytical reports from sexual-minority students, who are most affected by the policies he calls for. His work has included reports from teachers, but to my knowledge, he has not yet reported on student accounts.

Schools can be considered cultural sites[12] where dominant gender roles and heterosexist norms[13] are continually vouched for and privileged.[14] Although most schools may be viewed in this way in the specific context of the TDSB and its *Equity Foundation Statement*, this is not an inevitable or unchangeable role for schools. Teachers are often perceived to operate as cultural agents, endorsing dominant subjectivities in the practice of teaching in schools.[15] However, such a role for teachers is not inevitable, and teachers can play a role in developing different approaches, particularly ones that stress equity. A number of scholars have noted that a normative pattern of behaviour in schools is maintained in order to eradicate difference since difference is regarded as a potentially subversive element in school culture.[16] Michael Manley-Casimir has observed that patterns of normal behaviour are applied both to teachers and to students and are imbued in the practices and processes of teaching that comprise what he terms "the normative enterprise of teaching." According to Manley-Casimir, "education ... provides pupils with knowledge and ideals which those pupils are expected to learn and to follow, with rewards for successful learning and following, and penalties for failure to do so."[17]

Manley-Casimir's specific concern is inappropriate teacher behaviours since such behaviours may give rise to issues of liability. In this context, he observes that schools are concerned with "maintenance and inculcation" of "collective representations" that model ideal behaviour.[18] His conception of this process, however, remains largely neutral in terms of the kind of values being conveyed. Although he describes the practices involved in this inculcation process, he does not enumerate the cultural dynamics – for example, gender, sexuality, race, class, and so forth – present in this process, beyond a concern for sorting out acceptable behaviours on the part of teachers from unacceptable behaviours for a legal process principally concerned with adjudicating liability, even while he acknowledges that education is a cultural enterprise. Investigation of the ways that the official task of the school – educating students – is also integrated into a school's structure, processes, and outcomes has been left, primarily, to other theorists.

A long tradition in the literature of the sociology of education conceives of schools as institutions imbued with the value-laden purpose of socializing youth for a larger society. More recently, this literature has begun to assess the role of the education system in communicating and maintaining hegemony.[19] Government-funded education came into being during the Industrial Revolution in Canada and the United States, a time when growing urbanization, increasing immigration, the industrialization of commerce, and changes within the family all combined to provoke broad societal concerns about moral and civic order in general and about turbulent youth in particular.[20] Adolescence has not always been recognized as a discrete time in human experience. The concept of adolescence was effectively brought into existence with the arrival of the Industrial Revolution and the establishment of compulsory schooling.[21] Gordon West observes that compulsory schooling delayed adolescents "from participating in the social and economic life" of the wider community and instead submitted them to the practices of school so that they would be prepared to join society after being properly educated.[22] Accordingly, many historians and commentators have noted that "the basic function of education under capitalism [has been] the reproduction of class structure without the reproduction of class consciousness."[23] This is a point about which scholars Michael Mann and Paulo Freire theorized over forty years ago[24] – albeit with more emphasis on class and race and less on sexuality and gender. It is a theme that since that time has occupied critical sociologists[25] and a theme on which more recent theorists and scholars have also written[26] but with sexuality, gender, and the investigation of "normal" at the core of their research and writings. The research of such theorists contemplates schooling as a site in which the maintenance of a social order includes "taken for granted" categories that emphasize not only class and race but also gender and sexuality as norms of schooling. It is worth noting, again, that Coyt stands as an example of a school that consciously pursues an equitable framework – one that not only promotes equity but also asks students to interrogate their teachers and to reach for their own adaptation of social justice.

Wotherspoon's critical perspectives on schooling are grounded in an appraisal of the compound purposes of schools and the schooling processes: schools are a place where formal education and credentials "can be concretely defined and measured, but [they are] also characterized by more indefinite tasks associated with [their] human interactive and social dimensions."[27] He notes that notwithstanding that a principal theme of North American cultural scripts is that individualism yields achievement, schools also convey to students the importance of society's cultural expectations and also transmit to students the fundamental expectation that they will comply with these expectations.[28] As noted by critical sociologists concerned with the sociology of education, these themes can be communicated overtly or through the "hidden curriculum."

The term "hidden curriculum" was first put forward by Philip Jackson in 1968 in his landmark *Life in Classrooms*.[29] Many commentators have observed that the meaning of the term "hidden curriculum" is not necessarily readily apparent. Nonetheless, the term has been much scrutinized since 1968 and has achieved widespread use as the theoretical basis for investigating schooling practices. The concept of the hidden curriculum is that the enterprise of schooling is not limited to the communication of knowledge prescribed in the approved, official curriculum. The hidden curriculum transmits social meanings and promotes cultural outcomes through schooling practices and activities that occur within schools.

Roland Meighan has offered some conceptions of the hidden curriculum, and Michael Haralambos has offered a different approach to the hidden curriculum. In Meighan's view, "the hidden curriculum is what is taught by the school, not by any teacher ... [and] is coming across to the pupils which [may] never be spoken in the English lesson or prayed about in assembly. They are picking up an approach [to] living and an attitude [to] learning."[30] Prefiguring postmodernist approaches, Haralambos suggests that the hidden curriculum reinforces the power structures of society and "consists of those things pupils learn through the experience of attending school rather than the stated educational objectives of such institutions."[31] Others, particularly Samuel Bowles and Herbert Gintis,[32] stress the relationship of schools to the labour market and economic sectors of community life. More recently, Wotherspoon observed that the operation of the hidden curriculum and the informal interactions among educational participants "serve to construct and reinforce identities both within and beyond schooling."[33]

Some theorists, such as David Gordon,[34] have questioned how an imprecise term has gained such prominence, and they point to Benjamin Bloom for an explanation: "The latent curriculum is in many respects likely to be more effective than the manifest curriculum. The lessons it teaches are long remembered because it is so pervasive and consistent over the many years in which our students attend school. Its lessons are experienced daily and learned firmly."[35] In early treatments of the hidden curriculum, theorists and social scientists agreed on the hidden curriculum as a cultural practice of schools but debated whether the hidden curriculum prompted benign cultural outcomes that served society's larger interests – such as making a practical and valuable contribution to the workforce – and whether the impact of the hidden curriculum was, for those who were subjected to it, coercive. Most of the recent critical writing about the hidden curriculum has theorized and documented what Gordon describes as its negative and pernicious effects.[36]

Differences arose early between the proponents of a "functionalist" perspective, like Emile Durkheim[37] and Talcott Parsons,[38] and criticalists such as Michael Apple[39] and Madeleine Arnot.[40] Under a functionalist approach, schools were viewed as cultural vehicles conveying the necessary values and ethics of a so-called moral education, the ultimate goal of which was to promote a student who was likely to contribute to the greater good of society. These theorists believed in and advocated the promise of curriculum as the best possibility of learning for all students. Critical theorists, in contrast, among them Arnot and Apple, viewed the hidden curriculum as a virulent process that pursued a coercive agenda and imposed a system of values, activities, and morals in pursuit of what, in their view, was more appropriately termed a "hegemonic curriculum"[41] that served the interest of a dominant group. Pierre Bourdieu[42] pointed to the power that lurked behind the outward appearance of neutrality where the hidden curriculum was cloaked. As Melinda Miceli puts it, schools were powerful institutions because they "appear[ed] to be neutral transmitters of the best and most valuable knowledge."[43]

Drawing on the often cited work of W.M. Stanley, Miceli's research approaches the hidden curriculum from the perspective that the "false objectivity of the process," in reality, "promote[s] a hegemonic curriculum ... that simultaneously legitimizes the dominant culture and marginalizes or rejects other cultures and knowledge forms."[44] For many concerned with the effects of a hidden curriculum, it has been noted how, outwardly, the hidden curriculum constructs students' lives and identities as so-called individual subjects while promoting their homogeneity as a group. For Miceli and a few others, however, the educational practices of an informal curriculum that are of the greatest interest are those that play a significant role in transmitting cultural expectations about sexuality and gender scripts. For the most part, as Miceli remarks, current explorations of an unofficial curriculum focus on the ways that "upper and middle class, white and male culture, history, morals, behaviors, norms, and values are taught and enforced in schools through the power of a hegemonic process in which they are also naturalized, neutralized and made invisible."[45] Although some of these theorists have addressed gender,[46] few investigations have been undertaken in which the focus has been on the influence of hegemonic masculinity and heterosexuality on educational practices. James Sears,[47] Debbie Epstein,[48] and Kevin Kumashiro[49] are exceptions who have directed their attention to the hegemonic curriculum of heteronormativity, and Miceli's own study of gay and lesbian youth is another.[50]

Epstein, Sears, Jacqueline Mikulsky, and others have theorized about the ways that an informal curriculum's promotion of heterosexuality makes heterosexuality a part of what Mikulsky calls "the unspoken and assumed identity"[51] of most students. For Epstein and her collaborators, schools are places where the education of students takes place both in the "official spaces of curriculum and classroom" and through the "micro- and often very unofficial cultures of students, [where] teachers and others [are] connected with particular sites."[52] What occurs at these sites may be best understood as the transmission of "appropriate knowledge" by institutional practices in "all phases of education."[53] The relationship between the formal and informal curricula is indistinct. Sears and Epstein, who have worked together on many occasions to assess their efficacy, are worth quoting at length:

> All educational institutions, at whatever phase, have both formal and informal curricula. The formal comprises what is overtly taught, the content of the curriculum. The informal, or hidden, curriculum is much harder to pin down, since it consists of almost everything else ... In practice, they are intertwined and bleed into each other. Formal and hidden curricula are formed and understood in relation to each other. No formal teaching can take place outside the context of the hidden curriculum and the hidden curriculum draws on all aspects of the taught curriculum. Social relations, forms of pedagogy, curriculum content, micro-cultural processes and dynamics, even the life histories of students and staff, all contribute to the learning and teaching that goes on within educational sites.[54]

Our understanding of the intricate practices of these curricula, thus described, would be usefully augmented by ethnographic investigation, particularly in a Canadian context – especially as the effects of a hidden or hegemonic curriculum are complicated by the interventionist strategies set out in the TDSB's *Equity Foundation Statement*. What is needed is a study that asks queer students about their awareness of and experiences with the formal and informal heteronormative practices of schools in order to expose the codes of heteronormative cultural assumptions and the ways that the formal and informal curricula play out in a site ostensibly governed by a well-written equity policy that acknowledges and seeks to reverse the negative effects of heteronormative practices.

In a postmodern world, the challenge is to encourage greater numbers of theorists and researchers to show that "normative heterosexuality is enforced rather explicitly in the environment, or 'culture', of public schools," if not explicitly in the official curriculum.[55] That there is surveillance of sexuality and reinforcement of heteronormative codes of behaviour in secondary schools should not be startling. As Miceli observes, one might expect the pervasiveness and power of heteronormativity in high schools to be obvious to any observer who walks into a school, yet, as she also points out, whether this is true depends on what is normal in a particular context.[56]

A Particular Context: The Toronto District School Board

The hidden curriculum is composed of the unspoken social norms that are outside of the manifest curriculum[57] but that students are nonetheless expected to learn. Sexual-minority youth are compelled to negotiate the hidden curriculum of heteronormativity in the classroom, hallways, and even outside of school space when they communicate with their peers – and, sometimes, with their families – about their experiences at school.[58] In the classroom, teachers and students are likely to assume that everyone in the room is heterosexual.[59] Victoria Clarke and Elizabeth Peel observe that the assumption of heteronormativity persistently sits like a challenge to queer students, either to defy the assumption or to remain silent.[60]

Didi Khayatt and Anthony D'Augelli are among the scholars who have identified how heteronormativity functions to marginalize and alienate sexual-minority youth through silence. For Khayatt, silence about the lives and experiences of sexual minorities "envelops" schools, affecting queer youth in a number of ways: some are "terrified about what [is] happening to them amidst what seems like universal reticence" to discuss or acknowledge homosexuality, a silence and invisibility that come to control sexual-minority youth.[61] As D'Augelli puts it:

> When young people pursue an understanding of themselves, they do not encounter a literature affirming their lives ... They find themselves deleted from most relevant courses. They are the "invisible" minority, yet the "hidden curriculum" that devalues the existence and contributions of lesbians and gay men is quite clear. At a time when accurate information and affirming experiences are critical ... [they] find few, if any, affirming experiences in ... educational settings.[62]

In my own classroom experience, discussions among students about the practices of heterosexism and heteronormativity are typically begun with blank stares. To many students, heteronormativity is what they consider "natural," "normal," and "the way things are." To them, in fact, heteronormativity is not really a thing that is there to be acknowledged. This is a fundamental point made by Miceli:

> Heterosexual behaviour and language are integrated and normalized to such a degree within school culture that they have become the "natural," often translated into "neutral," high school environment. Because of this,

things like male-female displays of affection, discussions about same-sex
relationships, school dances, proms, anti-gay jokes and insults, and harassment of g/l/b [gay/lesbian/bisexual] students are not viewed as "explicitly
heterosexual."[63]

What exactly is being silenced? Epstein and Sears point out that "many kinds
of knowledge are dangerous ... because they destabilize established common-
sense world-views [and] because they pull the veil away from oppression,
discrimination and suffering, making for uncomfortable confrontation with
these issues ... because knowledge is ... a form of power."[64] As Epstein, Sears,
Miceli, and Eric Rofes assert in their writings, most students and teachers are
oblivious to this oppression and what a marginalizing experience school is
for sexual-minority youth. For many, these formal and informal practices
that assert the hegemony of gender practices and heteronormativity are
regarded merely as "the way things are."[65] For sexual-minority youth, however, this environment leads to what Epstein and her collaborators have
called "silenced sexualities."[66] How heteronormativity is deployed in schools
and pervades school space is the question to be addressed by queer theorists and educators such as Sears, Rofes, Epstein, Sara O'Flynn, and David
Telford. For these scholars, particularly Epstein and her collaborators, heteronormativity is an issue of power. As for the challenge confronting policy
makers and queer educators, they note that the strategies and frameworks
of heteronormative power "constrain what people do and understand and
constitute a pressure towards the construction of particular kinds of identity."[67] And yet, as Miceli points out, administrators, teachers, parents, and
students often perceive such heteronormativity in schools in the mould of
the "normal high school environment."[68] It is left to the students and teachers in this book to articulate the ways that heteronormativity amounts, in
fact, to a form of oppression that threatens their safety.

Epstein, collaborating with Richard Johnson, has been careful to distinguish between homophobia and heterosexism, and this distinction is
important in assessing the effects of the hegemonic curriculum of heteronormativity. That homophobia, based on fear and hatred, may play out alongside heterosexism is predictable, but they are not synonymous. Discussing
the relationship between heterosexism and homophobia, Bruce MacDougall
notes that the limits on "homosexual expression and visibility" in the classroom are brought about by heterosexism. For MacDougall, "the intense indoctrination in heterosexism" in schools is the most important factor in the

perpetuation of homophobia.[69] Epstein agrees, observing that heterosexism locates sexual-minority youth outside of the "norm" and defines them as "other."[70] Recognition of homophobia, then, does not sufficiently engage with notions of "otherness" or the role of "othering" in defining social difference, and it does not acknowledge how, in many cases, this "othering" leads to bullying and, at the same time, has significance for reconceptualizing safety. Programs and intervention strategies that are designed merely to address homophobia are limited. They uphold the perspective of violence against queer kids that, first, insists on viewing violence as an event that implicates individuals, not the larger culture, and second, limits notions of violence to physical violence. Equally, such programs may focus upon the queer student as "other" and do little else to address additional ways that oppression is expressed in the institution of schooling (or anywhere else).[71] Heterosexism, in contrast, is broader in scope, recognizing the cultural esteem accorded some and the way that others are accorded disadvantaged standing in the same culture. This social "othering" is accomplished by a range of structures and activities, as well as by an intricate set of values, attitudes, beliefs, moralities, and images that works in intricate ways to support the heteronormative order and the heterosexist interests that govern it. In fact, as Kevin Kumashiro notes, "different forms of oppression (such as racism, classism, sexism, and heterosexism)" are enacted in schools in "multiple and contradictory ways."[72] Heteronormativity, then, is not just part of the hidden curriculum – it is also overt. Gust Yep captures well how heteronormativity operates in this compound way:

> Heteronormativity is everywhere: It is always already present in our individual psyches (e.g., our thinking), collective consciousness (e.g., community values), social institutions (e.g., marriage), cultural practices (e.g., wedding rituals), and knowledge systems (e.g., education). In spite of its prevalence, heteronormativity remains largely invisible and elusive to most people by presenting heterosexuality as a natural state and a social "given" with a sense of rightness, moral rectitude, and a projected cultural ideal ... This sense of heterosexual moral superiority, cultural achievement, and social privilege permeates all aspects of social life.[73]

The outcomes for sexual-minority youth have been much theorized and documented. One consequence for sexual-minority youth of being dominated, ignored, or subordinated is the control of knowledge about them.

Philip Jackson's early theorizing about the hidden curriculum offers a general template for understanding how oppression operates in school space;[74] it has been left to others to develop the approach and to consider its appropriateness as a means to appreciate the hegemonies of sexuality and gender. Kumashiro considers how these informal practices are enabled by the control of knowledge in the case of the queer "other":

> Researchers have suggested that the "knowledge" many students have about the Other is either incomplete because of exclusion, invisibility, and silence, or distorted because of disparagement, denigration, and marginalization. What makes these partial knowledges so problematic is that they are often taught through the informal or "hidden" curriculum, which means that, because they are taught indirectly, pervasively, and often unintentionally, they carry more educational significance than the official curriculum.[75]

How the queer "other" is defined depends upon the construction of a heterosexual ideal against which this "otherness" is juxtaposed. Associated with heteronormativity, dominant gender codes are promoted and reaffirmed in the values, morals, and structures that inform heteronormative schools.[76] These structures affect all youth, heterosexual and nonheterosexual. There is a sizable body of literature theorizing and documenting how girls are denied cultural independence, authority, and equality. Madeleine Arnot and other scholars make clear that the hegemony of masculinity defines girls and encourages them to define themselves and to find their cultural worth in relation to the dictates of hegemonic masculinity.[77] Boys are inducted into an order and become subject to a cultural arrangement that imbues them with power and authority but does so at the expense of their emotional lives as well as exacting other costs. In short, boys and men are often shortchanged by a culture that bestows power and privilege that often obfuscate the oppression of hegemonic masculinity. Yep captures the ubiquitousness of heteronormative influence:

> Heteronormativity affects everyone, but in different ways and to different degrees. Because heterosexuality is a patriarchal institution, women living inside the heteronormative borders (i.e., heterosexually-identified women) are subordinated through culturally idealized conceptions of marriage and motherhood. These conceptions propel women to enter relationships with unequal power and to engage in unpaid labor in the service of men. Heteronormativity also affects men who are heterosexually-identified.

Heterosexuality constitutes men as "real" men (i.e., "real" men are aggressively heterosexual). As such, it keeps men living inside the heteronormative borders fearful of being emasculated and deprived from a range of gender performances, possibilities, and life pleasures through a lifelong labor of "proving" their manhood ... Most straight men are afraid to be sensitive, tender, and emotional because of the fear of being perceived or labelled "sissy" or "faggot" – an ever-present threat to their manhood.[78]

From one perspective, hegemonic masculinity imbues males with power and prestige at the expense of "others," but it is a weapon against both. The codes of hegemonic masculinity are intolerant of those who reject or fail to live up to the demands of gender, boys or girls, and in schools are almost always intolerant of nonheterosexuals. These codes not only bestow upon boys a power to act but also demand that they do so. These codes are a social burden for everyone, as hegemonic masculinity regulates the lives of all students.

Drawing on Adrienne Rich, Howard Buchbinder, and other theorists, Didi Khayatt observes that "although many hegemonic principles operate to maintain male supremacy, one of the most fundamental is heterosexuality."[79] As Khayatt puts it, "Heterosexuality ... depends upon the power differential which characterizes male/female relations, and therefore on the differences which justify this power."[80] She links these differences to institutionalized "gender role" practices whereby masculinity functions as "the measuring rod against which femininity is judged (and found wanting)."[81] In this conception, masculinity "becomes the determinant, the relevant descriptor, and as such, the defining ingredient of power."[82] The place of homosexuality is clear:

Homosexuality both in men and in women – but for different reasons – threatens the hegemony of masculinity. Gay men, stereotypically perceived as "effeminate," generally jeopardize the gender roles because they, often purposefully, blur the distinctions between masculinity and femininity ... Lesbians threaten masculine hegemony as well. They challenge gender roles, they become financially independent, and they remove themselves from being sexually available to men – a prerogative that heterosexual men believe is rightfully theirs.[83]

Regardless of whether oppression is based upon gender, race, class, or some other category of difference, Kumashiro and others point out that individual

students respond to oppressive treatment in a variety of ways.[84] Since
Benjamin Bloom, many critical theorists have disagreed with his insistence
on the "consistency" of the hidden curriculum.[85] As David Gordon puts it, a
good deal of the response of theorists throughout the 1980s and 1990s has
been to consider contexts "where students have read the hidden curriculum
and resisted it."[86] Some students accommodate the demands of the dominant values at least enough to "succeed" academically while maintaining a
connection with their "otherness."[87] Others resist the dominant heterosexist
norms, practices, and values operating in schools. Drawing upon Antonio
Gramsci's notion that "hegemony is never total"[88] and invoking Michel
Foucault's observation that "where there is power, there is resistance,"[89]
Epstein and her collaborators observe that "it would ... be a mistake to assume that there is no room for manoeuvre" in schools.[90]

Nonetheless, as Kumashiro emphasizes, notwithstanding the "apparent
differences between those students who 'succeed' and those who 'fail' or
simply fail to distinguish themselves," the important and single commonal-
ity between them is that they "all experience oppression."[91] Of course, there
are ways that students resist cultural expectations, whether externally or
internally felt. The effects of resistance – for example, to official cultural
expectations – raise a further research inquiry that is acknowledged in this
book but that deserves a separate, more in-depth inquiry. To what extent
can and does such resistance result in furthering the dominant subjectivities that the resistance is intended to subvert? Nonetheless, however courageous, exhilarating, and astonishing individual resistance may be and often
is, it would be a wrongful return to the misguided philosophical under-
pinnings of Elmer the Safety Elephant, misplacing the responsibility of resistance, to focus too much on the responsibility of individuals: change is
not their burden. Kumashiro outlines the mission of resistance well and
makes clear that the struggle is not one for individual shoulders: "Challenging
oppression is not an act of 'individual overcoming' where students change
only themselves; it is an effort to change oppressive ways of doing or learning any of the subject matters that are currently being repeated at the institutional level in many schools and society."[92] Mary Rasmussen makes the
point that the regulation of sexuality in school space raises the issues not
only of "safe space" but also of "queer space," a place where potential resistance may find expression.[93] Kumashiro's observation that oppression occurs
in a variety of forms, playing out in schools in "multiple and contradictory
ways," is an apt description of resistance, also a complicated concept.
Rasmussen has this to say about the multiple and contradictory ways that

school space operates: "Members of school communities possess a variety of sexual and gender identifications. They are compelled to rub up against one another within and around school settings, thus they are all complicit in the production of all manner of sexed and gendered selves."[94] So-called resistance theorists claim that students are much more alert to the messages of the hidden curriculum than some other theorists acknowledge. This view is best laid out by Paul Willis.[95] His ethnographic investigation of working-class students following graduation demonstrates that the students possessed a plain awareness of the hegemonic purpose of their school and, specifically, of the hidden curriculum.[96] There is, however, no one coherent or accepted account among critical theorists that explains what is meant by resistance,[97] how it works, and to what extent it may operate, and it is well beyond the scope of this section of the book to investigate resistance in further detail. As Gordon notes, despite the differences among theorists about the workings of the hidden curriculum and the role of resistance, it is important to bear in mind that the hidden curriculum is a "social text" and that "to be of meaning, this text must be read and interpreted by the students."[98]

Extending the work of Kumashiro, Rofes, Miceli, Rasmussen, and others, we can see that the oppression of sexual-minority youth raises the issue of safe space in schools and, in view of the cultural muscle of the hidden/ hegemonic curriculum, issues of equity and social justice. The recent emphasis in these conversations on the production of a heterosexual hegemony in schools has prompted theorists such as Miceli to address "heteronormativity as an important and powerful social force" that is perceived "to coerce, oppress, and control the lives of individuals."[99] Miceli argues for further analysis on the ground based upon an analysis of "the power and social force of heteronormativity at work in the lives and experiences of g/l/b youth."[100] The importance of this task cannot be overstated.

The *Equity Foundation Statement* of the TDSB can be used to combat multiple forms of oppression, particularly of sexual-minority youth. The *Equity Foundation Statement* has received attention in historical accounts but remains largely ignored by empirical researchers, possibly because equity continues to be viewed apart from issues of school safety. There is an important need to unite them. Many theorists, researchers, and policy makers dealing with issues of bullying, hegemonic curriculum, or hegemonic heterosexuality,[101] as well as literature dealing with the law or policy and program interventions, consistently call for policies that the TDSB already has in place, ignoring the thirty-year efforts of teachers, educators, and administrators to deliver them. It is also important to present the voices of sexual-minority youth and their allies as a means to develop the argument that safety must be conceptualized in terms of equity in order to address the specific safety needs of sexual-minority students. This goal also underscores the value of further research in this area. Such exploration will inevitably lead to a consideration of which plural normative orders are at work and how these other orders interact with and complicate the formal equity policy in place at the TDSB, as well as the safe-school provisions of the *Education Act*.[102] By listening to the voices of sexual-minority youth, we will better understand the social text of the hidden curriculum and be able to respond to David Gordon's call for this text to be construed by the students themselves.

5

Obstacles to the Implementation of Equity Policies

———

> This is the way I am. I was meant to be this way. I was a learning experience for my mom. She used to be very homophobic. I was meant to help someone.
>
> — MIKE

How safety is conceived is a pertinent factor in determining the extent to which equity is pursued in a particular school. In a significant way, this book is about the structures that can be used to achieve social justice for sexual-minority youth in secondary schools, but equally it is about the structures that complicate and sometimes impede the achievement of social justice among these sexual-minority youth. These social structures can be viewed as twofold. First, there are those structures that include formal law, construed broadly to include policies, legislation, regulations, codes of conduct, and so on. Second, there are those social structures that many would view as unlegalized social structures, which include social organization of class, race, gender, and heterosexuality. For sexual-minority youth, who are characterized by their nonconformity and repudiation of traditional gender roles, all of these social structures must be taken into account when assessing how effectively, if at all, this group can obtain social justice at school sites. These social structures may, in fact, have an interactive aspect.

The implementation of equity in schools is dependent not only upon the extent to which and the ways that policies are implemented in schools but also upon how they are affected by other cultural factors and social structures at play in schools. Participants pointed to a series of such factors, which I sort into three groupings. In some cases, these factors were seen as obstacles to implementation; in others, the issue was effectiveness once implemented. The first group of factors affected policies by rendering them, in the view of the participants, less effective. A second group of factors made policies more effective in circumstances where the identified factors were *present*. Third, participants indicated that when law and policies were used to respond to isolated incidents, the reach of policies was limited and the larger school culture was not likely to change. When law and policies were used to attempt to transform culture, their reach was greater and the larger culture was more likely to change.

The Ideological Iceberg

Halfway through Joey's presentation, in which he came out to his school as gay, there was an audible gasp in the audience, and then the inevitable murmur that ripples over a crowd when they realize something iconoclastic, if not shocking, is being said. And then quiet. When I asked Diana Goundrey, the guidance counsellor at Crestwood Collegiate and Vocational School, to tell me how she interpreted the silence, she thought for a moment and then said, "I would describe it as a respectful silence." Then she laughed, "Wonderful, complicating equity. We have it, but it's not straightforward." Joey was very humble about the presentation and quiet about his feelings – he did not want to talk about the experience afterward – but very satisfied with his choice and with his contribution to the celebrations of Black History Month by making a "gay statement." Diana described the experience for Joey and for the school this way:

> The issue is not a lack of well-written policies, we have those, but
> of other factors, one being an emphasis on law and order responses
> and a de-emphasis on equity and social justice. What oppresses
> most of these kids is the need to play it straight. Nobody's going
> to punch Joey out over this. But what will they be thinking? What
> line is drawn around him? I hope none. I think Joey occupies a
> certain status in the school where that won't happen. He's close to
> graduating, but that's not true for kids coming in the door. That
> wasn't true for the kids who showed up in Grade 9 in September

and were gone by December. The [*Equity*] *Foundation Statement*[1] will be the real harbinger of safety for queer kids and gender rebels, but it will take time.

"Law and order" responses are certainly necessary. Tim McCaskell, an equity officer with the Toronto District School Board (TDSB), told me, "You have to have your rules-and-consequences pieces. But you need your equity piece as well." McCaskell told me that "the rules-and-consequences part, the part that is often being aimed at in policy discussions, is only dealing with the actions of individuals." Asked to elaborate, he put it this way:

> Having policies around harassment and bullying is certainly not enough. You've got to have regular educational work to dismantle and constantly challenge the kinds of cultural values, the kinds of stereotypes the kids will be learning from the rest of their environment, in school and elsewhere, and you've got to have all this systemic stuff in place, not only in terms of harassment but in terms of these values being promoted. That's the situation for many schools.
>
> However, the board policies now in the TDSB, that were won over a huge political struggle in 1999, are probably, I think, the best in North America, if not anywhere. I mean they're really very, very comprehensive. There's always room for tinkering, but generally that piece is good. The problem is the implementation, it's not happening.

In many ways, McCaskell's comments struck me as a direct response to a question that had been posed rhetorically to me by Ryan, a fifteen-year-old gay student at Triangle, a high school program of Oasis Alternative Secondary School that offers courses exclusively to queer students in Toronto. Ryan described what had happened at his previous high school when a gay or lesbian student was verbally or physically harassed, but more tellingly he did so by outlining for me, vividly and memorably, the shortcomings of response-based policies that fail to implicate cultural values supposedly shared by all:

> Well normally the school would say, "Oh, I'm sorry, I'm sorry, it won't happen again," and then they would react. But they don't mean it. I mean, it doesn't change anything. I live with my Dad.

My mother left us a long time ago. When I do see her, she never
asks me how I am and you know why? Because she doesn't want to
know. If she knew, she might have to do something. That's what it's
like at schools. They don't want to know what's going on every day.
They'll deal with physical or verbal things, but they don't want to
ask you how you *are*. What would be the ramifications for school
policy if they listened to students?

On a different day, in a different conversation, McCaskell provided the answer. In his view, the structure of schooling would change fundamentally if
schools implemented the TDSB's *Equity Foundation Statement*, a document
intended to deal with more than just the "physical or verbal things." He is
worth quoting at length:

> When you're talking about a system of oppression, you've got
> to think of it as kind of an iceberg. You've got individual actions,
> and with that, there's the physical bullying, the name-calling, the
> beating-up piece – because of the dominant ideas. Queers are
> second-rate, queers are unnatural, queers are different. If a student
> calls somebody a fag, they get hauled in. They get disciplined,
> actually. It's dealing with individual actions.
>
> But think of this as an iceberg and this is the part that's above
> water. If that's the piece that's in place, the "law and order response"
> piece, you're pushing down on this iceberg. It just pops back up.
> You're not really changing the values that gave rise to the bullying.
> So there's got to be an educational component, a continuing
> educational component because it's inevitable that, without it, the
> bullying will be inevitable, and you're only dealing with individuals.
>
> So, secondly, there's the systemic piece – what policies are in
> place, what curriculum is in place. The ideas that people have they
> learned from the system; ideas then inform actions.
>
> These pieces are all interrelated, of course. The system shapes
> individual actions – what they allow to happen and what they
> don't allow to happen.
>
> Thirdly, actions of people in power shape the system. People
> learn from how they see people being treated. So we've got this
> kind of circular system. So there's got to be a political component
> that deals with the systemic stuff. Those three areas all have to be
> dealt with, something transformative.

Sian is white, female, and in the same grade as Joey. Less deliberate than Joey, she is a bundle of energy, oblivious to all punctuation, except exclamation marks, when she speaks:

> Oh my God! Joey did it! He wanted to come out for Black History Month and the reason – and the reason he wanted to do it is because it's pretty much a heterosexual Christian assembly at this school, and so we wanted to represent black queers. So Joey is like, "I will write a poem," and he wrote a poem talking about all this oppression, how his brothers and sisters are putting him down.
> Everyone knows him 'cause he's just a wonderful person. He's extremely involved in the school and everyone's like, "Oh my God!"

When I ask Sian to elaborate on what she means by characterizing the assembly as "Christian" in past years, she is very perceptive in drawing a distinction between homophobia, heterosexism, and heteronormativity. It is a familiarity with queer theory that I have noted before in many of the participants:

> No, it's not homophobic, I wouldn't say. It's not really hostile or stupid and based in fear of queers. It's more that they just assume that everybody is the same. It's so important that the humungous heterosexualness of things gets attention, too, and that's what's so cool about Joey's poem. It's about him, but it makes people think about themselves because now they have to ask themselves if they feel any different about Joey now and why that is. It's not just about queers, you know. The straight kids and teachers, too, need to think about their own gender prisons. It's not always because they're homophobic but that sometimes everything is just so heterosexual and that's damaging, too.

Sian is one of the students at Crestwood who helped to found a Gay-Straight Alliance, which in her school is called Closet Space. Sian tells me, "I don't know if Closet Space helps with dealing with heterosexism; it's so strong at this school, but it's helpful in providing a refuge from it."

When I interviewed Peter and Murray Corren in Vancouver, they spoke about the importance of implicating heterosexual students in educative programs on the grounds that they are implicated in the regime of oppression in schools. By this, they meant not just "teaching" heterosexual students, as

Kevin Kumashiro would say, about the other but also addressing the social construction of all sexualities and genders and looking at the ways that privileged students participate in this oppressive regime.[2] This was a subject about which they had been thinking for some time. As much as both stressed the significant importance of equity policies that called for the presentation of queer realities in the curriculum, they preferred policies that also encourage heterosexual students to contemplate their own social construction. Murray spoke first:

> It's interesting that you bring that up. When we were, initially, in negotiations with the [British Columbia] Ministry of Education to settle the curriculum human rights complaint, the director of governance was in attendance at that initial meeting, and he looked at me and said, "I don't really understand what this is all about." And I knew it was a leading question. And so I said to him, "Well, here's a metaphor that I believe works really well to explain why I think this is important. Public education provides both a mirror and a window to students in classrooms. The mirror is there to reflect back to them their realities. So the curriculum reflects students' realities. It also provides a window onto the world about those who are different from you and their realities. So queer kids sitting in a classroom, or children of queer parents sitting in a classroom, have the right to look into that mirror and see their realities reflected back to them. And straight kids sitting in that classroom have the right to that window into a world which up until now has been portrayed as being immoral, objectionable, sick, criminal – and also, at the same time, to be a mirror on their social realities."
>
> So it's a two-way process. And so we're here in this human rights complaint not only to provide an educational environment that is supportive of queer kids and queer families but also to provide those kids who come from heterosexual families, who are themselves heterosexual, to learn about the realities of queer people – but also their own realities in terms of their own sense of masculinity and femininity and that it's cultural – because homophobia and heterosexism comes out of that.

For the Correns, Tim McCaskell, Carla at Elizabeth Coyt Alternative School, and most of the students and educators with whom I met, the curriculum should include an acknowledgment of queer lives, queer realities. Murray Corren told me that he thought queer realities should form a part of the curriculum in the early grades and continue throughout all grades:

> It depends on the age level. At an early age level, just simply talking about the whole variety and models of family configurations we have in our society. It's okay to have two moms or two dads.
>
> First of all that they're there and that it's okay. You start with ground rules like that. And then dealing with the name-calling from a very early age. Providing children with a clear rationale as to why it's not appropriate. Teaching children about being socially responsible.
>
> And when they start to move into the intermediate grades, teaching them about the consequences of social injustice in our society. At that age, they are able to understand it and know what the effects of social injustice are. So that by the time kids get to high school, you can begin talking about sexual diversity to the point where, I believe, sexual-health education needs to deal with every kind of sexual diversity and, inevitably, social justice across the curriculum.

Peter agreed, buttressing Kumashiro's observation that "oppression ... is not always easy to recognize"[3] by offering this succinct comment about the heteronormative school environment: "What you think is normal is culturally normal, or you've been influenced to think that way. We had to get at that in our settlement."

Peter Corren also stressed the importance of dealing with the issue of having someone to "look up to":

> But you also have to get into the issue of positive role models. The contributions of gay and lesbian people, past and present. You don't have to make a big deal of it. All you do is you have those conversations that there are people from all walks of life who have contributed to science, technology, and art ...
>
> And you've got to look at the differences between urban and rural areas. Kids in rural areas feel very isolated. If they can make that connection to people like themselves, it builds up self-esteem and all sorts of things.

George Smith investigated the experiences of gay male students in Toronto high schools in the early 1990s. Because of the difficulties of accessing classrooms, most of his interviews were composed of adults who were recent high school graduates. In his work, a research project undertaken in tandem with Didi Khayatt's exploration of the experiences of lesbians in Toronto-area high schools,[4] Smith described the ways that "antigay activities ... [were] a normal, everyday part of school social organization."[5] Smith argued that verbal and physical mistreatment experienced by sexual-minority youth was grounded in what he labelled the "ideology of 'fag.'"[6] Drawing on Smith, Lori MacIntosh has observed in her own fieldwork that "this ideology saturates the school environment and sets the parameters for homophobic harassment."[7] For MacIntosh, the power of heteronormativity works like this:

> Assumptions of student and teacher identities as heterosexual, examples expressed through heterosexual narrative, and curricula seeped in gender normativity are all characteristic of the ways in which non-normative sexualities are "inadvertently" excluded from curricular agendas and various social justice reforms ... There is a denial of the normalcy embedded in the construction of knowledge and a desire to believe that homophobia is simply a matter of ignorance. We subsequently assume that it is homophobia that must be understood, leaving heteronormativity as a live incendiary device – and curriculum its tripwire.[8]

When I spoke with Dalton, he was in his final year at Crestwood. At the time of our interview, Dalton was very involved in queer politics in Toronto and by his own assessment "probably was not your typical queer kid in high school" simply because he had "always read and been politically aware and active." As Dalton put it,

> I think queer kids, generally, are probably more aware of the heterosexist nature of schools than straight kids. Anybody who is trying to get by in an oppressive atmosphere or culture would tend to be, I think. I was maybe a bit less afraid of being "outed" in high school. In fact, I was out, but that was because I had a boyfriend and I didn't want to pretend that I didn't.

Dalton and I met downtown at a café in the Annex in Toronto; it was one of the few interviews that I did not conduct on school property. I picked up on his use of the word "heterosexist" and asked him to elaborate on the general culture of schools. He explained,

> High schools are pretty heteronormative all the way through and homophobic, for sure, particularly in the early grades. But even the students that may think they're not homophobic, there's no question that they're very heterosexist. And why would they not be given the heteronormativity of the school in general? The curriculum, dances, clubs, the posters you see on the walls, the movies they show in class, sex ed., sports, the teachers, all of it. Heteronormativity is subtle, it just runs along like an engine you forget is running, like sitting in your car and not remembering the motor is on – but the heterosexism of school is pretty blunt. Take dance posters. The pictures they would use to inform you of the dance. Not only did they tell you where, what day, and what time, but also who. There was always a photograph cut out from some magazine of a male and female, so that heteronormativity sort of skews all the day-to-day things and makes life in schools pretty heterosexist.

In our discussion of "heterosexism" and "heteronormative space," I asked Dalton whether he was familiar with the Triangle program. Triangle, Canada's only high school classroom for sexual-minority youth, is one of three programs that comprise Oasis Alternative Secondary School in the TDSB. Triangle describes its mission as "providing a classroom where Lesbian, Gay, Bisexual and Transgender (LGBT) youth can learn and earn credits in a safe, harassment-free, equity-based environment, and developing and teaching curriculum which includes and celebrates LGBT literature, history, persons and issues."[9] Dalton, like all of the sexual-minority students I met, was quite familiar with Triangle:

> Towards the end of my high school years, after I'd come out to myself and knew a little bit about the community, I would have become much more aware of the Triangle program. But I always knew that the Triangle program was there and – well, it's not exactly a utopian place for queer students, but it was a refuge. Some queer students who find themselves in really awful situations, not just heteronormative or heterosexist complaints, but where all of that has just led students to really pick on and bully somebody,

so they have to get out. It's a transitional program for students
who weren't surviving in other places and needed a bridging
element, after which they were supposed to go back into a regular-
stream high school. But I never would have considered going into
a program like that myself.

Earlier on in my high school, from Grade 9 to 10, it wouldn't
have occurred to me that – because I wasn't fully out to myself –
it wouldn't have occurred to me that I could belong in a gay/
lesbian high school.

But views on them in general? I think the Triangle program is a
really crucial support for students. I wish more school boards had
similar programs. I think it's an interesting possibility.

There were few queer students who did not talk about the pressures for
sexual-minority youth in simply walking the hallways. I met Len through
Lorna Gillespie at Trimble Collegiate Institute. An older student a year away
from graduating, Len, like Dalton, conducted himself with a lot of confidence and, interestingly, also described himself to me by saying, "I'm not
like a lot of queers in school, I would say." He summed up the dilemma of
hallways as succinctly as anyone:

> In my early years, I avoided hallways because they were really ruled
> by this dominating self-validating culture in this school. The dom-
> inant culture was not violent, I wouldn't say, not violent or overly
> aggressive, or homophobic, but it was definitely very heterosexist.
> And [with] the cool kids hanging out and walking through that
> hallway, [it] was always a little bit uncomfortable for me.

This social regulation was raised as an issue by many queer students and
was, as Len put it, "sometimes blunt, sometimes not." Sometimes the blunt-
ness was oppressive and, in Len's words, "even violent." As he explained,
"heterosexism and heteronormativity, for me, sometimes it's difficult to
know how to distinguish them."

At Earl Grey Secondary School several students used the school newspaper to complain about the school's recently formed Gay-Straight Alliance
(GSA). As Terrence, who with his friend Sam had helped to create the GSA,
told me, "I think they were trying to rally the troops against us. The usual
methods weren't working." In the view of many students and teachers, Gay-
Straight Alliances were important but also problematic. Murray Corren

explained why GSAs were important: "They are extremely important. Kids need to know that there are those there, be it teachers or whoever, who are there to support them and provide them with a safe place where they can go just to be themselves." "Being yourself" has limits at some schools. Murray told me, "One administrator didn't like the word 'queer.' He asked, 'can we use a different word?' Teachers were tearing down posters."

As an equity officer with the Toronto Board of Education for several decades, Tim McCaskell had witnessed the birth of GSAs in Toronto:

> They're happening. We tried to get one set up in a Catholic school, and we got permission to do so. They are difficult. When I was there, what we had was a lesbian/gay kid support group for the whole system, and we got maybe a dozen or so kids that would come to a central area of the school. Because when you tried – in those days anyway – to set up anything to do with "gay" in the schools, during school time, people tended to be too terrified to show up.
>
> Now calling it a Gay-Straight Alliance helps alleviate that a little bit because it doesn't necessarily mean that you're going to be gay if you go there, but it certainly means you're under suspicion.
>
> But what I've found has happened is that you usually get kids in the upper grades who are finally beginning to come out and whose contact with the ghetto in the outside world has given them a bit of self-confidence, and they will find a teacher that will be the staff adviser and will get one of these things set up.

Diana Goundrey, one of the advisers to Crestwood's GSA, described the school's treatment of sexual-minority students:

> There are teachers who have taken a really active role in making students feel comfortable. They deal with homophobia and queer issues in class through the curriculum. So that happens. I've had parents come and comment on how they wanted their kid to come here because they saw that little poster. One of my colleagues said that, also. That was one of her – one of the reasons she decided to stay at this school, because she saw the posters and felt immediately comfortable.
>
> And there's our group. There's Closet Space. And everybody in the school has been completely welcoming. When we decided we

were gonna do this club, it was just like great, okay, another club to add to the list. We were included in a – I don't know what you call it – like a club fair, let's say, where Grade 9 and 10 kids – where kids can go and look at all the different clubs, and everybody had things set up.

And we were set up there, and it was like we were a club like any other club. I think it was alphabetical, so it wasn't like we were stuck at the corner or something. We make announcements. It's just like any other club. It has been really good.

McCaskell pointed to one problematic aspect of GSAs that was raised by a number of interviewees, but like them, he nonetheless underscored their importance:

GSAs tend not to be – somebody needs to do some real research – they tend not to be very long-lasting. They tend to last only like a year or so because these are kids in the upper grades, and when those kids graduate, then where do you get somebody else to keep the thing rolling? And the teacher who's going a little bit out there to actually support such a group may just withdraw as well.

Now I have heard of a couple of schools now that are just beginning to keep them going the same way that the football club keeps going or the chess club or the debate club or whatever. So we may be moving into a new era. So they're kind of an interesting and important strategy, I think.

Jeffrey White, one of two leaders of the Triangle program, offered a nuanced assessment of GSAs:

There's a couple of things that I think around these things. The Gay-Straight Alliance, it's a great idea, but who's going to them? It's mostly white, middle-class students and it tends to be mostly female. Most of them probably identify as straight, and they want to support their one queer friend who's too damn afraid to show up at the group because they all know it meets on Tuesdays in Room 309 and, if you go to that room, you're labelled, you're othered, and the rest of the school culture is like most school cultures: you get moved into a different position within the school now. So if the school doesn't sort of allow for that kind of safety and protection, then are you gonna go to that meeting? Hell no. So other schools have started creating groups like Over the Rainbow to try and create a way without saying Gay-Straight Alliance.

And, certainly, Over the Rainbow at Coyt is more expansive in its approach, seeking broader aims of social justice as its primary goal. White continued:

> I worry about students who don't feel that they can access those meetings because within their ethnic background there's so much other issues of homophobia, transphobia that they would be afraid to attend, or because they might be the only person of colour showing up at this meeting, when everybody else is white, so they'll still feel very marginalized within that group.
>
> And there's a lot of socio-economic issues. Who can stay after school and participate in the club? "Well, I need to work 'cause I'm helping my mom pay the rent and keep food on our plates." So there's issues that way, too, that can impact some of these groups. So yes, I think they're a great thing, but shouldn't we be doing more of this stuff within the actual curriculum and addressing the heteronormative cultures of our school so that all students have access to them?

For Diana, at the end of the day, notwithstanding the limitations often associated with such groups, the GSA is a powerful force of "resistance in [her] school to the general school climate." Diana's assessment of the power of the Closet Space posters was far removed from Gabriel (Gabe) Picard's elegiac appraisal of the lone "Positive Space" door knocker tucked away in his high school in Thunder Bay. Diana said,

> When I see those Closet Space posters ... I'm amazed. And I'm amazed at where I see those in the school. If I go into the metal shop, it's hanging there. Or if I go into the auto shop, it's hanging there. It's the first thing you see when you walk in the front door of the school. I know that's maybe a small thing – but it means a lot to kids.

Terrence and Sam, two Asian Canadian gay males, were both seventeen when I met them. In their last year of high school, they decided to establish Earl Grey's first GSA. They approached Mr. Taylor, a heterosexual teacher in

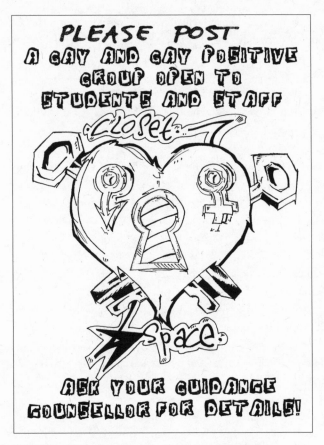

FIGURE 7 Closet Space poster, Crestwood Collegiate's Gay-Straight Alliance

their school, to enlist his support, which was generously extended. Unfortunately, the "blunt" forces of heterosexism responded with counter-resistance. For weeks, a debate raged in the pages of Earl Grey's school paper. The following article, by "C.B.," was titled "Just Not Right":

The emergence of the Gay-Straight Alliance at the school has certainly brought a degree of tension and discomfort in the community. Although I truly believe the GSA has been well received and the community has been very respectful, the whole idea and some of the actions taken have made me personally and many others think about their views on homosexuals. I encourage everyone to think long and hard about what is being preached. The introduction of the GSA has definitely made me think long and hard about

homosexuals in the [Earl Grey] community and homosexuals in general.
Before the presentations I was indifferent about homosexuals and thought
they should be treated equally and that they can do whatever they want to
do because it will not affect me. However, after thinking hard I have become
more opinionated.

Homosexuals should not be discriminated, they should be treated as
human beings and should not be made fun of or disadvantaged due to their
sexual preference.

Moreover, they should not be discriminated for their (in some cases)
eccentric actions around their peers. However, why do people have sexual
preference? Gays do not just enjoy the company of other men. The purpose
of choosing sexual orientation is to have sexual interactions with one another. I would like to use the example of gay men to illustrate my point. By
no means am I a scientist or know exactly what the functions of the sexual
organs are but it is clear the only two sexual organs for reproduction are the
penis and the vagina which only when used together produce offspring. I'm
not going to get into the specifics on gays, but they have only one sexual alternative, it just does not work, and the possibility of reproduction is scien-
tifically impossible! Whether you believe in a god or not everyone can agree
this sexual interaction is not right, the interaction is physically wrong and
those who conduct themselves in this manner should definitely not be supported. I don't mean they should be reprimanded or physically or verbally
abused. Homosexuals can/should still maintain friendships with straights.
They should feel comfortable in our community and accepted but they
should know that there [sic] actions biologically are improper and you cannot argue otherwise. Just as straight humans must cope with and accept
gays, gays must realize and cope with the fact that their sexual actions are
not condoned by society ...

Everyone should look down deep and share what they truly believe, it
will be much more constructive than the GSA telling us what the right and
wrong ways to act are.

Some time after the ruckus had died down, I sat with Terrence for one of
several formal interviews-conversations that we conducted. He looked back
on the episode and summed it up this way:

> I've seen this before. People start out by saying, "Well, gay people
> and lesbians shouldn't be discriminated against, I'm not a bigot,"
> and then they go on to do just that, clinging to their privilege. This

was a big thing in our school, as you know. It was very heterosexist. But at the same time, there's no denying there are a lot of
kids who want to be cool and not be seen like that. But I have to
say, our school is more privileged than a lot of other schools, and
things are often more polite here. This was as rude as it got. Which
is still bad, but I think at other schools where things are maybe
more run by street code, putting up with or even liking the idea of
having a GSA wouldn't be seen as an attempt to be cool, it could
get pretty bad. I could see lots of kids being afraid to go. Like in a
small town or a more rural school. Even here, lots of times it's girls
who show up at GSAs because they have a queer friend and they
want to go.

Sam recalled that the letters in the student newspaper went back and forth
for weeks. Together, Sam and Terrence had penned a first response, titled
"Just So Misinformed":

The publishing of C.B.'s article in last week's [newspaper], entitled *Just Not
Right*, has certainly brought a multitude of mixed emotions to [our] community. While C.B.'s opinion should be respected, his argument is flawed
with misconceptions. Before I share my own view on the issue, I'd like to ask
the school community to put things into perspective. Any time there is a
reference towards sexual orientation that you have trouble relating to, imagine that reference applying to yourself. Then you will be able to forge your
own opinion on the issue at hand, as opposed to being influenced by the
argument's face value.

Even before the Gay-Straight Alliance was revived, I knew that there
would be misconceptions concerning its role in the school. I was afraid that
people would feel that the GSA was trying to force ideas of what's "right"
and "wrong" into their heads, to change their opinion. The GSA's mandate
was never to tell the school community how to act[,] it was only to provoke
self-introspection within the individual and discussion within the school.
As a representative of the GSA, I'm hoping to provide an alternate view to
the issue, inspiring thought and discussion.

He raises a point worthy of discussion – physiologically and biologically,
the penis and vagina do "fit." He is also aware that the reproductive systems, as inherent in the name, are for reproduction. Does that mean sexual
intercourse is for the sole purpose of reproduction? Absolutely not. The

reality is that few people have sex only for the purpose of reproduction. Most even try to prevent it from happening by using contraceptives. Frankly, the majority of people have sex for pleasure and sexual gratification, not for procreation. Furthermore, some heterosexuals also participate in other sexual acts that do not necessarily involve the interaction between the male and female sexual organs – oral sex, for example. The heterosexist belief that straight, penis-to-vagina sex is the only acceptable way to have intercourse is, in a word, misguided.

Also, according to C.B. he feels that homosexual relationships are purely for sexual reasons. As I mentioned before, let's put things into perspective, through the eyes of a heterosexual. The following is a direct quote from his *Just Not Right*, with words referring to homosexuality reversed and referring to heterosexuals instead: "Straights do not just enjoy the company of the opposite sex. The purpose of choosing an orientation is to have sexual interactions with one another." This statement simply is not true. Heterosexual relationships are not based solely upon sex. Love, a genuine care for another person, exists in heterosexual relationships, and the same applies for homosexuals.

I would also like to address how C.B. seems to believe that sexual orientation is a choice. Sexual orientation is not a conscious decision; people do not consciously decide to be gay or straight – they are who they are, and that cannot be changed. Also, it can be agreed upon that gays have been (and still are) discriminated against in various societies. Given that, who would make the conscious decision to be gay and be discriminated against, living a life of doubt, fear, rejection, and possible loneliness? Homosexuality is also not limited to humans either. There have been many documented cases of homosexual animal behaviour. To cite a specific example, Roy and Silo are two male penguins at the Central Park Zoo in Manhattan. In the past seven years, they have been inseparable, and have been seen to entwine their necks, vocalize to each other, and have sex. When offered female companionship, they refused. They've even raised their own chick, Tango, taking good care of it ever since it was just an egg.

Reading the noted article, it really brought to my attention how misled the community could be. It further strengthens why the Gay-Straight Alliance is here. We are here to inform you with all the information we can and THEN you can devise your own opinion. We merely want everyone to be aware and more informed of a topic that is so quieted in most societies. When putting yourself in the others' shoes, how does it feel to be told that what comes naturally to you is wrong? How does it feel when someone tells you that what you truly believe in is wrong? Is this truly tolerance and acceptance when someone tells you that who you are is wrong?

The student who caused the uproar, C.B., wrote several more letters, not exactly apologetic, but each succeeding response was written with less and less confidence as the letter writer became, in Terrence's words, "kind of isolated in a spotlight." The school's official response was to stand behind Sam and Terrence and the GSA. Sam told me,

> There's no doubt we had a lot of institutional support, but there's also no doubt that we got a lot of "looks" to let us know what some people thought, and what they thought was that they didn't like the idea of a GSA at this school. So even though C.B. was isolated, there's no doubt that that isolation was official and that even now, things are resuming to the way they were before. Some of the parents complained, too, but the administration told them to take a hike.
>
> So even though Terrence and I knew the school was officially behind us, especially Mr. Taylor, you knew that some people didn't. But I think the important thing is that you knew the official position was "the GSA stays," and that's important not just for Terrence and me but also because you want the up-and-coming students who might be thinking of taking it over some day, maybe next year, to see that. And you especially want the straight hetero kids to see that.

Predictably, echoing Tim McCaskell's concerns about GSAs, both Terrence and Sam worried about their GSA's future after they graduated, but they both expressed to me that the commitment of the club's staff adviser, Mr. Taylor, would ensure its continued survival. I would agree. In my conversations with Mr. Taylor, he expressed his commitment to making sure that the GSA continued after Terrence and Sam left. Informants at other schools, however, have been less optimistic. One teacher told me, "These things go as the students go – it really depends on who, if anybody, wants to take it on."

I had thought that the final word on the issue of Earl Grey's GSA was the following observation from a teacher at Earl Grey who was so angered by the response of some students and parents that he decided to come out to his students and to the school. In his words, "If these two boys could do it, I felt that I needed to and that I needed to stand with them. Coming out has always been the best way to resist the heterosexism and homophobia that otherwise keeps us silent and invisible."

However, over a year after interviewing Terrence and Sam, I ran into Sam one night on Bay Street in Toronto. He told me that he was studying design and that he was overwhelmed but really enjoying university. I asked him to look back on his experience with the GSA and the debate his actions had inspired in the school newspaper. We talked for a few minutes about the "heteronormative citizenship"[10] Terrence and Sam had tried to address:

> You know, it's interesting. It seems to me, now, that there was
> much less homophobia there and much more protection of
> heteronormative citizenship in response to what we were doing
> than I wanted to see at the time, or could see. I wanted, I think,
> to see this as something that C.B. was doing because he was
> homophobic. And it's funny because it wasn't homophobia that
> caused Terrence and me to want to start that group, it was just the
> general hetero nature of the school. I hadn't really been aware of
> a lot of homophobia at Earl Grey, it was the hetero culture that
> we found we had to do something about.

Azmi Jubran had been marked as "queer," probably less because he was believed or even assumed to be homosexual and more because it helped to declare the heterosexuality of his tormentors. As Diana put it, "If a boy calls another boy a fag, he's not just defining 'the fag,' he's defining himself as straight." Jubran had suffered the day-to-day social consequences of being a targeted queer person without actually being gay. The British Columbia Human Rights Tribunal[11] found that Jubran was entitled to protection under that province's human rights legislation, only to have the trial court,[12] upon judicial review, reverse the decision of the tribunal. Jubran remembered how he felt when the trial judge ruled that there was no protection at law under British Columbia's human rights legislation for the "reality" of his heterosexuality, notwithstanding that he had been socially constructed as "gay":

> I don't remember half the stuff I learned in high school because at
> the end of it, I didn't get the same opportunity that the students
> who harassed me got, and it's really unfair. I made a legitimate

complaint, a complete, legitimate complaint, and to have a judge
tell me basically, based on a certain technicality, oh, look here,
look under fine writing, you should've looked at that sort of thing.
To say that just because I'm not gay, I do not get protection? He
might as well have kicked me in the nuts. I had a sick feeling, I
really did.

My lawyer, from the beginning, had a feeling this was gonna go
all the way, that they were gonna fight it all the way to the Supreme
Court. So she told me, "Be prepared that this may happen," and I
said to her, "Okay," and of course, they – after the decision came
out, I had a call from the legal-assistance society, and they asked
if I wanted to appeal, and without a doubt, I said, "Yeah, let's do it,
of course. There's no way I'm gonna back off now."

For a person to seek protection from discrimination under human rights
legislation, the discrimination must be founded upon the actual or perceived
applicability of one or more of the enumerated or analogous grounds set out
in human rights legislation. The trial judge could not find such applicability;
however, under a social construction of reality reflecting Jubran's day-to-day
experiences, the Court of Appeal extended the protection of the legislation
to him.[13]

This decision was founded upon three findings. First, following guidance
provided by the Supreme Court of Canada (SCC) in *Robichaud*,[14] the Court
of Appeal made clear that the provision in the province's human rights legislation[15] that Azmi Jubran was relying upon – as quasi-constitutional legislation – was to be broadly interpreted in order to give effect to the underlying
purpose of the legislation, namely, the elimination of discrimination. In
Robichaud the SCC stated that "the Act must be so interpreted as to advance the broad policy considerations underlying it."[16] In *Montréal* the SCC
confirmed that it was also "inappropriate to rely solely on a strictly gram-
matical analysis, particularly with respect to the interpretation of legislation
which is constitutional or quasi-constitutional in nature."[17] The chambers
judge employed a narrow interpretation of "sexual orientation," holding that
Azmi Jubran, a heterosexual, had not been discriminated against on account
of his sexual orientation by victimizers hurling homosexual epithets at him
– even as they physically abused him.

Second, asserting the long-held principle established by the SCC in
O'Malley, the Court of Appeal agreed with the tribunal, which had considered Jubran's harassment in light of the principle that "it is the effect of

the conduct, or action, not the intent of the harassers, that is relevant in determining whether discrimination has occurred."[18] In consideration of the fact that human rights legislation was intended not to punish victimizers but to provide the victimized with a legal remedy for the consequences of the victimizers' conduct, the Court of Appeal found that Jubran could seek to bring himself within section 8 of the British Columbia *Human Rights Code*. This section of the code offered protection from discrimination in the provision of public services – here, an education – on the grounds, in this case, of "sexual orientation." These two factors together had the cumulative effect of extending to Azmi Jubran the protection of the province's human rights legislation. In my view, what the court understood was that Azmi Jubran had been socially constructed as gay. A social construction, or construct, is any experience or event "devised" or "constructed" by people in a particular social group when they agree to behave as though the construction exists or to follow culturally specified, agreed-upon, or conventional rules. One instance of a social construction is social or cultural status. For all of his harassers' protestations to the contrary – that they had never "believed" Jubran was actually gay – they subjected him to the *treatment* that they agreed queers deserved.

A final point needs to be noted about the Court of Appeal's legal reasoning to impose liability on the school board based upon the actions of students. The school board's principal objection was that, notwithstanding the harassment Jubran received, the school board was not responsible for the actions of students. However, under *Ross*,[19] school boards bear "the duty to provide students with an educational environment that does not expose them to discriminatory harassment."[20] In the Court of Appeal's view, the North Vancouver School Board did not meet its duty because it failed to provide the teachers at Jubran's school with training to deal with homophobic bullying and harassment. In this regard, the Court of Appeal agreed with the tribunal, which had cited *Ross*, that "a school board has a duty to maintain a positive school environment for all persons served by it."[21] Even though the board did not incur liability due to the actions of the harassers, as would have been the case if the harassment had been conducted not by students but by teachers, the Court of Appeal, citing the tribunal, made clear that the board's "obligation to maintain a non-discriminatory school environment for students ... [gave] rise to the School Board's duty respecting student conduct under the [British Columbia *Human Rights*] *Code*."[22] The court concluded that "the School Board did nothing to address the issue of homophobia or homophobic harassment with the students generally, nor did it implement a program designed to address that issue."[23] Therefore, the board's failure to perform its duty to train the teachers to deal with homophobia at the school and the effect of this failure on the conduct of students, particularly Jubran's homophobic harassment, gave rise to the school board's liability.

Jubran told me that he enjoyed the process in the Court of Appeal and related to me how his experience at the court had been so different from his experience before the chambers judge:

> So we did the Court of Appeal, and that was amazing, being in the Court of Appeal, because it wasn't just technical. They were talking about how society is, how it works right now, what is accepted and what isn't right, and I had a good vibe, I really did. Actually, I had a really good vibe at one point during the appeal. While the school board lawyers were putting forward their part, they basically – Justice Ryan stopped them and said, "Well, okay, I have a question for you because I recently read a book," and so we're not talking about law here, we're just talking about everyday life, just simply reading a book here, and she said, "Well, I was reading this book about a German guy during World War II, and the Nazis knew he wasn't Jewish, and yet they persecuted him as a Jew. So are you going to say to me that he is not being discriminated against?"
>
> The school board had nothing to say to that whatsoever, and I think at one point their lawyer said, "Yeah, I guess they were," or I think maybe she admitted to it somehow, and after that, I somehow had a feeling – well, it was just like a point of relief, I don't know. It was just amazing. It was simply out of a book. It was nothing on the paper, nothing in law. It was something that was just basically sort of like common sense really. This is how it had been for me and the judge got it.

Space, Teachers, and Challenging the Curriculum

Ryan is fifteen years old. He lasted less than four months at his high school before seeking a transfer to Triangle. Ryan is tall, slim, and dressed in baggy pants, a baggy shirt, and a baseball cap worn backward. He has very long hair, particularly at the front, with bangs in his eyes that hang down almost to the middle of his nose – his mother says he looks like a sheepdog. Ryan thinks he "looks gay," but I would not describe Ryan as looking gay; rather, seeing him on his skateboard in the street or on the bus he rides with his skateboard under his arm, most people would likely see him as a "skater kid" before thinking he was gay. Only later do I notice that Ryan is wearing eye makeup and fingernail polish:

> I'm trying to make up for the credits that I lost this year in Grade 9 and get next year's Grade 10 credits. Or most of them, 'cause there's some that they don't do here at Triangle, like drama or art. Yeah, they don't do drama or art here. And then I'll go back to mainstream school in Grade 11, I guess. But I don't plan to take off the makeup.

Ryan told me that he thought "gender and heteronormativity was more important to straight students than bashing queer students." Ryan's perspective interested me because most of the students with whom I spoke were in upper years. Most of the lower-year students I encountered were in mainstream schools, cognizant of the price of not fitting in. Ryan had already transferred out of such an environment to Triangle. Ryan told me about the following incident that happened in his Grade 9 English class, an incident that I found startling because the same thing had happened to me when I was in Grade 10. In my class, the books were Pearl S. Buck's *The Good Earth* (1931), for girls, and Alistair MacLean's *The Guns of Navarone* (1957), for boys. Here is Ryan's account:

> Bashing queer students is what comes after. It starts with everybody doing the boy thing, the girl thing, the "het" thing. Then to prove that they're normal, they'll look around to bash a couple of queers.
>
> Let me tell you what happened in Grade 9 this year. The English teacher was saying to us, "Okay, you have two choices of which book you can read." I can't even remember what they were. And she said, "The girls will want to read this one, and the boys would want to read this other one. Okay," she says, "which book do you want?"
>
> And then she went through the entire class list, calling out everybody's name one by one, and I remember thinking, okay, so now we've got all this gender pressure on us to choose the books she's laid out for us by this boy-girl rule and there's – I remember thinking, you know, I really feel this pressure now to choose the boy book. I really resented that she did that, and I resented even more that we all succumbed to what she basically set out for us to do. Now why do we all know to do that? And why did we do it? There wasn't one person, male or female, including me, who didn't. Not one.

James, also at Triangle, a year older than Ryan, told me why he left his original high school:

> I found the expectations of sexuality and gender to be more of a problem personally than bullying. My sexuality I could hide. That is not a good thing and I am not saying it's a good thing and I would be unhappy if someone took what I am saying to support that. But hiding kept you a safe distance from being bullied. But the *expectations* of gender and being straight, I couldn't escape and couldn't hide from that. Just being a boy brought you into contact with their power. If you were a girl, it brought you into contact with their power and it defined you. What do you do with that for four years?

Ryan described what finally drove him to Triangle:

> I really couldn't take it there anymore. It was really hard not only to be out, with all the pressure to conform to the straight structure, but you kind of get harassed in the hallways. You'd have people yelling at you, and you just wanted to be left alone. And I had kind of gotten – I'm not sure if it was mugged, but on my way to school for some reason, this guy started throwing snowballs at me and I ignored him. And then after I kept ignoring it, he crossed the street and then decided to smash me into a fence and start shoving snow down my clothes. And well there was a suicide type thing and I had to go to the hospital. I'd been thinking about it before I came to Triangle. I didn't really feel like staying at my school after that. It was really hard not only to be out, but you kind of get harassed in the hallways. I had people yelling at me and coming up to me and asking, "Yo, guy, why are you so gay?" and I just wanted to be left alone. So I just tried to get away as fast as I could.

After our formal conversation-interview had ended, Ryan continued to talk about his physical appearance. He said to me that even his friends, who had no problem accepting that he was gay, would nonetheless make comments about the fingernail polish and eyeliner that he wore. During the interview, I had specifically asked him, "Was there anything about what you wore or said or about how you presented yourself that would encourage people to think you were gay?" And he had said "no." When I pointed this out to him,

Ryan said something very interesting: "I think most of it was more homo-phobia and the gender-binary system because everybody had an extreme problem with the nail polish or the eyeliner. I had some friends who had no problem accepting that I was gay but would make comments about the fingernail polish and eyeliner."

As I walked Ryan outside, he emphasized again that he thought crossing the gender line of what was appropriate for boys was of more importance and greater significance in the minds of some high school students. Why did Ryan think his friends felt the need to comment? "To make themselves feel more secure," he said. Then he waved and took off down the street on his skateboard.

I had been struck by Diana's excitement about the Closet Space posters hanging in the metal shop and the machine shop at Crestwood. I decided to go for a walk through the school, and as she had indicated to me, there were the posters. The issue of school space as gendered space or school space as heteronormative space was raised by many of the sexual-minority students – or, if the issue was raised by me, it was a subject on which the students had much to say. Some school space could be read as threatening, and some school space could be read as safer, depending upon the degree to which the space was "masculine" or "heteronormative" or "heterosexist." Strikingly, with the exception of Diana, all of my informants identified machine shops, woodworking shops, and metal shops as some of the most threatening spaces in schools – second only to school gyms and physical-education classes. Diana told me,

> The most supportive people have been the tech guys. I'll go down-stairs and I'll call the auto guys and say listen, I need a float for the Pride Parade. They'll joke. They'll say, "I don't know if I can find any gay tow trucks. I'll see." But they'll do it. They'll make jokes or whatever. But they'll do it.
>
> I think things have just changed, and they've realized, because some of them have been victims. They've had – and they see kids get picked on because they're not macho enough. So they're pretty cool about that.

I spoke with Kyle, a student at Crestwood, and relayed to him what Diana had told me. Kyle was dismissive of Diana's observation. "That's because she's a woman. The tech guys, the phys ed. teachers, they treat females dif-ferently. They're happy to do her a favour because she's pretty. What do they say when she leaves, I'd like to know. That little poster provides cover." Jubran told me that his shirt had been set on fire in a shop class and that he had been kicked between the legs by a female student in a gym class.

When I asked Kyle whether there were any spaces at his school that were more gendered, more threatening, or safer than other spaces, he confirmed that there were but pointed out that the school space was sometimes gendered in unexpected, even contradictory, ways:

> Yes, I definitely did read space like that. Sometimes, I was wrong. A space where I was wrong was in the art house. It's a slightly separate building, a separate entity in the building. It's perceived to be the only place in the school that represents school identity in a positive way. But there was a course taught in there by a real straight guy, and it was a junior course, but it didn't engage me. The art house wasn't really a gay space once I investigated it, even though on the surface people probably thought it was. And the students wanted it to be.
>
> On the other hand, drama was only because of the teacher. Not the students. There the students were real closety, whether because they didn't want to get typecast or what, I don't know. So you had to watch out because of the students. Then there was that art space. I wouldn't say that the art space, in general, was queer space because of the students who made it up. It wasn't very comfortable, again, because of the students. So these spaces were both perceived one way, positively, I think, because of art and drama, but occupying those spaces was different.
>
> I avoided spaces where I didn't want to be, areas where there were young students, where these hetero issues seemed more immediate, and sort of the students who were the least academic. Students doing very masculine things like shop or woodwork, which to me was more threatening.

Len, who had earlier identified the hallways in his school as being heterosexist, talked to me more about the "rule" or "regulation" of space by his school's heteronormative citizens:

> Like I said, I avoided hallways because they were ruled by this dominating culture in this school. There were certain areas of the school and certain people that I instinctively avoided, because they

were very dominating, even by how they looked at you – there was a dominating culture in my school and they were it and they let you know.

And the cool, straight kids would hang out and sort of patrol their space, and so walking through that hallway was always a little bit uncomfortable for me. They didn't even say anything. They were there and they looked at you and let you know you weren't part of their heterosexist geography because you were queer.

The vocabulary used by the students to describe everyday occurrences in their schools never ceased to astound me. John Allen has explained that "geography ... is about power and [that] political geography is about the use of power to administer, control, and fix territorial space."[24] Allen also points out that power is "exercised at someone else's expense."[25] I asked Len whether he felt the "straight" students had power that he did not and, if so, what the source of this power was and how it was exercised. His consideration of the expression of power in hallways captured, in terms of day-to-day occurrences, how in theory queer citizens experience marginalization as a result of spatial practices:

I think it was more of a situation in which they had social power. They had a certain prestige within the school, and that comes about through, among other things, normative gender and sexual presentation. I think the students who are perceived as cool feel the need to maintain that status. And the way they interacted with each other was also part of this – whether that power came from displaying signs of affection in the hallways or talking about the other gender in certain kinds of sexualized ways.

That personal gender presentation was really normative, so the guys all looked and dressed a certain way. They all had this swagger and would wear baseball caps, pants a certain way, and talk in a certain way to their friends. A lot of hashing around and things like calling their friends by their last names – a certain way of talking, dressing, of moving.

The women I would say the same thing. All sorts of normative, very feminine presentation. They exuded their sexuality. It was a very dominant kind of sexuality. I think being heteronormative and sexist and even homophobic was part and parcel of it. And it goes on without most of them consciously thinking about it.

Was Len paying a price because of the "rule" of the straight kids, and if not, what about sexual-minority youth generally? I was interested in knowing whether this power had been exercised against him personally. He said,

> It hasn't been. But I am not sure that anyone would. I have a kind
> of citizenship in the school. No one has ever called me a "fag" ever.
> Nobody ever called me "queer," and I actually did date a few girls
> and I am a very popular student, well known throughout the
> school. I am, you know, involved. So, you see, I have a significant
> role in the school culture that afford[ed] me a visibility even when
> I wasn't "out," even though I didn't identify myself as gay the way
> some students do.

Len was a very articulate informant. Like Dalton, he struck me as mature beyond his years, and like Dalton, he attributed this to the fact that he was involved in a relationship and took strength from this relationship against those who might have moved against him: "Once I started showing up with my boyfriend, well, people must've known then! But I still don't think anyone would have dared cross me just because of who I am in the school. It's too late to get me. I'm established. So I don't feel I've paid that price. However, that doesn't mean I don't feel something."

Unlike at Sylvia Avenue and Burton School, there are no courses at Len's school dealing with gender and culture. Nonetheless, Len had read widely on his own: he was perceptive and generous enough to distinguish between his personal experiences and his position in the broader cultural landscape of his school. He is worth quoting at length:

> When you're queer, you're differentiated the minute you walk
> down the hallway or enter the classroom. You can't relate and they
> don't let you relate. In the halls, it's the students; in the classrooms,
> it includes the teacher and the curriculum. The upside to that, I
> think, is an awareness of how the school and the world works,
> which gives you a target, allows you to know what to change. Now
> can most queer kids do that when they're fourteen years old?
> When you're fourteen years old, it can be crippling, but you're very
> aware that all of these trappings are just that. They're trappings.
> That's why it's important that there are students in upper grades,
> like me, like others, and teachers, who can maybe speak out or just
> make themselves known by being out, just through their presence,

to change things, maybe, but also for those fourteen-year-old
students in Grade 9.

But school, for me, is still a very oppressive experience because
of the expectations of gender and sexuality. I think for queer
students, there's a real tie, a real relationship, between being gay
or lesbian and gender – sexuality and gender. In fact, the most
oppressive part of high school for me is the expectations placed on
me because I was a boy, these straight kids I was talking about, this
whole straight culture. I just find that so restricting and more than
just restricting, I feel it as a weight. A weight that I felt was going
to crush me, maybe until I met my boyfriend – and brought him
to school.

Although Len attributed much of his experience to his secure social position within the school, he made it clear to me that he had witnessed incidents of physical and verbal bullying in his school. He explained to me how such incidents were handled, a description I heard at each school I visited:

Security was the front man. They would physically stop it, catch it,
and then take the offender to the VPs, whose full-time job it was
to mete out student discipline. Our VPs are one black male, two
white females. They respond in the typical fashion, following
the rubric of what they needed to do. In other words, get rid of the
offender. Once students were suspended ... well, they were gone.

Suspending students, I would say, is not entirely effective
because it was treating the problem too close towards the end
of the spectrum, ignoring the start and focusing on the end of a
problem. That's too close to the end, but it's what most schools do
to show they're doing anything. That's my main criticism. There
are not enough resources, money and otherwise, put into dealing
with all of the systemic problems.

I asked Len about these systemic problems: How, if at all, was it possible to improve the experiences of queer students in schools – was there anything the school could do officially? He said,

In terms of what the VPs think is their "official" role, I think they
spend a lot of their minute-to-minute energy dealing with "look at
what you did, this bad thing, this is what's going to happen to you

now," instead of saying, "This is what's happening in the school,
this is a huge problem, let's look at our equity obligations." It
doesn't fit into their day. Look at how the system of education is
putting all these people in the same classroom and then not doing
anything to educate them about each other. Even though we have
this mighty equity policy.

Unprompted by me, Len raised the issue of the *Equity Foundation Statement*.
Like most of the queer students I met, he was aware of the *Safe Schools Act*[26]
but also of the TDSB's equity policy. I asked him his opinion of these policies
and whether he thought they could bring about the kind of experience he
would like to see queer students encounter in schools. He said,

> Yes, I do think these policies could improve schools the way I'd like
> to see them improved. Unless I'm wrong, I think the equity policy
> talks a lot about school climate or environment or something like
> that. And that's what is the big thing for me. The general climate.
> But general climate means you have to think about "the general
> climate" and that means thinking about straight kids, too. They're
> the ones most responsible for the climate.
>
>   I think that my experiences are the result of how straight kids
> think and act about themselves ... I don't want to generalize, but
> I think that gay people are automatically more attuned to the
> demands of gender, the demands of heterosexuality, than straight
> kids are. So somehow you have to get at that straight culture, at
> how straight kids thrash around and present themselves. I mean if
> somebody hits somebody or even calls you a fag or a dyke, that's
> not allowed. And everybody knows it's not allowed. So they've got
> that covered. The climate stuff, not so much. How straight kids
> present themselves, not so much.
>
>   But to me those are two different things: first there's the culture
> and second there's the homophobia. And so, somehow, the policies
> have to get at both of those things, and I think they do, with the
> homophobia, or the emphasis being on school safety, or they're
> trying. I don't think the schools even think about the other part.
> And they should. Change the way gender plays out in sports, in
> phys ed., in the shops, in the masculinized spaces of the school,
> the homophobic teachers. Start studying gender and presentation

of gender in the curriculum. That's what I'd do. That's where I'd
start. The policies are saying what's needed to be said, but they have
to lead to changes in the curriculum, changes in the hallways. Why
does the school dance poster have a picture of a boy and girl on it?

I was not surprised to hear, again, of school dances. School dances and the
images used to promote them were raised many times by interviewees, and
each time they came up, I thought of Sharon Dominick's classroom, walls
covered in images from current magazines. It was not surprising, either, that
Len's definition of bullying, when I asked him for one, was broad: "I'll tell
you what I would consider bullying against me. If someone inhibited me
from doing something I wanted to do, or if someone inhibited me from being who I wanted to be ... so if someone was an obstacle for me, I would
consider that bullying."

At an anti-bullying conference I attended, I spoke with a vice-principal
who blamed a good deal of the lack of implementation of the equity policies
on vice-principals:

> It's political. The vice-principal's office is a political office. Nobody
> who's in there – I shouldn't say nobody, but I will – wants to stay
> in there. They have an eye on a higher office. Nobody wants
> trouble. Nobody wants to rock the boat. Implementing equity
> rocks the boat and draws unwanted attention to your school.
> That's not the way to get ahead.

At the same conference, I asked a guidance counsellor for his take on the
political nature of the vice-principal's office:

> There are some very good policies at the TDSB, but sometimes they
> don't get carried out at a particular school because they're given to
> the VP to deal with, and then the VP has political aspirations, and
> wants to go further ahead in his or her career, and doesn't want to
> have anything controversial going on, and that is an impediment
> to a particular school's being transformed to a more progressive
> place.

When I relayed these opinions to Diana, the guidance counsellor at Crestwood, she said,

I think I would agree. But I don't think people actively sabotage
the equity policies. I think what happens is they don't have time.
They don't see it as a priority. They see safe schools as a bigger
priority, and they don't see that equity is a part of safety, that it is
just as important, because if you've got equity, then you've got
safe schools. So sometimes it's that. It's just lack of priority. And
sometimes, it's just lack of time.

Len spoke of the lack of resources as part of the difficulty with "giving
teeth to equity." This was a complaint I also heard from Jeffrey White at
Triangle, who said the TDSB "needed to put its money where its mouth
was." When I spoke with Jeffrey, he had only recently taken over running the
Triangle program. Since then, he has dealt with hundreds of students who
have arrived at Triangle seeking safe havens and searching for the equity
that does not exist at the schools from which they have fled. Jeffrey said,

The TDSB has this wonderful equity policy that's written down,
there it is, but who's implementing it? Very few people. There's
no money behind implementation of the policy, so all of the
principals are aware of it, but it can just sit up on a shelf because
there's no money. So equity's not getting done.
Students come to Triangle and start learning about queer
realities. One student heard about the equity policy and said,
"What? If I knew this was in place, I would've gotten my parents
behind me and we would've done more at the school to really
have the school do something." And, of course, I'm aware of Gabe
Picard's case in Thunder Bay right now, where a school has been
taken to court to demand it. Here, we have resources because it's
our mandate.

I showed Lorna Gillespie several publications I had accumulated in my
travels through schools, all proclaiming how to promote equity and positive
spaces for queer students, among others. When I asked her where they
came from, she laughed: "These look like those wonderful publications from
the equity office that we never see because they land in the vice-principal's
office and get buried. Nobody has any time or money to implement any of
that stuff." I asked Lorna whether implementation of equity would be improved if these publications went to the guidance counsellor or to the

school library or to the teachers themselves instead of to the vice-principal.
She said,

> No, because teachers don't see equity as part of their job. So the
> number-one reason equity doesn't get addressed is simply that
> they would say it doesn't relate to their subject. They truly believe
> that those concerns are just not part of what they've been hired to
> do. That's an excuse. I think it's relevant to any subject. In fact, the
> *Equity Statement* says that.

Lorna took a broad view of curriculum reform, convinced that the reforms
needed to begin in the early grades but also needed to be a mandated part of
the curriculum. In her experience, the first obstacle to successfully teaching
about gender and sexuality was convincing teachers that equity was part of
their job:

> Well, we definitely have to start early. And it needs to be part
> of the mandated curriculum. Because otherwise, teachers aren't
> going to do that. I mean there are very few elementary teachers
> who are going right out and dealing with this topic, even if they
> might want to, because they would be concerned about parents.
> They definitely would be concerned because so many people think
> that you don't talk about these things until a certain age, right?

When I asked Lorna about what could be done in high school, she said,

> Well I think we need to do workshops for teachers first, and I'm
> going to try to push for this next year. I think we need workshops
> for the teachers – for teachers, for staff, and for students. We
> actually had one once where somebody came in to talk to the
> teachers, just the teachers, about what school was like for queer
> students, and the teachers at the back of the room turned their
> chairs around with their back to the people who were presenting
> and read the paper and ignored them.

I asked Lorna whether she believed this was a conscious political statement
on the part of the teachers. She said, "Well, it had to be. You have a guest
speaker, you don't turn your back to them."

Lorna identified teacher homophobia and unease with approaching these subjects as the second obstacle preventing effective implementation of the TDSB's equity policy. Lorna was not the first informant to point out that many teachers were homophobic. There was not one student I met who did not experience homophobia from at least one teacher. There was not one educator I met who did not find himself or herself surrounded by homophobic colleagues. For example, at Azmi Jubran's human rights hearing, the principal testified that he had never seen physical and verbal harassment of the kind to which Jubran had been subjected, yet Jubran told me that a good deal of the bullying that he experienced occurred in front of a teacher and/ or with a teacher's approval:

> Many things happened in front of the teacher. Apart from physical
> and verbal stuff, there were notes being passed around about me.
> I specifically remember one. A student wrote a – not wrote, drew
> – a picture of me and another male holding hands, saying, "Oh
> isn't this great under the sunlight?" or "Isn't this romantic?" and
> passed it to me. The teacher saw it, and basically all the teacher did
> was say, "Whatever you're doing, stop it," and went on with the
> calculation on the board. He didn't care.

I was reminded of what Michael, a Grade 12 student, had said to me at an anti-bullying and anti-homophobia conference: "I mean my teacher is up there gay bashing. Why wouldn't I want to stay in the closet where it's safe?"

Brian is a very large, strong-looking sixteen-year-old male student at Triangle. Prior to Triangle, he attended a TDSB school in the west end of the city. Brian made an interesting point about the irony of equity policies, noting that the very target of equity – the privilege and prestige enjoyed by some – is precisely the aspect of themselves that those imbued with advantage do not wish to give up and, in fact, cling to jealously:

> When I was at that school, I did a parenting course and they
> were talking about marriage. Do your ideal marriage. And I put
> a guy. And the teacher, she would refuse to mark it. The teacher
> refused to mark it. And she even went to the principal. And then
> I was getting mocked by the teacher and the principal – like I
> was – where me and my friends ate lunch was right in front of
> the principal's offices in the hall. They knew what they were
> doing.

FIGURE 8   Note written by a student and passed to Azmi Jubran during shop class, Handsworth Secondary School, North Vancouver, BC, Wednesday, 22 June 1997

Somebody would see me standing there outside the principal's office and yell, "What did you do now, gay boy?" and then when the principal, when she called me in, she heard them, so she said, "See, your attitude, because you're out, you provoke those kind of remarks." And that's what she said to me. And she knows my history about my dad, about how my dad died when I was twelve years old. So she made a comment that sticks to me to this day: "It's because of your dad, he didn't get to teach you certain stuff." And I'm like, "I'm gay 'cause my dad ...?"

I think it bugged them that I didn't fit a stereotype. I mean, to me, I'm the worst fashion guy and I don't pretend to have good fashion. It's like this t-shirt and a sweater. And I don't know anything about it. Plus my school was such a heterosexist place. You're not gay because you're not fashionable, you don't talk gay, you're not feminine, you're not everything the stereotypical gay guy is. So that made them uncomfortable to think that they couldn't tell who was gay and who wasn't. Students and teachers, they weren't interested in equity because equity is a direct threat to their status in the school.

Lorna made a similar point, referring to what she called the "inherent conservativism" of teachers. "They are a conservative bunch," she told me over lunch. When I challenged her characterization as overly broad, she nodded, thought for a moment, and then explained,

> Well, I just think it's a social-class thing. Teachers tend to be white,
> they tend to be middle-class, they tend to come from families that
> are relatively privileged, and so they've gone to university, they've
> done the humanities thing, and they don't know what to do, so they
> decided to be a teacher. That's a general statement, for sure. And
> what do whites do with their power? Not much. Because they're
> conservative and equity is a threat to them. And the students
> sometimes are just as conservative and just as desperate to hold
> onto their big-man or big-chick status.
>
> So I think there's a number of things. One, they just don't see it
> as part of their job. Two, they're conservative or homophobic. A
> third reason is that they may just be ignorant. I think most of them
> don't even think about doing it. It's not like they think, "Oh I would
> like to do this but I'm scared." And, fourth, they're afraid if they do
> make a bid towards equity, they won't have the support of their
> fellow teachers because we know how conservative teachers are
> and maybe unlikely to offer the kind of support that's needed to
> encourage other teachers to step up. And last, if they are aware
> of equity, it's a threat to their own privilege. And I think some of
> them want the status quo to continue in their students – in some
> of their students.

Despite an equity policy that specifically calls for equity in the school curriculum and environment, and despite official calls in support of a safe and equitable climate for sexual-minority youth in this policy statement and other supporting documents, concerns about parental and community reaction are present. Lorna continued:

> Most schools want to avoid it. Like in my class, every year, there's
> a big hoopla when we discuss homophobia, homosexuality, queer
> theory, the whole bit. Other teachers wouldn't touch that with a ten-
> foot pole. They're scared that the parents will say something, and
> in thirteen years I've had one parent say something. They just don't
> have a political commitment. They don't see their job as political.
> They think it's the dissemination of information and that's what

you are as a teacher. They don't really understand what I consider
to be a teacher to be their idea of a teacher.

I asked Lorna whether the administration, which might have more knowledge of the equity policy than many of the teachers, ever stepped in and
encouraged the teachers to pursue equity concerns in their classrooms. "I
have yet to see it," she said. When I asked whether there were any other
reasons the administration did not take a proactive role, she explained,

> Well, they're former teachers. And they're former teachers who
> want to become bureaucrats, so now you're going even more con-
> servative than maybe the other teachers. If you're a teacher and
> you want to move to be a VP, you're not dedicated to the teaching
> part in my view. You want to make more money; you want to have
> more power. And you certainly do not want to rock the boat.
>
> If you're a VP, you're headed for principal. Once you make princi-
> pal, you might want to go further to be a superintendent, but I have
> to say I don't think that's necessarily always true, but sometimes.

Referring again to the publications that come from the TDSB equity office,
I asked her to explain what happens when the publications arrive in the
school. She said,

> Let me put it this way. If the school board plunks a new program
> or idea in the school and says, "Here, this is what you should do to
> be proactive about gay and lesbian and trans issues," what's going
> to happen? Well, either nothing is going to happen or teachers like
> me are going to pick it up and push.
>
> If it was just handed to the admin, zip for the most part, al-
> though we do have a VP right now who just went with me to that
> forum down at the St. Lawrence Center on gender identity and
> sexual orientation that I told you about. She's definitely on board,
> but I don't think she has the guts to actually do anything right out.
> I'll let you know.

Lorna spoke from experience – she had been teaching for over twenty years:
"These kids are so much more conservative than I am. I was born in 1953,
but sometimes they act like *they* were born in 1953. I say, 'I'm over fifty years

old and I'm so much more with it and radical than you are. What's wrong with you?' But times have changed – I'm a '60s girl."

Doing More than "Zip"

Kevin Kumashiro has identified four possible approaches educators have taken to combat oppression through the curriculum – each of the four approaches conceptualizes oppression in different ways.[27] Only two of the approaches are intended to address both the formal and informal agendas of school curriculum, what Michael Warner has characterized as "heterosexual culture's exclusive ability to interpret itself as society."[28] First, there are educational approaches aimed at providing "education for the other."[29] Under this approach, educators recognize that schools are "harmful spaces"[30] for sexual-minority youth and others who are "othered." The goal has been to improve the experiences of these students so that, in the case of queer students, queer realities and identities are acknowledged and reaffirmed and false assumptions about sexual-minority students are tackled. For queer students, a primary purpose of this educative approach is to view schools as unsafe spaces, to deal directly with the discrimination and physical and verbal harassment faced by queer youth, and to ensure that schools can be therapeutic and safe spaces.

A second approach seeks a curriculum that includes education about the "other." In this conception, all students receive information about sexual-minority youth. This requires an investigation of what society deems to be normal and also a consideration, in Kumashiro's view, of the dangers to sexual-minority youth when heterosexual students conduct themselves armed only with partial knowledge about sexual-minority youth.[31] However, critics Gerald Walton, Susanne Luhmann,[32] and notably Deborah Britzman have pointed out the problematic that accompanies educative approaches focused purely on the "other" (which Kumashiro acknowledges in his third and fourth assessments of educative approaches), in which heteronormativity dodges critical investigation.[33] School knowledge in Britzman's view must be expanded to include heterosexual students so that their own sexuality and notions of gender are scrutinized. Failure to do so may expand knowledge about queer realities and queer lives – and this outcome is very valuable – but this knowledge is received by heterosexuals in their normative positions. These normative positions remain unchallenged and, in fact, are reinforced, thereby ensuring the continuity of each student's individual heteronormative experience and at the same time valorizing and sustaining the heteronormative experience of schools generally. Drawing on Britzman, Gerald Walton puts it this way: "Pedagogies of inclusion and diversity are problematic because curricula that purport to be inclusive actually produce new forms of exclusivity through reliance on constructs of normalcy."[34] Kumashiro prefers an approach that critiques students' privilege and, in some cases, leads to "unknowable" consequences – where what students question and critique leads to unexpected and unpredictable places and knowledge.[35]

A more transformative approach would require that heterosexual students themselves be implicated in curricular reform. This point is highlighted in the conceptualization of "school knowledge" as a "social product," as described by Jean Anyon in her assessment of the schooling of working-class children. Although focused on a different context, her explication also functions as an apt reading of the production of heteronormative scripts and knowledge:

> An examination of school knowledge as a social product suggests a great deal about the society that produces and uses it. It reveals which groups have power, and demonstrates that the views of these groups are expressed and legitimized in the school curriculum. It can also identify social groups that are not empowered by the ... social patterns in the society: they do not have their views, activities, and priorities represented in the school curriculum.[36]

The heteronormativity that governs most heterosexual students normalizes their position, with the inevitable outcome that information about queer youth is received by heterosexual students from a normative cultural stance. This is the point made by Len, Dalton, and Carla – that the curriculum should implicate heterosexual students by investigating their own gender and heteronormativity.

Kumashiro identifies a third way to approach anti-oppression education – education that is critical of privileging, on the one hand, and of disadvantaging the "other," on the other hand. Citing the research of educators who have theorized about oppression, Kumashiro underscores the need to comprehend oppression in schools by examining how and why heteronormativity is privileged and how and why sexual and gender rebels, or nonconformists, are marginalized as "others" – including how this dual process is legitimated and sustained by "social structures and competing ideologies."[37]

The fourth and most transformative method pointed to by Kumashiro is education that is intended to "change students and society." This approach targets and identifies oppression that occurs when "ways of thinking that privilege certain identities and marginalize others ... are cited over and over. Such citational processes serve to reproduce these hierarchies and their harmful effects in society."[38] The stereotyping of sexual-minority youth results in their marginalization, discrimination against them, and threats to their safety.

The maintenance of heteronormativity through spatial practices was considered by many students to be as harmful as or even more harmful than the threat of verbal or physical harassment. Notwithstanding this perception that the dominant arrangements of school space favour "straight space," the official school policies of the TDSB stress equity. Queer bodies and voices are ignored or excluded. Even though the TDSB's *Equity Foundation Statement* was considered by these participants to be adequate or more than adequate – a policy statement that Tim McCaskell described to me as "the best in North America" – spatial practices in the hallways enforced and reinforced heteronormativity. Len referred to the hallways, school entrances, and other "official spaces" of his school as "boy/girl land" and confirmed that queers navigated these spaces as "others." Like Len, Peter Corren viewed curriculum change as a key method of transforming the geography of heteronormative space:

> First of all, if you don't have curricular reform, both ministry man-
> · dated and approved curricular reform, teachers who might want
> to do this work in their classrooms – some will go ahead and do
> it anyway – but others are reluctant to do so because of fear of
> parental backlash and fear of backlash from their colleagues. And
> they won't be able to turn to the curriculum and say, "Here, it says
> in the curriculum I am to do this." If it's there in the curriculum, a
> teacher then can say, "Do you know what folks? I am required to
> do this." And there is nothing that anybody can do.

Diana agreed: "Because it's not part of a mandated curriculum, policies can sit without being voiced. But the vision has to be larger." As with most of the people I interviewed, I told Diana about Gabe Picard's story and about his notion that the vision had to be as large as changing a culture. She was impressed by his courage and shook her head at the response of Gabe's principal: "You can't change a culture, Gabe."

The Correns disagreed with the view of Gabe's principal, which is why they filed their human rights action in Vancouver. Murray Corren pointed to the value and importance of formal laws and policies in transforming the culture but underscored that "hearts and minds take longer":

> I think the fact that we now have things "in law" and in policies gives a legitimacy and a stamp of recognition that without it, we would probably have a much greater struggle. The fact that legal cases have come to the courts and human rights tribunals have, first of all, very much brought the issues to the fore in the public discourse, but secondly, the gains that we have made, puts a stamp on it that says, this is what this country is about, this is who we are as Canadians, living in a pluralistic democratic society. And when the Supreme Court of Canada makes the pronouncements that they have around our issues, I think a very strong and clear message goes out to the general population – that this is who we are and this is what we value.

Peter, Murray, and I discussed how the fear of school violence in the discourse surrounding safe schools had permeated Canadian conversations about safe schools, but we noted that Canada, nonetheless, seemed further ahead in making real strides for sexual-minority youth in schools and for gays and lesbians generally. Peter compared the struggle for equity in schools for sexual-minority youth in Canada with his conception of the struggle in the United States:

> I'd like to say that one of the things that makes Canada Canada and not the United States are all the strides gays and lesbians have made in the past twenty years at law. My only regret is that most of those advancements have come only as the result of legal challenges and that there hasn't been the political leadership to move us forward, of being proactive.
>
> If we can get the education system right, as you've implied, this is not going to be a quick change, but if you can bring up generations that are accepting and understanding, in the long term, it's only going to bode well for everybody.

Tim McCaskell spoke to me about oppression running through many levels and institutions of society. As someone who worked for thirty years in the TDSB's equity office, he was well positioned to comment on the struggle to bring equity and social justice to sexual-minority youth:

> We're talking about a long period of social transformation. The educational system is a very important piece, but it's not the only institution in the world. There are all sorts of others that have similar oppression going on. And so that's different kinds of work in different kinds of areas.
>
> If you deal with this in the education system, you'll be able to combat things that are outside of your control outside it, but one would hope that people in the legal system, in the media system, in other kinds of institutions would be doing similar work so that after a while these things would begin to be mutually symbiotic and reinforced.

Conclusion

Three themes emerged from participants regarding the implementation of the TDSB's equity policy:

1 Participants indicated that the following factors obstruct implementation:

   i programs stop at the vice-principal's office:

     a the vice-principal's office is political – does not wish to be seen as courting controversy (equity perceived as controversial);

     b administrators tend to be conservative and favour status quo rather than effecting change of any sort;

     c administrators tend to be teachers who have been less interested in the teaching part of the occupation;

   ii funding from the TDSB for implementation is inadequate;

  iii teachers may be homophobic – hostile to idea of equity for sexual-minority youth;

   iv teachers do not see ensuring equity and social justice as part of their job – they see their job as disseminating information, not changing culture;

   v teachers fear lack of support from other teachers;

   vi heterosexual students are not implicated;

  vii few or no "out" teachers or supportive teachers are present to act as models for sexual-minority youth – discourages students from taking an active role in seeking social justice in schools.

2 Participants indicated that the *Equity Foundation Statement* is more effective in circumstances where the following factors are present:

    i   teachers work to support gay, lesbian, bisexual, transgendered, and queer (GLBTQ) students despite administration indifference or lack of support or interference;
    ii   GSAs are present in school;
    iii policies include GLBTQ content in curriculum, reflecting queer realities and experiences;
    iv   students hold conferences at schools on bullying of GLBTQ students and life experiences of queer students;
    v   GLBTQ realities are reflected in school culture (e.g., drama, art);
    vi   heterosexual students are implicated in curriculum on social construction of gender and sexuality;
    vii queer teachers are out to provide practical role models for students.

3 Participants indicated that when policies and legislation, such as the *Safe Schools Act*, are intended to respond to isolated incidents, schools are more likely to follow policies. However, in terms of addressing a broader conception of oppression faced by sexual-minority students, this approach is not effective since the larger school culture is not likely to change.

In January 1998, Ontario premier Mike Harris amalgamated the Toronto Board of Education with five other Metro Toronto school boards to create the TDSB. Jobs were cut and programs scaled back. Statistics were no longer kept on the number of harassment/bullying complaints. No longer was anyone taking down the details of what were, for sexual-minority students, day-to-day experiences throughout high school. Therefore, only by collecting empirical evidence and giving voice to the subjects studied is a vivid picture – or any picture – likely to be captured and presented on behalf of students frequently subjected to homophobic bullying and the oppression of the hidden curriculum.

The hidden-curriculum theory exposes what students learn beyond what is taught from books: knowledge is transmitted and received through other school structures beyond the formal curriculum. In this regard, hidden-curriculum theory shares with legal pluralism a revelatory function. However, legal pluralism offers us something further. Hidden-curriculum theory is not employed to discuss how multiple normative orders compete with each other, particularly state-issued law. In particular, discussions about the hidden curriculum have not been employed by scholars to address the specific issue of why law on the books alone is insufficient to achieve equity or to construct safe schools, broadly conceived – in other words, to combat what hidden-curriculum theory successfully tells us is going on in schools. Legal pluralism, then, can be used to explore the competing nature of multiple influences that hidden-curriculum theory does not.

The hidden curriculum permits us to see how existing inequalities based on gender and heteronormative sexuality are reinforced in schools in various ways, including through the social structures of the classroom, learning activities, textbooks, spatial practices, and extracurricular activities. Revealed, these social outcomes can be addressed through programs, equity policies, and legislation that acknowledge the cultural by-product of schooling. Legal pluralism shows us that programs, policies, and state-issued law alone, although important determinants of students' experiences, may be insufficient to effect a transformation of school culture without also taking into account other normative orders operating within youth culture. The objectives, approaches, and practices of equity can be, and are sometimes, influenced and complicated by other normative approaches to the social regulation of student space. Legal pluralism suggests that the best way to take these other normative influences into account is to introduce equity policies and programs at an early age.

Kumashiro has indicated that oppression is "not always easy to recognize" and that it occurs for sexual-minority students in multiple and often contradictory ways. This oppression can result from bullying, whether it is physical, verbal, situational, or cyber-based, as acknowledged by most scholars, but also from heteronormativity, heterosexism, and homophobia, as underscored by the students and teachers. Approaches to making schools safe have tended to ignore the equitable aspect of safe schools. Equity policies intended to address heteronormativity, which is a great source of oppression for sexual-minority youth (and leads to violence when transgressed), are complicated by the factors discussed earlier in this chapter. It may be that the only or best means to recognize the complicated ways that oppression is expressed in the educational context is to ask the students. As Ryan said to me, "What would the ramifications for school policy be if they listened to students?"

6

The Long Arm of the Law?

───────────── Mapping (Other) Normative Orders
in Youth Culture

> When it comes to the point when somebody has to say some-
> thing, they're thinking, "I don't want to be that tattle tale." Here's
> something to think about. There's two options, you think. This
> person's in trouble and I have to get them *out* of trouble, so do
> I say something? Or do I want to get this person *in* trouble? And
> that means saying something. And you can't do one without the
> other, so there really is only one option ... shut up!
>
> — ANNA

Sharon Dominick is at the front of her class at Sylvia Avenue Collegiate and
Vocational School. Every class, Sharon spends five minutes settling down
the students. I am struck that the students call her "Miss." They seldom, if
ever, call her "Miss Dominick" – simply "Miss." In response to a long look
from Sharon, a large girl who is loudly confronting another student turns to
Sharon: "But *Miss*, she won't give me back my pencil case." The room is
never completely quiet. When the students are finally quiet enough, Sharon
explains the exercise she has planned for this class: "We're going to work
briefly on the 'F' word." This brings an instant reaction from the entire class
– a lot of "ooohing" and a few whistles. "The one that means '*gay*,'" Sharon
clarifies. "The what?" one of the students asks. It is Wayne. Wayne makes

sure he is heard from in every class. "Oh, *that* 'F' word. Fag. Oh, sorry, Miss, I was just sayin.'"

Sharon responds, "Well, you can just say in a note to me why I don't want to hear that word. I went out of my way to say 'F' word, and you went out of your way to use it." Wayne rolls his eyes, but this scenario has played out before and it will play out again. Sharon walks over to the board, where she has already written questions for the assignment. "I want you to work through a couple of questions that are on the board. You remember these words 'connotation' and 'denotation'? Yes? Do you remember what 'connotation' means?" After a brief discussion and general agreement that "connotation" means "social meaning" or "implied meaning," she reads the questions to the class:

Okay, number 1, "What is the connotative meaning of the 'F' word?" Okay, so what is the *social* meaning or *implied* meaning of that word? You may have multiple meanings. And there are multiple parts to the question. Okay, so, "A. What is the *factual* meaning of the word?" You may want to look up the history of the word. You can use the dictionary and you can use the computer.

Some students are already pulling out books and papers. Other students ask to borrow paper or a pen as Sharon continues:

And 'B' part, "How does the word get used in today's culture?" For example, does it appear on the Internet? And then, here's a question about the word "queer."

There is much laughter and comment from the class at this. "Miss, you said it."

"Miss, you said the word."

"It's okay to say *this* word," Sharon explains. "Why do some people want to *reclaim* the word? What does that mean – to *reclaim* the word? We talked about this before." No takers. "It means to use it in a new way." Sharon continues:

And the next question is, "Why are some people uncomfortable with re-claiming?" What do members of your *group* think about using the word today? And I want you to come up with reasons. I want all of you to participate. You can't just say, I agree, or I disagree.

There is a lot of rumbling from the class and some grins at private and whispered comments. Sharon ignores them. "Any questions?"

Throughout Sharon's explanation of the exercise, my eyes scan the students, trying to take in the range of reactions, but my attention keeps coming back to Barry, who is very still and very quiet. Barry is the student who usually wears a perpetual grin across his face and swoops across the classroom, comfortable in his impersonation of the "Jack" persona from *Will and Grace*. On this day, I have the sense he is trying to be invisible. There are no signs of Jack McFarland.

The next day, before class, I notice that Barry is early and sitting with three female students. They are practising reading aloud the work they have prepared for class. "Jack McFarland" is in full evidence. Whatever he is reading, the girls are all enjoying it, and the four of them periodically have to stop since they are laughing so much. I notice that Wayne enters the classroom. He sees them and moves to another part of the room. I also notice that, once seated, Wayne stares hard at Barry – waiting for Barry to notice that Wayne is staring at him. When Barry finally sees Wayne, Wayne rolls his eyes, shakes his head, and turns his back. The message is clear: don't be so gay. Barry's demeanour changes; he becomes still and quiet. His friends, who have had their backs to Wayne, are unaware of the message that has just been sent to their friend. Sharon and I have both noticed.

An hour later, class is almost over. Sharon is taking volunteers. Many of the students have put up their hand, anxious to read their work. Barry has not been one of them. He has sat quietly throughout the class, his hand down, despite his early arrival that morning to practise his presentation. I am thinking about Barry when I become vaguely aware of what is happening on the other side of the classroom.

"I have a question about that guy sitting at the front of the class." Wayne is speaking. I have come to realize this about Wayne: what bothers Wayne eventually comes out. Wayne conducts himself as though he occupies some sort of leadership role in this classroom, but whether this leadership exists only in his own mind or only with respect to a few students, I have not yet decided. However, in this moment, I do begin to realize that his question is about me. "Who is he again?" Wayne asks.

Sharon jumps in: "I've introduced Donn already. Weren't you here?"

"I don't know," Wayne answers with a grin, and this is met by some laughter from the students sitting around him – but just a little.

I sense that a number of students do not wish to support this sudden questioning of my presence in the room, and they do not smile in solidarity with Wayne – a possible indication of the breadth of Wayne's classroom leadership. Sharon seems unperturbed, her usual bearing in all circumstances. Sharon has seen and heard it all before and is used to repeating information to her students. I have started to become accustomed, as well, to the extent to which students respond to subjects or questions that interest them, holding them up for another inspection.

Sharon says, "Donn is a law student who is studying high schools and the law. And he's our guest." As I have already made clear, Sharon and I have arranged, as a safeguard for the students I meet with and interview, not to identify specifically my interest in the bullying and harassment of sexual-minority students.

Wayne looks at me a long time as he thinks about this – at least, it seems a long time to me – and I am pretty sure I know what he is about to ask. "I don't get it," he says. "What does *schools* have to do with the *law?*" There is that question – again.

Theories and Forms of Law: "Regulation in Many Rooms"

Building on the view of interviewees that both bullying and safety need to be conceptualized broadly in order to address the specific needs of sexual-minority youth, and using hidden-curriculum theory as a point of entry into understanding why sexual-minority students regard equity as important in making schools safe from heteronormativity, this section employs legal pluralism to argue that policies and law reform that respond to bullying alone are not enough. Legal pluralism demonstrates that the effects of formal law and policies need to be measured, rather than assumed, and that the law of the state (i.e., the law "on the books"), although perhaps the most visible, public, and high-profile form of regulation, may not be – at least as currently written – the most significant determinant of students' experiences and of the outcomes of equity and social justice.

For many people, including perhaps most lawyers, law exists only, or primarily, in the form of appellate-court decisions or as directives promulgated by elected representatives in government; however, there is a group of critical scholars for whom the study of law entails a much broader approach than simply focusing on state-issued legislation, policies, and judicial opinion. Other mechanisms of social regulation can be as potent and can engender the same kind of responses in a community as official legal controls. This focus on the everyday is at the root of the research undertaken by scholars who employ the theory of legal pluralism. Legal pluralism is used in theoretical and empirical research to navigate an investigative course through multiple regulatory processes, including the state's promulgation of formal law, but it also includes other modes of analysis aimed at investigating other normative orders present in a culture.[1] Legal pluralism is the socio-legal theory that law, in a broad sense, is issued in all social and economic contexts – for example, schools, the workplace, and families. Legal pluralists look beyond the state-centredness of common conceptions of law (i.e., formal, state-issued law in traditional studies of legal phenomena) to argue that not all law is uttered by legislators or by courts. As Sally Merry has noted, legal pluralism at one time referred almost exclusively to the interests of cultural anthropologists in setting out the social effects of intersecting or overlapping systems of laws among indigenous peoples in Africa, Asia, and on other continents.[2] The interest of these researchers was concentrated on European colonial laws and local customary law and conventions.[3] British and French colonialists laid down a European model of law over local law, integrating both to the extent that local law was not "repugnant to natural justice, equity, and good conscience" or "inconsistent with any written law."[4] Merry characterizes this form of legal pluralism as "classic legal pluralism."[5]

However, as the aims of researchers who grounded their work in legal pluralism expanded, different conceptions of legal pluralism took shape.[6] One helpful definition of legal pluralism that Merry proposes is the occurrence of any two or more legal systems coexisting in the same cultural space. In this conception, legal pluralism is concerned with the ways that compound legal systems emerge, change, and are perceived to be interconnected with one another.[7] The legal norms may or may not issue from the state – often, there are multiple sources. Legal pluralism directs researchers to consider, in addition to traditional law, other forms of social regulation and normative ordering that operate throughout society.[8] Thus – and this is Merry's preferred definition – the pluralist form of investigation, by exploring other legal orders, studies "the extent to which other forms of regulation outside law constitute law."[9] Researchers, therefore, contemplate traditional sources of law (i.e., constitutional documents and conventions as well as laws created by legislators and by judges) but also embrace other legal orders.[10] From the perspective of a social scientist employing legal pluralism, law is a "system of thought by which [particular] forms of relations come to seem natural and taken for granted ... in support of their categories and theories of explanation."[11]

The configuration of legal pluralism that has been put forward by Merry and adopted by some researchers has not been received without debate.

Much, although not all of it, has centred on whether normative orders other than state-issued law really can be equated with law or comprise a legal order.

I am less interested in debates about whether other normative orders amount to law or legal orders and am drawn to a consideration of these cultural influences as complicating forces that attract equal or greater loyalty in the day-to-day lives of the individuals whom formal state-issued law seeks to govern. Brian Tamanaha explains the attraction of legal pluralism in action this way:

> What makes this pluralism noteworthy is not merely the fact that there are multiple uncoordinated, coexisting or overlapping bodies of law, but that there is diversity amongst them. They may make competing claims of authority; they may impose conflicting demands or norms; they may have different styles and orientations. This potential conflict can generate uncertainty or jeopardy for individuals and groups in society who cannot be sure in advance which legal regime will be applied to their situation ... This state of conflict, moreover, poses a challenge to the legal authorities themselves, for it means that they have rivals. Law characteristically claims to rule whatever it addresses, but the fact of legal pluralism challenges this claim.[12]

With respect to the problematic of considering these social forces to be law, Boaventura de Sousa Santos offers a characterization that is attractive and apt for the purposes of this book:

> Why should these competing ... forms of social ordering – from informal dispute-processing mechanisms implemented by neighbourhood associations to commercial practices, codes enforced by non-state armed groups, and so on – be designated as law and not rather as "rule systems," "private governments," and so on? ... This question can only be answered by another question: Why not? Why should the case of law be different from the case of religion, art or medicine? ... It is generally accepted that, side by side with ... official, professionalized ... medicine, other forms of medicine circulate in society: traditional, herbal, community-based, magical, non-Western medicines. Why should the designation of medicine be restricted to the first type of medicine?[13]

Emmanuel Melissaris has indicated that

the study of the legal must be directed towards the discovery of alternative perceptions of the world and justice and of different practices of solving practical problems by accommodating competing interests as well as meeting the prerequisites of substantive justice. The question of law and justice then becomes one concerning our *whole* way of life, how we perceive and place ourselves in our surroundings.[14]

The theory among educational theorists that an informal curriculum functions alongside an officially prescribed curriculum is similar in some ways to the theory espoused by legal-pluralism scholars since both are concerned with multiregulatory systems, but they give rise to two different conversations engaged in by two different groups of scholars. The hidden curriculum bolsters a normative order, whereas legal pluralism directs us to an examination of other normative orders that reinforce the production and consumption of heteronormative privilege in the educational context and the corresponding disadvantaged position of queer students.

State-promulgated law is the most visible, public, and high-profile form of regulation, but it may not be the most significant in terms of its social impact, particularly among students. I should add that I do not mean to suggest that official law is not up to the task of addressing the oppression of sexual-minority students and that ultimate solutions do not lie in looking to law for this achievement. My focus at this point in the study is on an assessment of current law and policies and on their effectiveness when considered alongside other regulatory influences presently operating at these sites. To understand what elements shape social phenomena and how these elements impact people's thoughts and behaviours, legal pluralism guides researchers to examine the multiple normative regimes in a particular social field (in this study, regimes that are involved in the production and consumption of heteronormativity, or equity, or social justice). The approach includes an engagement with formal state law at different levels (e.g., federal law, the *Charter*,[15] the *Constitution Act*,[16] and provincial legislation), with informal state law at different levels (e.g., policies of individual schools, policies of school boards, and administrative decisions), and with rules, codes, manners, practices, or normative systems developed and applied by non-state actors that operate in practice or effect much like legal controls.

To understand how to distinguish a legal-pluralist view of law from a traditional, or law-centred, approach, it is best to begin by setting out what is intended when referring to a traditional view of the law. The long-established law-centred view of what constitutes law reflects how the average person, even someone unschooled in any study of law, approaches law as it exists apart from society, politics, or economics, including all legal mechanisms, phenomena, and institutions. In this traditional view, law is a field of social control that is separate and autonomous from other areas of society (e.g., art, commerce, and leisure) and that operates in a designated location within society.[17] Under this approach, the law is viewed as something official, given, and delivered with cultural pageantry – it is a formal social activity that endows certain people with authority to act and to which the populace is expected to respond. Both Harry Arthurs and Marc Galanter characterize the formal approach to law as the basic "paradigm"[18] by which lawyers, judges, many law professors, and most of the community understand and measure law. The objective of laying down clear penalties for certain prohibited behaviours animates this basic paradigm of law: law promulgates sanctions to punish and/or to restrain violations.[19] In this representation, when law is enforced, it is the power of the state that is called forth to enforce the law's intent.[20]

As Leslie Green has observed, however, some laws have other functions. Law defines and regulates: it "draws lines and sets standards," for example, when it gives voice to zoning regulations.[21] The law tells us that to be recognized as a legal will, a testamentary disposition must conform to the requirements of provincial legislation dealing with wills – writing requirements, witness requirements, necessary signatures, even the order in which the signatures are appended to the document.[22] Here, the law merely dictates *when* a written document will function as a testamentary disposition, but no *obligation* to create such a document is imposed by the legislation. Traditionalists, purists, and certainly most lawyers, however, would likely point out that these examples are connected by distinct and unyielding restrictions on where the law is – and is not – found. In this perspective, the law is composed of a set of norms articulated by the state (i.e., the legislature and the common law), executed by state officials (e.g., police forces, tribunals, bureaucrats, and court orders), and administered by lawyers and judges in courtrooms.[23] All aspects of day-to-day cultural life, therefore, are governed by state-issued law: promises supported by consideration (or rendered under seal) are enforced and the security of personal and real property is maintained by laws developed by legislators and judges, professionals, and experts.[24] Despite acknowledging that the law obtains its power from the state, legal traditionalists have often argued that the law is free from the influence of any class or group of interested persons.[25]

Hence, as Arthurs points out, agreeing with Galanter, the sway and pervasiveness of this perspective on the law are evidence of "legal centralism."[26]

Scholarship that attempts to apprehend social behaviour, customs, manners, and conventions by studying formal law alone is confronted by the confines of this approach. Arthurs suggests several essential factors that limit conventional legal analysis.[27] First, not all cultural enterprises can be accounted for by formal law.[28] Moreover, some events, although outside the emphasis of conventional legal analysis, may be considered using a traditional approach.[29] Additionally, the "paradigm" of law fails to give reasons for the inability of formal law – the "marshalled powers of the state," as Arthurs refers to formal law – to achieve its intended outcomes.[30] Finally, a centralist position fails to account for "law-like patterns of social behaviour" that occur in the absence of the supposedly fundamental traits of official law.[31] In sum, legal centralism, it is argued, obscures or misses what plays out at other cultural sites.[32]

This view of law capitulates little, if any, ground to what legal pluralists would contend animates their more robust characterization of what constitutes law. Nor would a socio-legal scholar, armed with a pluralist approach, narrow the conception of what makes up "juridical space" – legal space is not limited to courtrooms but is sufficiently wide in scope to encompass any cultural site where behaviour is shaped and/or regulated. The truth of this becomes evident when it is appreciated that interviewees in this research indicated that some spaces were more tinted with regulatory characteristics than other spaces – even within the same school building. Arthurs suggests that "what lawyers practice and [what] academics teach" in law schools is not promulgated exclusively from parliamentary proclamation or judicial order; rather, law originates in "semi-autonomous 'legal fields,'" not in the separate, autonomous fields that characterize courtrooms and legislatures.[33] Arthurs notes that these fields include, but are by no means limited to, such cultural sites as workplaces, schools, hospitals, prisons, and neighbourhoods.[34] Although purists may disagree, legal pluralism informs us that each of these fields constitutes a location from which law also issues – where behaviour is regulated in similar ways:

> Thus, social scientists have not hesitated to propose new definitions of law which at least link it to other apparently similar phenomena. For example, it has been proposed that law consists "primarily of rules by which persons in society order their conduct, and only secondarily of 'norms for decision' developed by the courts and of legislation enacted by the state" ...

Thus, we can no longer ignore [the law's] economic function, its political content, or its social effects. Nor can we fail to address the ongoing processes by which different manifestations of law come into existence, shape and are given shape by events, and interact with each other. And finally, we must accept that law is much more diverse in its content, causes, and effects than our original paradigm proposed. This new way of looking at law we may therefore call "legal pluralism."[35]

Legal pluralism recognizes the large role of the state in governing the community and the influence of empowered actors to carry out the will of the state; however, where the decentredness of legal pluralism most markedly deviates from traditional law-centredness is in pluralism's rejection of the supremacy of both the state and its designated actors in marshalling a single, normative order. Of equal interest to the socio-legal scholar are actors in social institutions such as the family, churches, mosques, athletic arenas, coffee shops, the workplace, and schools, all of which also muster normative regimes and often do so in complicated ways. Julia Black expresses it this way:

Social problems are the result of various interacting factors, not all of which may be known, the nature and relevance of which changes over time, and the interaction between which will be only imperfectly understood ...

Government does not have a monopoly on the exercise of power and control. Rather it is dispersed between social actors and between actors and the state ... Regulation occurs in many locations, in many fora; there is "regulation in many rooms."[36]

Legal Pluralism in an Educational Context

Sally Moore describes another aspect of the semi-autonomous social field that is useful here. In Moore's view, this field

can generate rules and customs and symbols internally, but ... [a social field] is also vulnerable to rules and decisions and other forces emanating from the larger world by which it is surrounded. The semi-autonomous social field has rule-making capacities, and the means to induce or coerce compliance; but it is simultaneously set in a larger social matrix which can, and does, affect and invade it, sometimes at the invitation of persons inside it, sometimes at its own instance.[37]

The advantage of Moore's conception is that it shows that the semi-autonomous social field is not tied to the exclusive influence of any one cultural group – thereby expanding the breadth of factors that may be at play. Moore's conception of the semi-autonomous social field demonstrates an important principle in the context of law and policy approaches intended to address the problems of oppression in schools, and it illustrates, if only partially, why new legislation and policies or other programs to orchestrate social change (e.g., the *Equity Foundation Statement*)[38] do not necessarily result in the intended outcomes: "This is partly because new laws are thrust upon going social arrangements in which there are complexes of binding obligations already in existence. Legislation is often passed with the intention of altering the going social arrangements in specified ways. The social arrangements are often effectively stronger than the new laws."[39] Moore's approach is not based upon preconceived notions or advance "definitive conclusions about the nature and direction of influence between the normative orders."[40] The external legal system enters and operates within the social field but not necessarily before other influences or as the only, or even the most, notable influence. As well, Moore's approach accommodates resistance and the agency of the actors who animate the field – something called for in the conception of one form of critical legal pluralism, put forward by Martha-Marie Kleinhans and Roderick Macdonald, that resonates with my conclusions:

> A *critical* legal pluralism ... rests on the insight that it is knowledge that maintains and creates realities. Legal subjects are not wholly determined; they possess a transformative capacity that enables them to produce legal knowledge and to fashion the very structures of law that contribute to constituting their legal subjectivity ... It endows legal subjects with a responsibility to participate in the multiple normative communities by which they recognize and create their own legal subjectivity.[41]

The concept is not new and has been taken into account by educational scholars advocating critical pedagogy, such as Peter McLaren, who has observed that "the individual, a social actor, both creates and is created by the social universe of which he/she is a part."[42]

In sum, one of the implications of employing a legally pluralist approach in this study of sexual-minority youth has been to swell "the research framework" used to investigate a culture[43] – in this book, the heteronormative

culture of schools. Investigation of secondary schools as one of these semi-
autonomous social fields encourages an emphasis on the ideological aspects
of bullying.[44] This approach renders visible the hidden and informal practices that are inevitably positioned in schools. It is this visibility that requires
the actors in this field to acknowledge the ways that the effectiveness of
equity policies are negatively impacted not by structural obstacles to their
implementation but by the presence of other interacting normative regimes
that complicate the effectiveness of policies. The purpose of the *Education
Act*[45] and its *Regulations*[46] is both to govern the operation of schools and to
deliver education throughout the province of Ontario. Each province is governed by its own legislation. In turn, school boards, which are created under
authority of legislation, are authorized – indeed, asked to – articulate board
policies in order to implement the governance of schools as set out in legislation and regulations such as the Toronto District School Board's (TDSB)
Safe Schools Foundation Statement[47] and its *Equity Foundation Statement*.
However, the governance of students is influenced by other normative orders. The literature on bullying has not investigated the overlaps and gaps
between two regulatory forces: on the one hand, formal state law as an
active participant in a cultural process that seeks to end bullying and, on the
other hand, the normalizing culture of the daily life of schools with respect
to gender, sexuality, and other norms (e.g., safety and equity), which complicates and interacts with formal law.

Determining whether these other normative regimes constitute law in
the sense that the *Education Act* and its *Regulations* constitute law, as some
legal pluralists might argue, is beyond the scope and purpose of this study.
In fact, to engage in this debate would deflect the focus of the study away
from my research questions and goals. Nonetheless, by borrowing and utilizing principles of legal pluralism, the purposes of addressing the research
questions can be better accomplished, namely, a consideration of the ways
that state-issued laws and policies, particularly the TDSB's *Equity Foundation Statement*, are effective and to what extent their reach may be complicated or rendered less effective. The research questions, then, become
distilled to a focus on determining what role state-issued law now plays in
the educational context when measured against other forms of social regulation. For example, my project inquires into the ways students observe each
other and, despite some forms of resistance, execute the values of the
normative social order,[48] often violently. For me, the purpose of employing
a legally pluralist approach is to address the research questions by observing and assessing a culture – here, the culture of sexual minorities in the

heteronormative educational context. Rather than engaging in a debate about whether certain social structures of the classroom constitute law, I am using principles of legal pluralism to investigate this social setting in a way that produces new knowledge about how sexual-minority students are governed at this site and about how this governance might impact their goal of seeking social justice.

Let me set out how I am not using legal pluralism. Legal pluralism, in the context of this book, might well ask, "what are the norms of street culture?" or "what are the specific norms of the unwritten but understood student 'code' that dictates that 'snitches get stitches?'" This kind of investigation needs to be undertaken but is certainly beyond what I set out to study. However, the students reported that these norms exist, are clearly understood, and demand allegiance. In the opinions of participants, the proscriptions of the street – the norms of street culture – have priority over any equity program that seeks equity by, for example, asking the victimized or bystanders to report bullying.

The reasons for my approach to legal pluralism in this book are twofold. First, this study has the documentary purpose of identifying these other influences in order to broaden our understanding of the experiences of sexual-minority students. This research was undertaken with a consideration of schools as sites where teachers and school-based administrators function as agents of culture in an environment where dominant gender codes and norms of sexuality are reinforced, but this examination of schools as cultural agents has been complicated by a consideration of the anti-discrimination and equity policies of the TDSB. These policies recognize the role of schools as cultural agents but seek to create an environment equally secure for all students regardless of gender, sexual orientation, and other characteristics used pervasively in practices of social subordination.

Second, employing a legal-pluralist approach provides one means of gauging the reach of formal law into youth culture.[49] The purpose of gauging this reach is to conduct a critical-prescriptive analysis of current approaches and to underscore the complicated ways that policies are received by students. This analysis includes investigating how formal state law interacts with other normative orders in the educational context – such as religion. State law addresses certain problems in schools but is compromised by its failure to account for the perpetuation of social norms within youth cultures. It is the hegemony of these norms that inculcates the negative notions of difference that lead to homophobic bullying and other forms of violence. Sexual-minority youth are thus easy targets despite state law or school policy. In this context, my focus is on other normative orders identified by the participants:

1 Gender codes: The power of gender coding has been noted throughout this book, but by no means can rigid lines be used to divide the themes and concerns of each section –which is as it should be.
2 Religion: The power of religion is a theme that emerged over and over in my interviews with sexual-minority students. Interestingly, the subject was often attached to comments about race. Race was a subject that many of the participants found difficult to address (although some were quite free with their commentary on race), and in the next chapter I deal with race not as a separate category of meaning but in relation to religion.
3 The "anti-snitch" culture: In the opinion of the participants, whose peers often monitored their gender and sexuality, the problems with reporting incidents of bullying and harassment were tied to the presence and power of an "anti-snitch," "anti-rat," or "street" culture among their peers, male and female.

Legal pluralism directs us to pay careful attention to the rules that may be understood and adopted, if not codified, by a youth culture in its self-regulation and peer surveillance. It is in terms of these rules that the effectiveness of formal state-issued law can be better understood, although this approach makes no claims to comprehensive understanding. It is useful to recall Kumashiro's observation that "different forms of oppression (such as racism, classism, sexism, and heterosexism)" are enacted in schools in "multiple and contradictory ways,"[50] an acknowledgment of the sheer range of activities, functions, and processes that occur in an educational setting. These factors may or may not constitute law as understood within the approach known as legal pluralism, but they are nonetheless usefully investigated by employing principles of this socio-legal approach.

7

Barriers to the Effectiveness of State Law

There's the law and then there's what my mother says.

— SILVER

Code of Silence: "Snitches Get Stitches"

Obie Trice's second CD, *Second Round's on Me,* contains a song entitled "Snitch," in which other rappers are featured.[1] The lyrics leave no doubt about norms against snitching and the low social position of anyone who "tells":

Just don't, whatever you do, snitch
'Cause you will get hit
Pray I don't face you, yeah.

The words describe the "street justice" handed out to snitches, revenge that may be exacted against them. Perceived as "weak" and buckling under to the law ("when the heat's on 'em"), there is no doubt that those who snitch have betrayed the group, having gone from "cats" to "rats" in need of "decon."

The music video of the song depicts Trice, Eminem, Akon, and their gang committing a bank robbery. One of them, Rick Gonzalez, captured by the police, snitches, and the entire group is rounded up and sent to jail. At some point, after this group is released, Trice, Eminem, Akon, and the others hound the snitch, and the video ends with the Trice-led group finding Gonzalez and pulling a gun on him. Singing a refrain of the chorus, they shout at him: "You rat bastard!" The music video of the song was edited when it was shown on BET and MTV. On MTV even the title of the track was changed, from "Snitch" to "Mindstate of a Mobster," and the word "snitch" was deleted from the track.

At Sylvia Avenue Collegiate and Vocational School, Sharon Dominick spends a good deal of time analyzing the misogynist and homophobic lyrics of singers, particularly singers like Eminem and other rappers. Drawing on the work of Jackson Katz,[2] she tries mightily to get her students to consider the power of some rap music – and the damage behind its lyrical assault on queer students. Diana Goundrey at Crestwood Collegiate and Vocational School undertakes the same efforts at her school in her work as a guidance counsellor, both with students and teachers. Both Sharon and Diana are familiar with the "anti-rat" or "anti-snitch" culture that is also reflected in these sorts of songs. Diana has a list of complaints about the music that students carry around on their iPods. Foremost among her grievances is that hip hop music, in particular, dehumanizes women and homosexuals and, at the same time, depicts how acts of violence against them play out in a culture that vilifies anyone who turns away from this culture or informs on criminals – by relegating would-be rescuers to the outside social position of being a snitch. Safety at Diana's school of 1,200 is implemented by surveillance cameras, two patrolling security guards, and strict enforcement of the zero-tolerance policies against physical harassment. Diana was a founding staff member of Closet Space, a recently formed Gay-Straight Alliance at Crestwood. Diana sees "pockets" of equity being pursued on behalf of sexual-minority students at her school but sighs deeply at the obstacles in her way. Diana credits a growing number of teachers at her school for supporting equity and promoting anti-bullying programs in the school; however, she is most frustrated by the anti-snitch culture that pervades her school:

> Yeah, it's pretty bad. Snitches get stitches. It's a huge problem.
> There's so much of this gangster, this jail thing, right? We hear a
> lot of jail talk in a regular school in a way that you never used to
> hear. I notice it because I used to work with young offenders. So I
> know – I've seen that happen over the years. And this snitching,
> this rat thing, that's a real jail thing. So you don't rat. There's that

brotherhood amongst thieves, and all that kind of stuff. It's bad.
Bad and huge.

I notice that Diana talks about a "brotherhood," and I wonder whether she means that literally, but she shakes her head, firmly, even as I begin to ask. "No," she says, "it's both boys and girls. It's both."

For a queer student, high school is often a lonely, harsh, and dangerous theatre encountered in isolation. Ridicule, harassment, and the threat of physical or verbal violence from students make schools unwelcoming and hostile. As well, institutionalized heterosexism and homophobia are threats to safety and self-actualization. The Toronto District School Board's (TDSB) *Equity Foundation Statement* is designed to change the educational experience for minority students.[3] I asked Diana and my other participants to measure the effects that the anti-snitch culture that animates youth culture has on a school's ability to fulfil the promise of equity policies and programs. When I first met Diana, I noticed that she had a tendency to lower her voice from time to time, almost inaudibly. At first, I thought she did this when I asked her a particularly sensitive question, but in listening to her interviews several times, I have come to recognize the sadness in her voice that accounts for the drop in volume:

> At the beginning of the year, we had – I thought – again, this is
> merely an observation. Oh, this ... it's so sad. I thought we had
> more kids than usual who simply stopped attending in Grade 9,
> mainly boys. And there seemed to be no reason. It's not like they
> had poor attendance before that. There seemed to be no reason.
> They would just stop coming. And they would never give an
> answer as to why. I tried ... but ...
>
> I suspected that they were being bullied, and they just didn't say
> anything. Wouldn't. Couldn't. They just didn't want to come to
> school, and they just waited for the next semester, so they could
> leave. That's what I think. I have nothing to back that up. But it's
> just strange that these perfectly nice kids, and they were quiet and
> nice kids. And they just stopped coming. And I wonder if that's
> what it was. God, I could cry.

I pointed out that the policies are well written and that at this school the students at least knew the guidance office was interested in equity. Diana said,

Yeah, yeah, yeah. But. It's so huge, Donn. So big. Because if they
said something, somehow it would get out. Even if you say to a kid
look, no one's going to know that you told me this. I'm going to say
blah, blah, blah. Even *that* makes them nervous, because if it ever
gets out, they're going to get killed. Donn, they're going to get killed.
And they know that. We can't protect them. Doesn't matter what
the school says. Doesn't matter. Can we stop?

The subject of race came up a number of times in discussing barriers to
effectiveness. When asked to theorize about religion, families, gender coding, and the power of the anti-snitch culture in framing the decisions of
youth in the context of a youth culture, many of the students and teachers
raised the issue of race. If they did not raise it, I did. My assessment is that
most, but not all, of the interviewees were reluctant to discuss race, however
much they might have had an opinion on it. In many cases, the interviewees
emphasized that they were characterizing people based on tendencies of
specific cultures, not based on any biological drives. Accordingly, on the
second day I spent with Diana, I asked whether there was a racial component to the anti-snitch culture at her school. Diana hesitated: "I think so." I
asked whether this anti-rat culture also operated among whites. She explained, "Yes. But that is more of a Regent Park–gang neighbourhood kind
of thing. 'We're from Regent Park. We don't snitch on each other. We don't
do that.' That's more of a class thing than a race thing. So it exists for both,
but the reasons are different." I asked Diana whether the students might
want to see their school improved, to accept students and teachers who
speak up and report violence as a stand against bullying and the culture of
gangs that are associated with the school. Diana was waiting for me to finish
the question. "No," she said simply.

Larson attends Crestwood, a multiracial school of 1,500 students, in
which the majority of the students are, in his words, "brown." Larson tells
me that "there is a definite anti-snitch culture among black students." When
I ask whether it's racist to lay the charge at the door of any particular minority, he says,

Our school likes to claim that it's multicultural, but it's way not.
It's mostly blacks and East Indians. A lot of them are homophobic.
Because most of these people are immigrants and they are taught
that way, to be fearful of homosexuals and all that stuff. It's not

biology, it's not racist, it's a connection between homophobia and maybe culture and religion. Most homophobic in this school? Muslims. Walking down the hall, they'll indiscreetly say "fag" or whatnot. It doesn't bother me because I don't let it. But the snitch thing is a big black thing.

I ask Larson why he makes an association between blacks and anti-snitching. He explains, "You see it. Some of them wear shirts that say 'No Snitches' or 'No Snitching,' stupid things like that. Just like most everything, it comes from the media. They see it on a music video and they want to fit in so they adopt it." Larson is not the first student to argue to me that taking care of snitches is central to this construction of urban masculinity:

> It's not all of the students, but enough that you can see it. I'd
> say mostly the black guys are the ones who do it. I think it's just
> because with the type of music they listen to, especially rap,
> they're more drawn to it, those are the things that come up more
> often in that kind of music. The code is you handle yourself, or
> you stick up for your homeboy, but you don't ever, ever snitch.
> If you do, you deserve to die. I don't have any problem in saying
> these things. I'm a gay student who is subjected to violence, and
> I feel unsafe because of that kind of code of behaviour. I don't care
> if it offends anybody to hear it. I'd rather be alive and count on
> people to help than care if I offend anybody. If you were here every
> day, you'd see it, too. That's what's going on. And, of course, that
> kind of, I don't know, sociability gives rise to concerns about
> being too close, so they make their homophobia known to
> counter that.

This is precisely the point central to Jackson Katz's investigation of urban music. He has observed that "this hyper-masculine posturing – so dismissive of women – produces homoerotic tensions in the inner sanctum of hip hop maleness, which then requires Eminem ... (and other gangsta rappers) to verbally demonstrate their heterosexuality by attacking gays."[4] Homophobic epithets define this brand of masculinity as something different and apart from homosexual identity or presence. The victimizer declares himself to belong to a masculine hegemony that is removed from the homosexual group.

Len, at Trimble Collegiate Institute, mentioned how the codes of behaviour among students that discourage snitching also sustain the general culture of fear that, for both victims and bystanders, surrounds harassment and bullying in schools:

> A lot of students don't rat or snitch out of fear. They don't wanna be hurt by the people who are committing these crimes or whatnot. And those people are often in gangs. I would say it's really big among black students, particularly Jamaicans.
> Just fear. That anti-snitch mentality feeds the fear. There is a definite gang presence at this school. But there are students here who wouldn't be affected by the fear of a gang presence, and they would speak up. I'm one of them. I'd just go to the office, the VP.

Noel disagreed with the wisdom of reporting, although he came from a much more rural area before transferring to the Triangle program at Oasis Alternative Secondary School:

> No, I wouldn't do that. Not at my old school, I mean. Maybe in Toronto, you could count on some back-up, but at so many of these other schools, like at my school in North Bay, forget it. You can report it, but nothing's going to be done about it. They just don't care. That kind of behaviour, bullying, harassment, it's expected. It's boys being boys. And it's not addressed. I don't know what their deal is, but probably because they're the older-generation type of teachers. Where it's like they just don't care. And then there you are, the rat. Whether you're the gay kid or the kid who saw it, if you reported it, you're the rat.

When I spoke with Azmi Jubran, who in addition to being labelled queer was also ridiculed and chastised for being a "rat," he pointed out to me that many people at Handsworth Secondary School, a rather affluent high school in North Vancouver, faulted him for being "disloyal" to the school. Even students who might have felt sympathy for how he was treated, "iced him out" when he complained about it.

On Monday, 27 May 1996, Azmi Jubran was in shop class. Jubran claims that Trevor Howard, a student in the class, called Jubran "gay" and, when confronted by Jubran, admitted to doing so. As a result, Jubran punched

Howard in the face. Howard brought criminal charges against Jubran, from which Jubran was acquitted because the judge found that Howard had "invited Jubran to fight." Jubran told me that the judge was frustrated by the disingenuousness of the students who testified:

> I was found not guilty. They were all lying out of their teeth. They all lied out of their teeth. It was ridiculous. The judge even – the judge stated that he was disappointed to see that it was happening at the school, and that the school was allowing it to happen, and that no one was there to represent the school, and that basically that they were all lying, and he was disturbed and disgusted to hear it.

According to the "Chronology of Events" filed by Jubran in connection with his complaint to the British Columbia Human Rights Tribunal, Howard denied Jubran's version of events: "Mr. Mike Rockwell interviewed Trevor Howard who said that he had called Azmi Jubran 'gay' in the past, but did not in this instance. Other students, Brad Hummel and Cale Watson stated to Mr. Rockwell that Azmi brings it on himself and that it's all a joke."[5] In his testimony before the tribunal, Howard admitted to being aware of Jubran's bullying and harassment from Grade 8 through 10, the year that Jubran punched Howard:

A   All through eight, nine and ten.

Q   And when you say "all through," can you be a bit more specific about how often you saw that?

A   Maybe once every four months.

Q   So once every four months, at least, big boys would taunt Azmi with words like "gay" or "faggot" and he would end up in a fight with them; is that what you're saying?

A   I'm not necessarily saying that they were always the ones starting it, but, yeah.

Q   And would you go and watch those fights?

A   Not usually.

Q   So how do you know they took place then?

A   Because I saw enough of them to know that they were happening.

Q   Did you ever report those fights to the school?

A   No.

Q   Why not?

A   Because most of the time they happened after school, so it wasn't really
    important.

Q   But it happened on the school grounds, right?

A   A couple of times I believe it did.

Q   So you never reported that to the school?

A   No.

Q   Why not?

A   Student code of conduct.

Q   Which is what?

A   You don't tattle on people.

Q   So you thought it was a bad idea to talk to the school about what was
    happening?

A   No, I just knew it was a bad idea for me to talk to the school.

Q   And what did you think would happen if you tattled?

A   I never thought about it.

Q   Well, you must have had some notion of what would happen. You
    didn't do it.

A   Oh, a notion would be that the fight would be broken up but my whole
    grad class would not like me, or I'd have problems with the people who
    it was important most to be on decent terms with.

Q   And when you say people that were important to be on – so you meant
    your peers in general.

A   Yeah.

Q   No one in specific?

A   No.

Q   So even though you knew that fighting wasn't a good thing, it was more
    important that you be liked by your classmates?

A   Yes.

Q   And did you call Azmi names so that you would be liked by your
    classmates?

A   I guess you could say that.[6]

Gabriel (Gabe) Picard observed the same slavish devotion to peer approval on the part of students who might have spoken up on his behalf but
did not: "I think when you're at a certain age, you don't wanna be like, you
know, a snitch. You don't wanna tell on people, especially when you're that
age, because you're trying hard to be cool, or whatever you're trying to do.

And lots of the time there's no point in doing it. Because you tell and nothing happens."

, The degree to which Jubran was denounced for standing up for himself is disheartening. To Azmi Jubran, Christian Richardson was only "a name" from high school. "I didn't even know him during high school," Jubran told me. "I didn't know of him. He was a student. He was some elected official on the student council, kind of like a head of something on the student council." Nonetheless, their lack of familiarity with each other did not stop Christian Richardson from testifying on behalf of the high school in Jubran's human rights action against the school. "Essentially he came forward as a witness for the school board, and basically said he found it insulting that I was attacking his perfect school in his perfect world." In addition to testifying on behalf of the school, Richardson also wrote a letter to the *Vancouver Sun* denouncing Jubran's human rights complaint:

Azmi Jubran's problems reminded me of my own experience at Handsworth secondary school ("Persecuted" student wants district to pay for golf, Sept 13). I, like many other high school students, was bullied, called names and "persecuted" by those who thought I was different. However, the taunting was one of the many challenges high school and life put before us. Some students deal with math, some with bullies. The bottom line is that the administration can only do so much; the victim has to make an effort as well.

I am shocked that Mr. Jubran is suing the North Vancouver school district. While I remember the feelings and the loss of self-esteem, I fought through them and became successful. Essentially, this case is about revenge, pure and simple.

It appears that Mr. Jubran forgets that he is to blame for doing nothing for 13 months after graduation because he had "no motivation." Clearly, that is laziness. I could see him languishing around the house for a month or two – but 13?

His claims for roughly $520,000 in lost wages is a joke. Who's to say he could have been working at hotels right out of high school? Claiming green fees and golf lessons is a flagrant attempt to extort the school district for a luxury some people cannot even afford.

What schools need these days is a good old-fashioned dose of reality and administrators need to be thanked for a thankless job.

We all endured high school bullies. The question is, have we grown up and learned from them? Yes. Has Mr. Jubran? No.[7]

Jubran told me that Richardson, who was not involved in the events that happened in the case, was so "insulted" that Jubran had "ratted" that he was willing to denounce Jubran at the hearing:

> He was completely biased, and it was basically a full-on rant on me. And he had some information at the tribunal that was, I thought, quite significant. He came forward to say that there was an incident that had happened to him. He had been in band class when somebody in the band class was projecting words of homophobia toward him. Calling him gay and calling him a homo and a faggot, and of course, he does not identify himself as being homosexual. And funny enough, he went and complained to the principal, and the next day, that kid, that student that harassed him, was kicked out of the class. Well, I'll state that that was the action that I was looking for. Why wasn't I treated the same way? Because he was a big guy in the school and had a relationship with the principal and, therefore, I would say, [was] favoured more so than myself.

Clea Parfit, who represented Jubran at the tribunal, questioned Richardson about his motivation for writing the letter. This is an excerpt from his cross-examination, conducted by Parfit:

Q   Mr. Richardson ... I have a copy of ... the letter and I just want to ensure that we're talking about the same letter. It commences: "Azmi Jubran's problems reminded me of my own experience at Handsworth Secondary ..."

A   Yes, that's right, that's the article.

Q   Okay. In that article, you, would it be fair to say, take a fairly negative approach to Mr. Jubran's human rights complaint?

A   I wouldn't say negative. I would just say differing in opinion because in no way [sic] tried to add a negative spin to it. It's just my own personal opinion, you know, which is speculation.

Q   Okay. So you say you didn't – you did not add a negative spin to it?

A   My intention was not negative. However, you have to remember once you send a letter to the paper, they do a little bit of editing, too.

Q   Are you telling me that what appeared in the paper is not what you wrote?

A   Not entirely. It's – some of the words were changed around, but it's the same – it's the same – like I would – I would still take – take the author of it. Like, it's the same letter I wrote, just some of the words were switched around.

Q   Okay. In the letter, it's correct that you wrote: "I am shocked that Mr. Jubran is suing the North Vancouver School District."

A   Yeah. Yes, I wrote that, that's true.

Q   And you write: "Essentially this case is about revenge, pure and simple."

A   I feel it is somewhat revenge, yes.

Q   My question is, is that what you wrote?

A   Oh, yes, I did write that, yes ...

Q   And you don't know anything specific about Mr. Jubran's circumstances apart from what you've read in the popular media, is that right?

A   This is true ...

Q   ... And you were also under the impression that Mr. Jubran was claiming for $520,000 in lost wages?

A   No. That was a misprint of the Vancouver Sun, I wrote $23,000 ...

Q   And you describe his claim, which you understand to be for $23,000, as a joke?

A   Yeah, because that – whose [sic] to say flat out of high school he could have been working in hotels. I mean for 13 months, he chose not to work.

Q   And so you'll agree with me that if you're saying you're shocked by his complaint, that you feel his complaint is revenge and that you feel his claim for damages is a joke, you – I think you'd agree with me that that is, in fact, a negative spin, as you put it, on his complaint.

A   I – I wouldn't say negative, I would say it's personal assessment. I'm not trying to in any way say from a legal standpoint or – it's just my personal view on the situation. But that doesn't affect a fact that (indiscernible) occurred.

Q   And you then conclude your letter by writing: "The question is, have we grown up and learned from them? Yes. Has Mr. Jubran? No." That's the conclusion of your letter?

A   Yes, it is.

Q   And when you wrote your letter, you were pretty fired up in opposition to Mr. Jubran's complaint, isn't that correct?

A   This is correct, yes.

Q   And would you describe your letter as a rant?

A   No, I would not describe it as a rant. I think it's fairly well worded and I kind of don't really take kindly to it being called a rant. I took a great deal of time in making sure it was appropriate for the paper.

Q   Thank you ... and those are my questions.[8]

In his testimony before the tribunal, Mike Rockwell, the vice-principal at Handsworth Secondary School, acknowledged the anti-snitch culture among students and the difficulty that the ensuing silence of witnesses created for the effective resolution of incidents of harassment: "And often this would happen in an investigation, where [a victimizer's] friends may or may not have told the truth. But it's like there is a code of silence with peers and you have to make a judgment, I guess, about the truth because the stories are often differing."[9] Jubran was continually harassed for documenting and reporting his harassment to Rockwell. The transcript of one of his notes indicates the ongoing nature of the sort of verbal onslaught he received for snitching:

> I walked into the 10:30-11:30 AM English class sat at my seat facing away from Devon Carson and this is when he had said to me "Why did you tell on [Steve] on Sept 13." I said nothing he then kept on persisting to embarrass me in front of the whole class. He then told me "don't you think that's childish" I said I think you're being childish, then he persisted to embarrass me until a couple of girls (Mischa and Siobon) both I think told him to stop it. He then had listened to them.

Remarkably, Jubran's harassment for being a "rat" continued long after he graduated from Handsworth Secondary School, very publicly, in Vancouver's newspapers.

Two students who testified on behalf of the school at the tribunal, and whom Jubran identified as two of his victimizers, continued their assault with a letter of their own to the *Vancouver Sun*:

> As classmates of Azmi Jubran, we saw the harassment he encountered, especially during his early years at Handsworth secondary school (Student's mom weeps as she recalls bullying, Sept 14). But we do not feel that his complaint of discrimination based on perceived sexual preference is valid.
>
> In our high school, as well as in many other schools, "gay," "queer" and "faggot" were commonly used as insults regardless of whether the person was homosexual. They were used in the context as "geek," "dork" or "nerd." Many of the males in our school have been referred to as gay at one time or another; we are no exception. In no way did anyone mistakenly think Azmi or us were gay.
>
> Did the school do enough to stop the harassment after Azmi lodged numerous complaints? That is up to the B.C. Human Rights Tribunal to

decide. In 1996, the school made a list pinpointing the culprits who had harassed Azmi. All were taken out of class and disciplined. They were told that if further harassment took place, there would be harsher consequences. We remember incidents where students would insult Azmi, even after they had been spoken to. They were taken out of class that same day.

Azmi was definitely harassed, but in no way was he discriminated against. Unfortunately, he was the victim of a common problem within our school system – being bullied.[10]

Not conveyed in the letter is that, according to Jubran, two of the students responsible for subjecting Jubran to the "common problem" of bullying were the authors of the letter condemning him for taking action to end the harassment – by them.

The retribution theme is one that I heard at many sites. Noel at Triangle remembered what happened to students who were bullied and who then spoke up at the school he attended before transferring to Triangle: "If I told a teacher, they would have to address it. But I doubt it would change anything. They would just go up to them and tell them to 'Stop bullying,' which, you know, doesn't help, and if anything it provokes more violence." Benjamin at Burton School did not see much of the anti-snitch culture at his school: "No, we are more of an open-bitch policy, not a don't-snitch policy. If something happens, speak up about it, talk about it, which is unique. But that's the general culture here. It pushes out the snitch culture." Noel described the school he attended before transferring to Triangle:

> I used to go to a school in North Bay. Yikes. I know there were
> students, gay students, who were bullied. They had bad attendance
> records, they were withdrawn. They stopped coming to school for
> a while, or they dropped out altogether. It's so difficult to get them
> to come forward. Sometimes they just transfer out rather than
> admit what's going on. Same thing with students who see someone
> getting bullied – you cannot get them to come forward. Even here,
> in Toronto, not here, of course, but my friends' schools, forget it.
> Rat killers rule. You don't want to be the rat.

The anti-snitch mentality affects victims of bullying, as well as bystanders. For victims, there are concerns about being perceived not just as a "rat" but also as gay. As Noel told me, there are two people sharing the bottom rung: "snitches and fags." "If you're gay and you ask for help, guess what? You're both – a fag and a snitch." Trista, also from Triangle, agreed: "Yup, a fag and a snitch. Lowest." I asked Carla and Emma, both from Elizabeth Coyt Alternative School, and Lazy Daisy, from Burton School, how this operates for girls. All agreed that boys and girls are both governed by the anti-snitch code of youth culture. Lazy Daisy said, "At my previous school, stuff would happen to me, but I never said anything. Because I didn't want to seem like a snake and I didn't want to draw attention to myself about me being gay. Snake and snitch. Yeah, it's like someone who tells on everybody else. Plus, I'm gay? No thanks." In the context of the anti-snitch culture, the messages queer students receive are mixed. The TDSB's *Equity Foundation Statement* tells them that students should not have to pursue their education in this climate, and, in fact, their schools may be, even if sporadically, following at least some of the protocols of the policy. As Diana pointed out, however, the street says something else: put up with it, don't complain – if you do complain, you're a snitch. Or worse, you have identified yourself as a queer student.

Emma expanded on why the anti-snitch code, which governs students at many schools, does not dictate how self-governance plays out at Coyt:

> Oh, no, there's no anti-snitch codes here. It's very much a school
> in which the institutional theme of social justice commands something
> else, that we look after each other – especially seniors looking
> after juniors. We all look out for each other, so if there was an
> instance where someone's feelings got fairly badly hurt and they
> recruited a few seniors to go talk to this person, there would be
> no retribution for that. None. We'd say to that kid, "You're being
> insensitive and you should probably go apologize." We look after
> each other. That person would go apologize and believe me, they
> would never enforce an anti-snitch code because the social-justice
> theme is so engrained here, they'd know they did something wrong
> – and now it had been dealt with and it was over.

Carla agreed with Emma but offered a slightly different take on the extent to which Emma's view might be true in all corners of the school. As always, the students at Burton School and Coyt impressed me with their ability to articulate ideas that reinforced the need to transform the current culture into one that emphasizes education and equity. Carla said,

> Yeah. I know what you mean by a code of silence. No, not really,
> not here. It's really interesting, though. There's sort of an interesting

dynamic in our grade because we're larger. There's the people who do sports and then the rest of us, which is really interesting. It's not that we clash, but we just don't really interact much. Our classes are often structured half and half, but we just don't interact much 'cause we can't find much common ground. So, on the other side, among the people who play sports, who are on teams, I've seen that sometimes, the other group of students in our grade, just a little bit of loyalty to the team and don't turn on us, but I haven't found that within our group of friends. And, still, it's not much with the sports half, nothing that would interfere with anybody feeling that bad behaviour wasn't going to be or shouldn't be reported. But you can see how it might take root among people who felt they were, I don't know, part of a group, somehow, if that feeling were greater than the sense of equity or social justice we pursue here. But thankfully, here, the general culture of equity wins out over any code of silence.

This examination of schools pursuing equity and social justice has shown how effective students can be in changing other students' behaviour. The ways that the senior students educate the incoming students at Coyt about the school's institutional themes of social justice, both inside and outside the school community, comprise the most notable examples. However, in the same way, without this education and example, students can monitor each other and survey each other in ways that lead not just to bullying but also to the continuation of bullying through the intimidation and harassment that results from the normatives of an anti-snitch tradition operating in youth culture. These norms and standards bring about an applied form of justice for students who dare to contravene them. For many students, conforming to school policies or school ethics that require or encourage them to report bullying and harassment to school authorities is worse than the bullying itself. The code of silence that exists among students shapes and articulates the street policies by which students conduct themselves and judge others "on the ground." The kind of retribution that Obie Trice warns will be brought to bear on anyone who "rats" constitutes this street law's force of "reason."

Religious Codes: The Lion, the Witch, and the Wardrobe

In the context of Gabe Picard's plea that we change the culture of schools, critical re-examination of the organization of schools is essential. Instead of viewing current spatial and curricular practices as natural or inevitable, I examine the forces that shape behaviour in schools. As Benjamin Levin and Jon Young put it, understanding the status quo means comprehending "why things are the way they are, how they came to be the way they are, who benefits most from them, and how they might be otherwise."[11] Regarding the cultural expectations of students, the interviewees, as well as my observations in the field, suggest that students are both subjects and objects of disciplinary forces: their behaviours are regulated first by outside forces and then by means of a disciplinary power that is internalized.[12] They monitor each other, thereby epitomizing, to some extent, the values of a normative social order. Recall that when Barry, at Sylvia Avenue Collegiate, became aware of Wayne's "don't be so gay" scowl, Barry received the message – and processed it, governing himself accordingly. However, nowhere did the intricacies of group and self-governance express themselves more frequently or with greater punch than in my discussions with interviewees about religion and religious influence.

Peter Corren identified "religion" and "religious backlash" as "the foundation of nearly all of the opposition that we've experienced over the ten years of doing anti-homophobic work." He referred to Hamed Nastoh, a young man who jumped off the Pattullo Bridge in Vancouver, and the reaction to his suicide as an example of the obstacles religion and "religious influence" present to the cultural transformation that the evidence presented in this book suggests is necessary in order to resolve the problem of the bullying and oppression of queer students in schools:

> Hamed Nastoh jumped off the Pattullo Bridge, killed himself, because of bullying, in fact, homophobic bullying, and ... the [British Columbia] Ministry of Education ... decided to take on, to implement, some kind of initiative around bullying in schools.
>
> And so Lorne Mayencourt headed up the taskforce that was charged with going around the province to speak with administrators, teachers, parents, and students about bullying in schools. And when they produced their report, the report clearly stated that the most prevalent form of bullying going on in schools in British Columbia was homophobic bullying, that they had heard about it over and over and over again. Wherever they went and whomever they spoke to, they heard about the high incidence of homophobic bullying.

When that taskforce came out with its seven recommendations about what the Ministry of Education should do about bullying in schools, not one of those recommendations addressed homophobic bullying.

In the Correns' assessment, this kind of response, grounded in a fear of a religious backlash against queers, is clearly homophobic. In contemplating the forces they perceived to be rallied against their work, Peter said, "It's all this business of 'everybody needs to be respected.'" Murray agreed, adding, "Everybody needs to be respected and we can't focus on one group." Peter added, "And yet it's obvious where most of that bullying is coming from, and yet they don't want to deal with it head on. There is some sort of agenda or suppressing going on." Peter interjected, "I think it's parental backlash – not even parental. I'd like to go even further and say it's religious backlash, which is the foundation of nearly all of the opposition that we've experienced over the ten years of doing this work." Murray cited "Christian fundamentalist religion" as a powerful force pushing back at their work:

> The Surrey School Board case is a prime example of this. You only have to look at the makeup of the Surrey School Board at that time. There's Heather Stilwell, a right, right, right-wing Christian fundamentalist. Initially, she got that constituency stirred up. And then she started her work with the other religious communities, stirring it up with them as well. But I think primarily, it comes from Christian fundamentalists, and then they bring in – like George Bush does – and instil fear in people, enough fear, and then you can get them all on your side.

Peter described to me how fear could be used to misinform and to secure large numbers of parents in opposition to queer curriculum change and cultural change in the classroom generally:

> You misinform them about what the subject is, then you can mislead them, then you just bring them in like cattle. Because they do what they're told. The majority of them have no idea what this is about. But they're told to do it anyway because they just follow.
>   It's a vocal minority. And quite honestly, some of the comments out of ministry staff endorse that as well. They're sort of quite fed

up with this small minority giving the impression that they
represent the majority [and] making a lot of noise.

Other interviewees pointed to different religious groups as being the "most
homophobic" or the "most resistant" to supporting queer youth. I asked
the Correns about the religious community. Peter told me that in their
experience, this community was both "positive and negative." Murray as-
sessed interactions and responses from religious communities in this way:
"Any religious community, be it Christian, be it Muslim, be it the Sikh community, be it Judaism, we have seen people on both sides of the issue.
Unfortunately, those who object are the most vocal."

Religion was identified as a form of constraint that students sensed in
school every day and, like the hidden curriculum, was identified by some
students as a greater source of personal intimidation than physical bullying.
Sian from Crestwood described the problem that religious belief poses for
those looking to make things better for queers in schools by implementing
curricular or cultural change through policies:

> When people call me "lesbian" or something, I always just put my
> hand over my mouth and I'll say like, "Oh my god, not a lesbian!"
> That's what I scream back. But that's not changing anything, is it?
> Even if I rat them out. I don't know what would occur and I don't
> know if anything would actually teach them a lesson other than
> education or to just give up on the people. It's hard to get through
> to the world when you're a minority.
>
> It's not worth it to try to educate these people on the subject
> because you're not gonna be able to get through their minds –
> because there's always the religious barriers. And that's what's so
> frustrating. Sure, maybe, you can deal with verbal insults or even
> physical bullying – I mean you can punish them, you can even
> have clubs like Out of the Closet or stuff in sex ed. or whatever –
> but how do you get at what these kinds of people are thinking
> when they're cloaked in their religion?

I asked Sian how she thought queer kids would behave in high school given
the circumstances she described. "Like me," she said. "I'm not intertwined
in this school in depth and I don't want to be."

By the time I spoke with Silver at Triangle, I had heard a lot of pessimism
from queer students and others about breaking through the "religious

barriers" that Sian identified and that so many others agreed were impeding the effectiveness of equity policies and transformational efforts. Before coming to Triangle, Silver had attended a school of the TDSB:

> Like all the TDSB schools, they have "policies," but, I mean, put that in giant, giant quotes because I know for a fact that a lot of the teachers there are quite homophobic, whether it's in a subtle way or in a just outright way. And I know that if a student complained that there would be like some kind of, "oh we'll investigate it" because they have to with the *Safe School Act* and stuff.[13] And they'd bring the teacher in and be like, "Yeah, we had a complaint from this student. So just don't say stuff like that anymore." But I guarantee you that they don't actually – that they would never actually do anything about something like that because adhering to their religion is more important than adhering to bullying policies.

That Silver transferred to Triangle rather than remain at her previous high school reflects, perhaps, a greater optimism than was felt by Sian, who remained at Crestwood, choosing not to become "intertwined":

> There was one teacher at my school who took equity seriously, but the other kids were just not receptive and I think religion was a big part of that. Who knows? Maybe you're getting through to some people, I am sure you are, but in terms of changing the culture that we were talking about before, I think it's too late for most of them. Not for kids in Grade 1 and 2 but for most of these ones. But I think you still have to try. I wouldn't give up.

Noel, also at Triangle, laughed out loud when I asked him about what role religion played, if any, in the lives of students at his previous school:

> It's like there's a little religious book they all read and carry around with them, with a little paragraph saying about how if you were a gay person, it was against God to be gay. That God created man to reproduce and continue the line of mankind. If you are a gay person and you are attracted to someone of the same sex, you could not do that and therefore you had a different agenda than straight people. Same sex is bad because you can't procreate. Which, of course, is stupid, because we could if we wanted to and a lot do.

Brad, a teacher I met at a conference dealing with anti-homophobia and the bullying of queer students, talked with me about the role of religion in the lives of students:

> It's amazing to me. I'm forty-seven and I cannot remember religion being this big a part of my life or in the lives of my friends when I was in high school. And I was a religious teenager. But it's there, now, and it definitely leads to a disconnect between what the policies are trying to do in terms of equity and how students experience school carrying their religious beliefs with them. There's education and then there's schooling.

Len, one of the more articulate students I met, was typically succinct in describing why religion was a force that students expressing a queer identity confront:

> Religion valorizes heteronormativity and condemns queers. There's not much mystery or more to it. People who practice religion stop their thinking there. Can you call that thinking? Religion rejects queers when what it needs to do is embrace us and find a place for us in the church. I'd start with acknowledging that the priest is quite possibly queer himself.

For James Sears, Walter Williams, and other advocates for queer youth, rather than suppressing or denying their queerness as many religions demand, queers should be free to emphasize their uniqueness. The difficulty is that – notwithstanding equity programs that pursue these goals or foreground gender difference or variation in sexuality – religion, as a counterbalancing force, more often does not.

Many of my participants carefully made this distinction between schooling and education. For some, education was distinguished as the official curriculum, and schooling was more about the hidden curriculum. For others, education was about facts or information, and schooling was about processes that, in the words of one student, "a lot of teachers seem to have forgotten is going on." Jerry said to me, "The education part, maybe you'll remember, probably you won't. The schooling part, you never forget. Students take that with them for the rest of their lives." Jerry had been out of high school for two years and was very involved with the organization Teens Educating and Confronting Homophobia (TEACH). He was also an editor of a local gay newspaper. He added, "Schooling normalizes hetero-sexism and lets homophobia take root for some." When I asked queer students who were still in high school how schooling most pertinently affects sexual-minority students while they are in school, the students responded with similar answers – the process "marginalizes" them, "isolates" them, or "marks" them in some way. Jerry said, "Schooling empowers the straight kids. They learn they have the power, that they're normal, and if they do it right, then they're cool, too."

The Correns and I discussed, in everyday terms, how homophobia develops in the school system and the disconnect between official culture and youth culture. I asked them whether they had seen the film *Elephant* (2003), written and directed by Gus Van Sant. *Elephant* is a chilling film. Stylistically and thematically, it grips the viewer in the way it depicts the multiple intersecting cultures that coexist inside one school. Adult, official culture, as in many high school films, is mostly absent. The film depicts the cool, quiet formality of the hallways, library, locker room, and cafeteria – spaces of structured order that are more or less empty – and the ineffective attempts to control the anarchic tendencies of youth culture. The harmonious surface appearance is shattered by the eruption of the violent subculture that has been lurking there all along. The conversations of the students fill these empty spaces with a meaning that seems totally disconnected from the adult attempts to impose order and from the eruption of violence. Does *Elephant* represent a post-Columbine anxiety in schools in a useful way, in the same way that, say, *Blackboard Jungle*, a popular 1955 Hollywood film, captured anxieties about juvenile delinquency in the 1950s? Does the film provide useful representations of how life in schools is experienced? I raised these questions with the Correns, who had been working on transforming curriculum and classroom experience for over a decade. I suggested that the film represented not only the gap between official culture and youth culture but also the difficulties of bridging this gap. The disconnect between official culture and how students experience schools may be the greatest challenge facing advocates of cultural transformation. How do you get at youth culture? How do you penetrate youth culture? The response was one I had heard before. Murray Corren's answer to this question was quick and assured: "You start right back at kindergarten." Peter agreed:

> Oh, yes, absolutely. In the situation of elementary schools, it's on the playground. You're out there, you know that there are adults supervising, but normally you're far enough away that they can't

see or hear what you're up to. In junior and senior high schools,
it's in the corridors. It's happening. This is part of the process of
schooling.

Confronting religious fundamentalists and regressive political-religious
responses in their daily life in schools and in their community work has been
common for the Correns. They see that religion-based adult anxieties about
queer lives and queer realities are linked with how homophobia develops in
high schools. Once entrenched, homophobia, fuelled by religious discourse,
is difficult to tackle, exposing – as both homophobia and religious beliefs do
– the restricted effectiveness of equity policies intended to recognize queer
realities in schools and to address the heteronormativity of schooling. As
Trista, a female transgendered student I met at Triangle, put it:

> These are power-tripping teenagers, armed with religion, being
> defined by their religion, trying to define you. Never mind trying
> to find our place in society – their attitude is "we'll tell you what it
> is." And what it is is heterosexist and religious-based. And forget
> about any queer content in the curriculum. You're going up against
> God, for God's sake.

Peter and Murray Corren have a queer son and have witnessed up close the
effects of heteronormativity, but also of homophobia, on queer students.
Having a queer son is one of the reasons why the Correns have struggled to
have queer realities built into the education system and the process of
schooling. In their view, this requires an educative component in the curriculum as well as a component that addresses the heteronormative culture
outside the classroom. Murray said:

> From the perspective of how homophobia develops in the school
> system, a little girl comes to school in kindergarten and they might
> be doing a unit on family, and this little girl reveals that she has two
> mommys and the question comes up from other kids, "Well, how
> could you have two mommys?" and it's over and done with and
> kids move on.
> Well, by the time those kids reach Grades 3 or 4, they've heard
> in the playground, outside the classroom, the homophobic insults,
> they've seen it in the media, in the general school culture, and
> many of them have heard homophobic stuff at home, so by the

time they get to Grades 3 and 4, they start to realize – they've
gotten enough of the negative messages to tell them – there must
be something wrong.

Secondly, if you want to insult and hurt somebody's feelings,
that's a good epithet to use. Thirdly, if you happen to think you
might be gay or lesbian, you are going to shut down and remain
invisible around it.

Then when they hit middle school or junior high school and the
hormones are kicking in, then the verbal abuse can start to manifest
itself in physical violence. And then when they get into high school,
queer kids or those who were perceived to be queer, their lives [are]
unbearable to the point where many of them [can] just no longer
tolerate being in such a toxic environment, that they simply leave
school.

Like most of the students, teachers, and others I interviewed, the Correns
were far from ready – quite the contrary – to give up on the state's ability,
through law and policy, to provide protection to queer students from
physical bullying and to transform the schooling experience of queer – and
straight – kids. Murray Corren understood and valued the sway of formal
law and policy, which are, at once, symbolic, practical, and effective on the
ground, notwithstanding the influences of other normative orders, particularly religion, that may filter through and also find expression:

The fact that legal cases have come to the courts and human rights
tribunals have, first of all, very much brought the issues to the fore
in the public discourse is extremely important. But secondly, the
gains that we have made puts [sic] a stamp on it that says, this is
what this country is about, this is who we are as Canadians, living
in a pluralistic democratic society. And when the Supreme Court
of Canada makes the pronouncements that they have around our
issues that affect how schooling is carried out, I think, a very strong
and clear message goes out to the general population – that this is
who we are and this is what we value. From that, change is possible.

Change may also spring unexpectedly from the cultural "muscle" that religion tries to flex in schools. Religion, or a religious backlash, was identified
by the Correns, and others, as the greatest obstacle to bringing queer realities
into the curriculum or, in fact, to transforming a heteronormative culture

into a more equitable one; however, the argument can also be made that the determination of religion to suppress a freer sexual and cultural impulse than it prefers may also give rise to an equivalent response to oppose this impulse. The visceral force of religious might demands recognition and a response in return that provides a clear challenge that must be met. As Murray Corren noted, "We need to have things written 'in law' or in policies because it gives a legitimacy, a force, and a stamp of recognition which without, we would have a much greater struggle with these other issues, like the influence of religion." In this perspective, religious codes are positioned as dictates of a full-bodied normative order that is on equal or almost equal footing with state-written law. Investigating how religion functions within a cultural site, such as schools, in law-like ways is crucial when assessing the ability, or inability, of formal law and policies – which, in the TDSB, are sympathetic and purposively supportive of sexual-minority youth – to effectively address harassment and oppression of queer students.

At the time I was at Triangle, one-third of the students were transgendered. Trista addressed competition in the minds of students between formal policies and other normative orders, such as religion or peer codes, that also dictate how they "ought" to behave. She expressed an awareness of what faces sexual-minority students, and their advocates, who seek to wade into youth culture with the notion of changing it. She expressed ideas I heard time and time again from many interviewees. Trista is worth quoting at length:

> For straight students, when they think of queers, in their mind,
> they're just already programmed to say that it's wrong and to
> condemn it. Bullying is one step away from that. And that usually
> comes from very small boxes that they live in – let's call that
> religiously motivated, even indirectly, from their families – and it
> bothers them when they see somebody like me outside that box.
> So they bully, they threaten, they do whatever. Mainly, these are
> boys who are insecure, straight boys, but it's everybody. There
> I am with my long hair and gender presentation making them
> uncomfortable. I had my hair cut about six times at my other
> school, forcibly, sitting in class, on the bus, they would just jump
> me and cut my hair with scissors. Boys and girls both did that to
> me. Don't you think that's a kind of rape?
>
> Well, sure there was apparently a zero-tolerance procedure
> against what I went through, bullying and stuff, but the school

never really enforced it. A policy would be a deterrent in theory, but in all reality, only for some. I don't think it would stop just because there's a policy on paper somewhere. First, there is peer pressure, peer codes. And they would be more loyal to peer codes than to response policies.

Going through high school not only sets you up for your education, but it also finds your place in the pecking order, or at least that's what you think at that time, especially if you're straight. You know, it's kick or be kicked. So that's what you learn outside of just getting an education.

In this perspective, bullying is explicable primarily in terms of individuals or groups (straight students) committing wilfully oppressive acts to police the borders of a "box." However, Trista also attributed "reflex" bullying to religious motivation, conceptualizing this sort of oppression as deeply ingrained:

> And, then, there's religion. You will maybe change some of it, now, today, but only by starting early can you start to change things for tomorrow. You need education, you need to start early. I don't see any other way. It's too late for my situation. Religion got to them first and they're acting out of reflex. That's why I'm at Triangle – this is the kind of school maybe all those places should be like but aren't and won't be for a long time, if ever.
>
> I know what these kids bring with them from home. I used to dress up as a kid, and if I heard my parents coming, I'd hide in my wardrobe. They were super religious and I think they're worse now. I think they'd be happier now if I had gotten trapped in my wardrobe and never came out. Sorry, too late.

Brent, from Burton School, made an observation that picked up on Trista's point about the interplay of religious codes and peer codes, how a student with strong religious beliefs about queers and queer students can influence another student or group of students who may hold no religious beliefs:

> Let's say you're a religious freak who hates gays. Or not even a freak, but that's still why you hate us. Well, you can influence other students because the opinion most students care about is [that of] other students. More so than parents or teachers.

A lot of people are brainwashed very early by their parents.
Generally, this is from religion, specifically Muslim students, in
my experience. They're taught very early on that homosexuality
is wrong. If they show any signs of it, they will be ostracized [by]
their family and it's scary. I have a friend who is openly bisexual
and Muslim and it's a big deal. So that religious student comes to
school, hates queers, and their friends pick up on it because they
want to be friends with that person. You just get this whole
atmosphere of hate and intolerance, bullying and fear. It's really
complicated, actually.

I asked Brent to assess the ability of well-written policies and provincial
legislation to address the situation as he described it at his previous school.
In his view, their difficulty in doing so was due to a combination of poor
implementation and ineffectiveness:

My old school is supposed to have all these policies in place, but
they've never taken them seriously. Because the administration
doesn't care. They don't pay attention to the policies. If you have
the whole school more or less homophobic, then how are you
going to weed everyone out? There were one or two cool teachers,
but how are you going to get at that Muslim kid, or Christian kid?
It's way too late at this point. So if you're like me, you transfer here,
or you go to Triangle, or you survive somehow. We tell people that
educating themselves is the only way to get rid of homophobia,
yes. They don't have the means to. How are people supposed to
educate themselves if the policies aren't carried out and when they
are carried out there's a religious backlash?

I wondered whether it was possible for parents to be a part of the solution? I asked Len about his experiences with parents. Len is not only an
older student but also experienced in community organizations. He said,

Parents are more often part of the problem, as it is, I think. They
could be part of the solution. It's a tough thing because the school
board's place is not to be educating parents and not to be changing
parents' beliefs. The *Education Act* governs students,[14] not parents.
So, there's a lot of very, very tricky, thorny issues when it comes to
ethics and religion that school boards come up against when they

start dealing with things like homophobia education, and out there
sit the parents holding their Bibles or whatever it is.

Silver described herself as "queer, not lesbian." She regarded parents as "responsible" for "queer oppression": "I think that schools are scared of parents
and they take their lead from parents. There are good policies, like the equity
stuff, at least in Toronto, but I don't think a lot of teachers or schools want to
deal with what the parents will think of them. So the schools ignore [them]."
According to Silver, who is white, schools are influenced by the bigotry espoused by parents who hold religious views or "romantic" views of how "they
want their families to be." She tried to articulate the association between
religious views and how families view themselves and their members:

> First of all, there's a tremendous number of immigrants in a lot
> of schools from countries where you get killed if you're a homo-
> sexual. Very negative. A lot of West Indians are unbelievable. East
> Indians tend to be unbelievable, Arabs. They're very homophobic
> and they trace it to their religion and blah, blah, blah. And
> Jamaicans. They're the worst, I would say, in terms of homophobia.
> Unbelievable. But it's not just religion, it's how these parents think
> about what kind of kids they've given birth to or raised and what
> it says about them.

This was a theme or argument that had been advanced by other interviewees
in different contexts. The first time I heard this idea was in my interview
with Azmi Jubran. Jubran was adamant that the boys and girls who bullied
him were making statements about themselves as much as about him. Even
though Jubran is not gay, making homophobic comments about his identity
was a means for his victimizers to define themselves as "nongay." Silver told
me of the circumstances that led to her enrolment at Triangle:

> My mother was one of the first people that I told I was queer, and
> I sure wish I hadn't because she took it upon herself to tell every
> single member of both my mother's and my father's side of the
> family and then to lock me up when they were all appalled.
> First, she put me on a very, very high level of prescription medi-
> cations, and I wasn't even able to stay awake during class. And I
> ended up being taken to a psych ward for two to three weeks
> because of the drugs. I don't even remember how many days I was

there, and because I was gone for so long, one of the guidance counsellors actually went to my mom and said, "Do you think she's coming back or should we take her off the records?" And my mom's like, "Well, she probably won't come back. She's sick, so she's probably going to find another school, especially with what's happened here, so keep her on record just so it says she's attending school, but there's a good chance she's not coming back." So my mother saw me as sick, so she made me sick, but it was a kind of sick she could talk about. Better to be a drug addict than a queer.

I found out later that what my mother did was illegal. But there's the law and then there's what my mother says. That place, you needed two keys to open the main door. And there was a window on the door, but there's a curtain that's on the outside that they close. So if you're inside and they close the curtain, you can't even look out at all. You can't lift the curtain up. It was like a cage. Basically, that's what it was like. I was in there two to three weeks. All because I wasn't the kind of daughter my mother wanted, wasn't the kind of person any of them wanted in their family.

Diana Goundrey conveyed to me the challenge of doing equity or social justice work in the face of religious opposition: "You can't argue with somebody who says their religion justified discrimination against gay kids – it precludes any kind of an argument when someone says, 'Well that's just my religion. That's what God said, and that's it.' Where are you going to go with that? You can't go anywhere with that." Not all of my interviewees saw parents as the centre of the problems presented by religious beliefs. Diana did not. Although hers was a comparatively rare experience, Diana had not encountered any interference from parents:

I don't think it's necessarily reinforced at home always. I think it's just the kids. We never get parents complaining about it – when I showed [the film] *Billy Elliot* [2000], I had a boy who was extremely upset about it. Threatened to beat me up over it[,] actually. A whole incident came out of it at this school. I never got a phone call from his parents. His parents didn't have a problem with it. He did.

He was kicked out – he was moved out of the school. But yeah, that extreme Christian, born-again Christian – we had a couple of teachers who were like that here who were saying some pretty scary things to kids. Well this one that I was thinking of is gone, luckily. But you know, they actually mean well. They'll say, "Well, love the person, hate the action," or whatever. And it's like, "What are you saying?"

Diana, Sian, Len, and many of the other interviewees agreed that education stressing equity or social justice and little else is the means to counter the normative dictates of religious beliefs. In Len's view, the needs of parents and the needs of educating students are at odds – a difficult concept for parents:

At the start, I would focus most on keeping the parents who are problems away. And letting them know that they don't actually have the right to interfere in equity education and what the [*Equity*] *Foundation Statement* requires. Because sometimes you'll have parents pulling students out of workshops and out of classes where they're going to be doing anti-homophobia education. At least in the Toronto School Board, that's absolutely not allowed. And not all teachers and administrators are aware of that, right? But that education is compulsory.

But they try and often it is because of religion. It's usually either religious or moral reasons, which really means the same thing even if people don't know it – usually they're tied together. Eventually, I mean, it's certainly to be hoped that parents can play a role in educating for equity and for diversity. But I'd rather see school boards focusing their resources and their time on the student and staff first.

Even implementing strong equity programs and curricular reforms that focus on students and staff does not resolve the difficulty of penetrating so-called youth culture. When I asked Sian at Crestwood to address the specific question of penetrating youth culture, she said,

There's only one way to "penetrate youth culture" as we were calling it. Education is the answer, but it's too late for my generation. We need to be working on the kids in kindergarten. They have to have some actual books that aren't all about [Roald Dahl's] *James and the Giant Peach* [1961] because I don't fucking care about *James and the Giant Peach*. I want to know queers. It's horrible, so people need to relate to queers.

If people were exposed to queers like me, then I wouldn't get as many dirty looks. If people were exposed to queers, then we would love them more. And religious reasons, ugh. People can say that their religion doesn't believe in this, but we can say, "Well, we believe in no hatred, so don't bring your hatred in this school and call it religion," because they can have their religions and they can believe in that, but that doesn't mean that they have to act upon being hateful, that's unnecessary.

If it's not religious, all that other shit that goes on, with peer pressure and breaking rules because they want to or snitching, all that stuff we talked about – if at the heart of it, they know something about me, about queers, then they aren't going to ignore me, or hate me, or beat me up. They're going to know me and be friends with me because for all their lives it's been normal that I'm there. But it's not like that right now.

Sian indirectly raised the issue that some students may harass or oppress queers to rebel against policies that discourage it. I had not been expecting this response, but it was one that was also raised by Len at Trimble Collegiate:

I just think those types of messages, that "bullying is wrong" or "bullying queers is wrong," are not successful. And you want to know why? Students don't respect teachers well enough to think that what they're saying, whatever they're told to say, is really that meaningful.

I don't think the students to whom that message is being targeted respond well to any preventative sort of disciplinary messages. I think that the message needs to be already existing in stuff they are required to do, like curriculum, or culture in general.

The rules of the school are very ambiguous – they're in a book that you're supposed to be aware of. But most kids get in trouble without knowing specifically what they did. Students bullying know it's wrong, sure, but they don't know which or how many rules they're breaking.

In November 2004 an issue burst open in Toronto when some parents in the Muslim community objected strongly, publicly, and in great numbers to the equity programs being implemented under the *Equity Foundation Statement* in order to address the problems faced by queers in high schools.

Muslim parents at Market Lane Public School, in conjunction with the Toronto District Muslim Education Assembly (TDMEA), demanded that the TDSB exclude their children from classroom discussions of same-sex families. Below is a pamphlet that was distributed in connection with the protest and that appeared on the TDMEA website in 2004:

INDOCTRINATION AND THE PROMOTION OF HOMOSEXUAL LIFESTYLE AND MORAL CORRUPTION IN OUR PUBLIC SCHOOLS. The TDSB's Human Sexuality Program is a blatant attempt to indoctrinate and promote the acceptance of homosexual lifestyle and moral corruption in our public schools and society.

Core Mission of the Program:

- To promote an anti-homophobia environment via educational workshops and consultations with the Toronto District School Board for students and teachers in school premise.
- To act as a resource centre in areas of human sexuality, ensuring a selective curriculum to promote sex and moral corruption in our public schools.

Core Value:

- The TDSB boldly encourages the development of curriculum and support services that promotes sex and moral corruption in our public schools.

Services to Teachers and Students:

- The TDSB provides information and services on lesbian, gay and bisexual students, parents and teachers.
- Classroom and school-wide presentations available on lesbian, gay and bisexual issues.
- Presentations promoting homosexual, lesbian and bisexual lifestyles to students during regular classes under the guise of family studies, health, etc. or during "health week."
- Students are encouraged to approach their teachers (English, Health, Physical Education, Drama, Social Studies, etc.) with suggestions for sex presentations.

The TDSB encourages, teaches and trains youths to conduct workshops in our high schools and in our communities promoting homosexual lifestyle and moral corruption.

The TDSB is consciously promoting an anti-faith, anti-family, immoral and corrupt value system through the school curriculum in the name of education.

To review "the human sexuality program" in detail, please visit the TDMEA's website at http://tdmea.tripod.com or click here.

A big applause to the thousands who joined and supported the TDMEA at the protest![15]

Jeffrey White at Triangle recalled in some detail the board meeting convened to discuss the issue:

> Well, that was an incident last year that came up when Steven Solomon, who's the TDSB human-sexuality social-work person and outreach person, did a workshop at a school and there were some concerned parents who were identified as Muslim and they really didn't feel that this was properly something that the TDSB should be teaching at schools. So the TDSB's response was that they didn't want those of us who identified as GLBTQ going to this meeting. They felt that it would up the ante, and they wanted to go from an approach that we're a public school system and it is our job to tell students about all of these things and I think they actually referred to the *Charter*,[16] they referred to the *Human Rights Code* for Ontario[17] and sort of said this is what our society mandates that we teach.
>
> As a public school institution, we need to be doing this, and they actually broke down the amount of time in the year in curriculum time that was actually spent talking about these issues, and it worked out to less than 1 percent of influence.
>
> So they sort of went from that route and said that we do this as a public school, and no you can't opt out of this kind of educational information; however, you as a parent can then go home and say, "That's great they taught you that at school; however, our religion sort of says this," and you can sort of do that piece with your child and that's your right as a parent or as a believer in Christian teachings, Jewish teachings, whatever the religion may be. I agree with the TDSB's position on that. We are a public school education. We should be doing this work.

Students don't check their personalities or influences at the door. They bring all of those cross-sections of personality and who they are with them as students – so we need to be able to effectively address those in a respectful, appreciating way. It's called education.

The last word on this subject goes to Dalton at Crestwood. I asked him the same question I asked Len – are rules enough? Can law and policy alone succeed, even if everybody in the school is implementing them? His answer echoed Len's and Sian's:

No. Because caging the lion only aggravates it. If you're forbidding something, that only makes someone want to do it more. If you tell a teenager that they can't do something or this is prohibited and a big no-no, I don't think it stops them from wanting to do it. It just makes them want to do it more. I know, it's hard to believe that, but I see it, it's the way it is. So you need to educate people so that they don't want to do it, or it doesn't even occur to them to do it. That, of course, is connected to having queers at dances, less of a normative culture represented all around the school. But if it's part of "rules," that's how they respond, if it's part of the way schools are, it would be different.

Hamed Nastoh was fourteen years old when he died by suicide. He was teased relentlessly and bullied by classmates at Enver Creek High School in Surrey, British Columbia. Before he jumped off the Pattullo Bridge, Hamed Nastoh wrote a four-page note describing the homophobic harassment he endured and blaming the bullies at school for driving him to seek death as an escape. In his letter, Hamed wrote, "Every day, I was teased and teased. I always acted like it didn't bother me, and I'd smile when I came home, but I was crying inside."[18]

Following Hamed's death, his family gave many statements to the media – to deny that their son was gay. James Chamberlain, a school teacher in British Columbia, who has worked for years against homophobic harassment in schools, addressed a letter to the editor of the *Peace Arch News* in Surrey in which he described hearing about what had happened to Hamed Nastoh and referred to Hamed as a high school student "struggling to come to terms with his gender identity within a hostile secondary school atmosphere and non-supportive family environment."[19] The letter angered the

Nastoh family, and Chamberlain received a seven-week suspension without pay for implying in the letter that Hamed was gay. Hamed's father made this statement about media reports that his son was gay: "This word is against our religion – against everything we believe in. We hate this word. Why would they use it?"[20] Hamed's mother stated that it was these after-effects – references to her son as gay – that pained her family most.[21]

Gender Codes: The Game Is Afoot

Looking back on his early descriptions of himself as a gay man teaching in a classroom, Eric Rofes offered this self-assessment:

> I perform[ed] traditional masculinity as a teacher and, while this was usually the way I appeared in the classroom at that time, I certainly had moments where I was caught gesturing or inflecting in effeminate and queeny ways ... Including gender non-conformity ... may have undermined my intended project ... In my quest to show that I should be allowed to remain in the classroom as an openly gay teacher, I sacrificed parts of my identity that did not comfortably fit into the world's sense of what is appropriate conduct of a teacher.[22]

For queer students twenty years later, the issues are the same. At the Fifth International Gender and Education Conference, "Gender, Power and Difference," held at Cardiff University in March 2005, the following questions informed the call for papers:

- What differences does difference make to people's lived experiences and opportunities in education, broadly defined?
- What are the differences that make a difference?
- How do they interact with and shape each other?[23]

These questions turned in my mind when I contemplated the Gender Box exercise (see below), both as I witnessed the exercise play out in a classroom and as I thought about the exercise afterward. The questions set out above inform the complex issues of gender presentation, gender conformity, gender nonconformity, and resistance that queer students face every day at school even if they may not articulate them precisely. Rofes poses his own question:

> Are our voices and gestures, movements and inflections, which violate gender norms and expose us as queer, things we feel embarrassed about

even as we insist they have a right to exist without harassment or persecu-
tion, or do we understand them as critically important forms of resistance
to gender structures which reproduce male supremacy and reinforce patri-
archal power?[24]

Feminist writers have identified young women's engagement with their appearance as a basis of alienation from their bodies, and there is also growing
awareness of this issue with young men. Liz Frost, for instance, has recognized the crucial social importance among youth of "how to appear" and
"how to perceive others' appearance," emphasizing that these concerns are
"integral to the process of constructing identities."[25] Sian framed the issue
more bluntly than Frost but no less eloquently: "Is there a sign on my ass
that screams 'Dyke' because of the way I walk and talk? Or am I all girly and
acceptable as a sex fantasy? And how do I feel about that? It terrorizes my
girlfriend, but me not so much."

In my interviews, I regarded the students as active subjects and wanted to
hear from them about what it was like to be a boy, or a girl, or a transgendered person, or whatever gender they chose to identify with. I began my
interviews by asking the students to describe themselves to me in terms of
their gender and sexuality. I made no assumptions. The subject of gender
was discussed as frequently as sexuality, if not more. In fact, many of the
interviewees associated homophobia and bullying with transgressions of
gender more frequently than with sexuality. This is a point made by David
Plummer, who argues in his work that homophobia is a policing mechanism
for males anxious to be reassured of their gender roles.[26] In interviews with
young males, Plummer established that boys use homophobic epithets to
police and target transgressions of gender roles, not to target sexual practices and sexuality. His findings show that boys who use homophobic slurs are
seeking to be reassured of their own gender performance and that "homophobia targets boys who depart from the collectively authorized expectations of their male peers."[27] For boys, words such as "fag" and "homo" are
intended to police gender rebels and gender outlaws. Although such bullying
words may not be used by boys to police sexuality, the words are not without
meaning. Plummer's results show that "homophobic terms were never used
to refer to girls and were never complimentary."[28] He describes the significance of this kind of language for boys beginning in early boyhood:

It was shown that homophobia has its early roots in boyhood "otherness" –
specifically in being different from the collectively authorized expectations

of male peers, in lacking stereotypical masculinity and/or in betraying peer
group solidarity. In that sense, the developmental foundations for homophobia lie in gender – in the sense of failing to measure up to "hegemonic"
boys' standards rather than necessarily being "feminine."[29]

I found the Gender Box exercise, discussed in the following section, illumin-
ating. Because issues of gender are raised by participants throughout this
book, I have chosen to focus on the Gender Box exercise in order to illustrate how gender codes function as a normative order in the lives of youth
and in youth culture and thus as another factor complicating, often impeding, the effectiveness of equity work and access to social justice for queer
students. The hidden curriculum works to normalize binary oppositions of
gender. Through surveillance, students themselves participate in this process of maintaining the deep-rooted power relations of the discursive representations of gender and sexuality. The creation and maintenance of norms
depend upon the harnessing of a potentially free sexual impulse so that it
can be socially defined and organized.[30] In the growing body of academic
literature on the organization and construction of sexuality and gender difference, a discourse on power has emerged that focuses on discussions of
governance.[31]

In this book, rather than turning to so-called grand theories to explain
the lives of students "on the ground," I have positioned the students as authorities about themselves. It was up to them to attach significance to the
themes that emerged and to articulate what connections or associations, if
any, they made between them. There is an excellent study of boyhood undertaken by Rob Pattman and two other researchers in London, England.[32] As
Pattman concludes about his own methodology, allowing students to speak
positions them as authorities about themselves and their experiences.
Pattman's analysis of his own study applies to the Gender Box exercise: the
exercise does not show what it is like to be a boy or to be a girl but rather
reveals, to the extent that it is designed to do so, how boys perform, display,
and experience boyhood and how girls perform, display, and experience
girlhood.[33]

The Gender Box

Sharon Dominick engaged her students in two versions of this exercise – the
Gender Box and the Race Box. The Gender Box, as Sharon presented it to
her class, was a hybrid of other gender-inventory exercises developed by
others. One aspect was initially developed by the Oakland Men's Project in

the 1980s as an exercise called "Act Like a Man," which was intended to deal with the issue of violence perpetrated by men. Since that time, the exercise has been adapted by many groups. Sharon explained her version of the exercise to me by referring to it as the "Gender Box," but for the students she called it "Act Like a Man" and "Act Like a Lady." Sharon also added elements of the Bem Sex Role Inventory (or Bem Scale) to the exercise, a scheme developed by Sandra Bem that can be employed to understand how individuals utilize gender as a category for organizing all aspects of their lives. This is how the exercise unfolded.

Sharon divided the class into two groups – boys and girls. She asked the boys to make a list of all the traits or qualities that, in their view, were characteristic of what it means to "act like a man" in our culture. She asked the girls to make a list of traits that inform our culture's idea of what it means to "act like a lady." The intention was to discuss the two lists separately and in relation to one another. Sharon asked the students to "think about the messages that you get about what it means to be a man or what it means to be a lady." She moved to the walls of her classroom and pointed to the collages of advertisements that covered them, images of men and women selling products – "hawking" gender. "We've talked about this. You know this. Okay, let's go. Get into groups." Making a lot of noise, scraping chairs, and talking, the students split into two groups. I noticed that they seemed to enjoy the opportunity to split into same-gender groups – they struck me as enthusiastic, and I did not hear a lot of the grumbling that often greeted group exercises in which the focus was on a book being studied. Here the focus was on the students themselves, and they seemed to embrace the exercise.

Each of the groups was given a Bristol board, a magic marker, and a time limit of ten minutes. At the end of ten minutes, they had generated two lists. This is the list the boys created:

"Act Like a Man"

– tough	– provider	– cannot wear purple
– aggressive	– protector	– handy-man
– competitive	– humour	– cannot act girly
– built	– don't wear girl colours	– messy handwriting
– be a pimp	– works out	– men are richer than women
– sporty	– slang	– don't wear tight undies
– fearless	– drink beer	– groomed hair

- short hair
- baggy clothes
- clean/scruffy
- sit with legs open
- independent
- takes care of family

- can get really drunk
- physical fighting
- barbeque
- nice watch
- suits/ties
- mook

- take control of a stressful situation
- are allowed to burp
- big feet
- more about lust
- watch action flicks

This is the list of qualities the girls came up with to describe how society describes what it is like to "act like a lady":

"Act Like a Lady"

- clean
- sit with legs crossed
- makeup/lip gloss
- long hair
- fitting clothes
- polite
- hour glass
- smart
- emotional
- no hair on most [of] body
- quiet/shy
- homemakers
- clear skin
- skirts/dresses
- smell nice

- nail polish
- proper English
- manners
- takes care of herself
- dependent
- champagne – girly drinks
- don't get trashed
- know their limits
- gossiping
- if girl wears too much makeup, she looks fake or trashy-looking
- tight, fitted clothes
- must learn to cook
- not too many sex partners

- must obey parents more than men do
- wear girly colours like pink and purple
- women are more affectionate toward each other than men are, hugs and kisses, they show their emotions
- smooth skin
- let the men take power over problem
- don't burp/fart
- shorter than men
- smaller feet
- more about love
- watch sappy movies
- supportive emotionally

Sharon drew boxes around the borders of the Bristol board and then read the lists aloud. The students hooted a few times at some of the items on the lists when their teacher said the words aloud. Sharon encouraged the boys to comment on the list made by the girls and to hear from the girls about the boys' list. The students did not require much encouragement – they were anxious to speak up about how they viewed themselves and each other.

The boys felt that some of the qualities that made a man a man were "desirable," yet they noted that with being a man came obligations and burdens that women and girls did not have to shoulder. The girls felt the same way about being a "lady": they valued some of their traits but regarded others as unfair distinctions between boys and girls.

Here, Barry spoke up and pointed out that each list contained things that both boys and girls "had" to do and traits that they "had" to possess as well as things that were expressed in terms of negatives – things that boys "should not" or "didn't do" and that girls "should not" or "didn't do." Sharon wrote the word "normative" on the board and pointed out that this was what Barry was talking about and was an issue the class had discussed many times in its "culture jamming" exercises undertaken in connection with looking at advertising and media images of masculinity and femininity.

Several of the students had specific observations to make. A female student named Emily objected to the fact that so many of the other female students began with words that characterized how a "lady" was supposed to "look." She had argued for some of the traits (e.g., courageous, strong) that had appeared on the boys' list but had been voted down by her fellow female students. I noticed that there were no boys who volunteered that they had asked for traits that appeared on the girls' list. In fact, one of the points that emerged from the discussion about the boys' list was that the boys seemed to be very conscious of defining themselves in opposition to girls: the boys were what the girls were not. And the boys admitted to doing this – proudly, it seemed to me – whereas the girls made it clear that this was not how they approached their list. Rather, the girls were very incensed about the messages society sent about being female and were glad to have the opportunity to express their outrage. Nonetheless, a large number of female students did not feel this way and happily accepted the standards, which they were – proudly, it seemed to me – meeting or exceeding. Sharon led the students through a discussion that considered each of the traits on the lists.

In light of this discussion, Sharon asked the students to briefly return to their groups so that they could consider what had been discussed and could see whether they looked at their lists in a "new way." "Are there traits on your lists that you think are desirable for girls to have," she asked the girls, "in light of our discussion, or not? Same thing with the boys, please. Are these traits desirable for boys? Or are they traits that everybody should have?" The students returned to their groups, and while they were taking a few minutes to reconsider their lists, Sharon said to me, "Of course, I'm hoping they don't circle anything, but ..." I nodded and pointed out that the circling had already begun.

Despite a discussion showing the boys that the girls also valued courage and strength and that being "emotionally supportive" is a trait that everyone can express and for which everyone can be appreciated, both the boys and the girls held to the belief that it is more desirable for boys than girls to exhibit certain traits and better for girls than boys to display others. The boys circled the following traits as being valuable for boys who want to "act like a man":

- independent
- takes care of family
- clean/scruffy
- humour
- drink beer
- don't wear tight undies

Willing to concede some ground in the discussion, but unwilling to yield all of it, the boys modified "tough" on the Bristol board so that it now read "tough (to a point)." The girls circled these qualities:

- clean
- polite
- takes care of herself
- smart
- smell nice
- manners
- women are more affectionate toward each other
- supportive emotionally
- if girl wears too much makeup, she looks fake/trashy-looking

Here, the girls made a modification, striking out "fake" but leaving "trashy-looking."

Sharon made separate lists and drew a box around the lists. She asked the students why they had circled these particular traits. The girls who answered responded unanimously that it was important for girls to present themselves well so that boys would be interested in them but, at the same time, not to overdo their presentation by being "trashy." With the support of the group, Emily had circled "smart." Sharon made a note of their reasons on the blackboard. Sharon considered the boys' list and began by asking them why wearing baggy "undies" was important enough to circle. Jeremiah, a black sixteen-year-old student, yelled out, "So you're not called a fag!" The answer seemed to meet with much approval. Sharon wrote the response on the board. "I asked you and I'm writing it down," she said. There was no discussion of the "F" word. Sharon wanted to get behind their thinking. What followed was a further discussion of boys defining themselves in opposition to girls and in such a way as to make it clear to the world that they were not "homosexual." The discussion reminded me of Azmi Jubran and the kind of harassment he had endured by boys who wanted to define themselves in opposition to how they were socially constructing him – as a "homo."

The boys who spoke up indicated it was important not to be perceived as "gay" or as a "fag," and they would not relent on the point. When Sharon asked the boys how they would respond if someone described them in terms of the words the girls had circled on their list, the boys had no real problems with any of the circled items (although they laughed at "smell nice") until Sharon got to the issue of boys being "affectionate toward each other." This would definitely be perceived as "gay" behaviour. Some of the girls disagreed with the boys on this interpretation, but many of them agreed and felt that boys should not be as affectionate with each other as girls are with each other.

Sharon asked the girls and boys to make a list of words that would be used to describe a girl who failed to act like a lady, who performed outside the "box." How would people treat you? She also asked them to make a list for a boy who operated outside the box. The girls felt that a girl who failed to act like a lady would be regarded as a "slut" or a "whore," or as a "bitch" or "dirty." The boys came up with a list containing the same words that appeared on the girls' list. For boys operating outside the box, both the girls and boys in the class limited their lists to words disparaging a boy's or man's sexuality: "fag," "queer," "homo," "gay." I was not surprised by this. I had asked all of my interviewees to tell me what words were used to insult a girl and what words were used to insult a boy, and I had found the same results. With respect to insults for girls, the overwhelming answer was "slut" and, less frequently, "bitch." Almost exclusively, the choice with respect to boys was "fag." These answers did not vary by gender – both boys and girls understood that "fag" was the worst thing you could call a boy, whereas, for a girl, it was "slut."[34]

Although boys and girls challenged each other at some points during the exercise, it seemed clear that there was some ground that neither group was

willing to yield. Sharon asked the students to consider how they would respond to a friend who lived outside the box or who ignored the culture's
message of how to act like a lady or act like a man. The policing mechanism
suggested by the boys was violence. "I'd kick the 's' out of him," was one response, received with much laughter. The general consensus was that boys
or men who choose not to act like a man are "gay," and there was not much
sympathy expressed for what might happen to such an individual. A few of
the girls were willing to admire girls who throw social conventions aside
and live more independently than society encourages "ladies" to live – but,
as one female student warned, "not too much."

Having led the class through a discussion of the price that is paid by those
who choose to move outside the box, Sharon concluded the exercise by asking the students to consider what price is paid when we are asked to live our
lives "inside the box." The question seemed to startle the students. The boys
in particular seemed unwilling, publicly at least, to acknowledge that a price
is paid. It seemed from the few answers that the boys gave to this question
that the "price" of being asked to "act like a man" was not a price at all but
something that should not be questioned or regarded as anything other than
"natural" or "just the way it is." As Jeremiah put it, "So long as I can drink my
beer, I'm happy." Interviewing them on a one-on-one basis might have yielded different responses, but the exercise was a group endeavour. The girls
seemed more willing to entertain the social injustice of being asked to live
"in a box" but only some of the girls and, generally, within limits. It was also
interesting to hear boys of this age in a group setting deny that there were
any pressures on them, since, overwhelmingly, the students and teachers I
interviewed felt there was significantly more virulent monitoring of boys'
sexuality than of girls'.

In response to a question from Sharon, the students considered whether
gender is an inevitable expression of biology or a learned result. For the
most part, at the outset of the exercise, the students regarded gender as a
biological consequence – although by the conclusion, about one-third of
the students, mainly girls, conceded that gender could be a cultural consequence but only in some circumstances. When pressed, those students who
allowed for the possibility that gender could be learned tended to maintain
that only certain traits could be learned and that some were always biological. When asked to classify which traits might be learned rather than
biological, the students had difficulty doing so. As well, even when gender
was viewed as a cultural consequence, the students tended to regard the
"desirable" gender traits they identified as traits to which they were "entitled."

For all of these students, apart from the culture jamming conducted in Sharon's classroom, these were new and difficult concepts, suggesting that earlier introduction to these topics might yield different results.

Some weeks later, when I was at Triangle, I mentioned the Gender Box exercise to Trista, the transgendered student I had met and talked with on several occasions. She said,

> Well, gender to a lot of people is assigned at birth. I was born a male and to them that means being masculine. If I call you a fag, then that means I'm not one, doesn't it? And that affects, of course, the position of women, too. I think homosexuality is something to be hidden in places like North Bay, where I come from, because it's really the fact that it makes people uncomfortable about moving outside of what your particular gender is supposed to be about.

This was a common theme I heard from the people I met in schools and at conferences. Trista summed up the "gender box" in which she had lived her life for seventeen years:

> There wasn't one day that I could get by without having to be stoned just to deal with the shit that people put me through just because I wanted to move outside the box that you were talking about. Just awful, horrible stuff. They cut my hair, they called me names, they put a knife to my throat. But I never cried. I didn't have emotions. I pulled away and told myself it would all be over and I'd leave as soon as I possibly could. As soon as I got the chance, I was going to leave North Bay. And I did.

I do not wish to end Trista's story on a mournful note. By her own description, Trista is happy now at Triangle – she believes she is thriving *because* of Triangle:

> Triangle is an excellent idea. I think they should have one in every major city, only because, in this way, queer people, queer youth, could have a safe place to go and educate themselves and not have to deal with the crap that I went through and a lot of the other students went through. And this is why a lot of the students are here. They couldn't deal with mainstream high school. The religious

crap, the way the jocks are, their girlfriends, all of it. And that
gender box, yeah, all of it.

Gender codes are a part of the general heteronormative culture of schools
and of the heterosexism that results in the kinds of oppression that it is
hoped equity programs can work against. The normative ordering power of
gender codes is a present force in the lives of students that competes with,
or complicates, the power and effectiveness of policies. In other words,
gender codes and policies are positioned as competing normative orders.
Investigating how other systems of normative ordering within a culture
operate as "law," or in law-like ways, is crucial when assessing the ability, or
inability, of "formal law" – which can be sympathetic and purposively supportive of "queer youth" – to effectively address harassment and oppression
of queer students.

Heteronormativity and dominant gender codes are promoted and reaffirmed in the values, morals, and structures that shape schools.[35] These
structures affect all youth, heterosexual and nonheterosexual. Boys are inducted into an order and become subject to a cultural arrangement that
imbues them with power and authority, often at the expense of their emotional lives. There is a sizable body of literature theorizing and documenting
how girls are denied cultural independence, authority, and equality.
Madeleine Arnot has identified that the hegemony of masculinity defines
girls and encourages girls to define themselves, and to find their cultural
worth, in relation to the dictates of hegemonic masculinity.[36] From one perspective, hegemonic masculinity imbues males with power and prestige at
the expense of "others," but it is also a burden used against them.

How homophobic epithets are employed by boys demonstrates that
homophobic bullying operates as a means for them to affirm their conformity with male gender norms. The implication, as in the case of Azmi Jubran,
is that "we will define you and harass you for being gay whether or not you
are gay because whether you are gay is less important than asserting the fact
that we are not gay." I would prefer that the last words on this subject be the
voice of one of the students. Len captured the experience of the policing
mechanisms associated with hegemonic masculinity in a way that reminded
me of what I observed in Barry's classroom:

Another way that boys would monitor you and let you know when
you weren't behaving like a boy should behave is that they would

stare at you and you didn't know they were staring at you until you'd look over, and then you'd realize this person was already looking at you and then they'd make a face and look away. That happened to me a number of times and I used to think, so what did you just do? You'd been looking at me all this time, waiting for me to realize you're looking over here or for me to look up and discover you looking over at me so that you could then give me this dirty look and look away? It was so important to you to do that, that you've been looking at me for how long? A minute? Two minutes? Twenty minutes? Forty-five minutes? How long have you been waiting for this opportunity to judge me and let me know that I'm not passing? I'm not doing what I'm supposed to be doing?

Despite the role of normative youth culture in impeding the effective implementation of state-issued law and policies aimed at ensuring equity for sexual-minority students, the actions of individuals "on the ground" can help to counter normative orders. This reality was affirmed by a letter of thanks that Sharon Dominick received from a former student:

Douglas Allington
March 26, 2007

Dear Miss Sharon Dominick,

Over the years, you have been a great teacher and someone I can depend on. Personally speaking, if there is an award for best teacher in the world, I think you would be a perfect candidate for it. Not only do you make the time to help your students, but you also take the time to talk to them as a friend, not just a teacher. And that is how I think every teacher should be. Many teachers can learn a thing or two from you. *Cough* Mr. Turcott * Cough.

This letter is a thank you for all the times you have been there to help me when I needed it the most. Especially in the tenth grade with all the problems I had being called the F word and when I got suspended. You were very supportive, and you still are. If it was not for what you did for me about my suspension, I would not have had someone in this school I could trust and seek advice from.

I hope you never go to another school. That school would never be the same without you there, and all of your cool posters and ads and pictures!!

It's a joy just walking by and seeing what new things you have put up to help the students "culture jam" and get out of the "gender box."

I hope to see you again. Thank you.

Sincerely,
Doug Allington

8

Conclusion

Doing Equity

This study of safety in schools in practice has been undertaken with the conviction and guiding philosophy that sexual-minority students are the most knowledgeable experts on their own experiences and lives and that sexual-minority youth and their allies are best situated to address the fundamental research questions of this book. In particular, I interrogated how bullying and threats to safety are understood and defined by sexual-minority students, and inquired into how sexual-minority students report that safety is pursued at their schools. I then asked sexual-minority youth and their advocates to consider how these definitions and understandings might be translated into law reform that reconceptualizes current approaches to safety and bullying.

The issues and concerns raised by sexual-minority students and their advocates around making schools safe for queer students are emblematic of much bigger questions about how schools should respond to shifting incarnations of safety in Canadian schools. Sexual-minority students defined safety for themselves much more broadly, in most cases, than did their own schools. Students felt that safety had to be defined in a way that made room for significant impact on the school culture in general, not just as something that was pursued in response to incidents of violence.

Students and teachers offered a critique of current approaches to safety by pointing to the need to conceptualize safety in terms of doing equity.

These students acknowledged that for many, if not most, students, including students in smaller cities and in rural settings, concerns about physical and verbal violence were significant and likely more immediate. A smaller number of students made a distinction between equity and social justice, depending upon the level of commitment demonstrated by a school to changing the school culture. The distinction between equity and social justice in the view of some students was contingent upon the extent to which a school was proactively trying to change the school culture – to address, for example, the heteronormativity of official and unofficial space in schools. Many of these students viewed heteronormativity as more immediately threatening to their personal identities than the fear of physical or verbal harassment. Therefore, all of the students I interviewed conceived of safety along these lines regardless of how they perceived safety was being pursued at their particular schools.

Although all of the students I interviewed believed that safety should include equity, the majority of students said their schools did not conceptualize safety in the same way. For most of these students, their own schools displayed a "fortress mentality" toward safety by emphasizing security and safety in response to a culture of fear, not equity. At most schools, there was a disconnect between how the students conceived of safety and how they experienced safety from day to day "on the ground."

I found two schools where the students felt that equity and social justice were a part of how safety was conceptualized. At the first of these schools, the students indicated that the pursuit of safety focused on equity by emphasizing equality and incorporating queer realities into the curriculum and into extracurricular events, such as school dances and assemblies. The students felt that the administration at this school tried to give more weight to the *Equity Foundation Statement*[1] than the *Safe Schools Act*.[2] At the second school, a larger school of three hundred in Grades 9 through 12, the students believed their school pursued safety in terms of social justice. The students at this school indicated to me that they were aware of the Toronto District School Board's (TDSB) *Equity Foundation Statement* but felt that this document was just "a starting point."

In sum, for many students throughout the schools of the TDSB, the greatest threats to personal identity and physical safety were linked to the heteronormativity of school culture and to the physical, verbal, and situational violence experienced by sexual-minority youth. The heteronormativity that governs most schools and normalizes the position of so-called straight kids meant that the information that heterosexual students received about sexual-minority youth was received by them in their normative positions. To address this, students recommended a mandated curriculum that included a study of the social construction of sexuality and gender.

Most students described their schools in one of two ways, such that their school could be put into one of two groups. The first group, accounting for the largest number of schools, conceived of safety in terms of security. For the second, smaller group of schools, control of student identity was paramount. For both groups of schools, safety meant responding to physical violence as it occurred, with the greatest preventative concerns being to keep weapons and unauthorized persons out of the schools and to monitor the actions of students in the schools. The rules were developed to foster a safe school environment at these schools. Equity policies were secondary to concerns about violence and the presence of gangs in the schools. Schools in this category, as well as those that might be classified as schools where identity was controlled, perceived their own students as threats. Most of the schools I visited fell into this category.

Informants indicated that these classifications of schools were not being offered as rigid descriptions of schools but were, rather, a useful means by which to view the general organization and understanding of safety as it played out "on the ground" and as it compared and contrasted with the students' own definitions and understandings of safety.

The interviewees, both students and teachers, made a number of suggestions for improvement that emphasized equity and positioned safety as consistent with human rights principles. They conceived of safety policies not only as responding to injustices, like complaint- and incident-based systems do, but also, and more important, as being proactive about achieving social justice for sexual-minority students. The proposals that were ultimately favoured by the students captured the major themes that emerged in discussions about safety:

1 the importance of school boards and schools conceiving of safety broadly to include not just physical violence but also verbal and relational or attitudinal violence;
2 the importance of conceptualizing safety as a proactive pursuit of equity and social justice (several students mentioned that it would be helpful if the *Safe Schools Act* had been called the *Safe and Equitable Schools Act* or if the TDSB's *Equity Foundation Statement* could be incorporated into the provincial *Education Act*);[3]
3 mandated curriculum change to reflect queer realities and queer lives;

4 curriculum change that also implicates non-sexual-minority students so
   that queer content is not perceived as a part – a lower or different part
   – of an undisturbed hierarchical arrangement of privilege;
5 a rereading of bullying in ministry law and policies to include cultural
   antecedents of bullying and to subvert social hierarchies rather than
   maintaining normative gender scripts;
6 sufficient funding to implement equity;
7 teacher training and workshops so that teachers feel the support of their
   colleagues and administrators;
8 more generally, the recognition of schools as valuable sites from which,
   in multiple ways, to dismantle the power and privilege that some enjoy at
   the expense of others.

Participants agreed that although the legislature and policy makers may face
significant challenges in drafting reform that acknowledges and protects
sexual-minority students in these ways, they were very much aware that
nothing less than a transformational process would bring about these changes. The guiding philosophy of this study has been to listen to the voices of
sexual-minority students, grounded in their own experiences, in an attempt
to understand how they perceive what most threatens their personal identities, as well as their physical safety. In the pursuit of safe, equitable, and accepting schools, this approach is one means to measure the effectiveness of
current law and policies where they are in place and to justify the construction of relevant law and policies where they are absent. Only with this knowledge can more effective reforms be imagined.

Implications of Legal Pluralism for the Safety and Acceptance of Queer Students

Sally Merry has articulated five ways that the research framework of a legally plural approach enriches investigation. Each is relevant to this study and
worth setting out. First, legal pluralism frees the research framework from
the ideology of law-centredness and legal centralism, which denies that it is
an ideology, and from the inclination to conceive of all legal ordering as
having been gained from state-issued law.[4] Legal pluralism encourages an
awareness that other systems and forms of ordering may be animating the
social space, notwithstanding that they may interrelate with state law. Legal
pluralism stresses "rival" and sometimes oppositional normative orders outside of state law and recognizes their "mutually constitutive relations" to
state law within the same socio-legal field.[5]

Second, having rejected legal centralism at its core, legal pluralism demands that an essentialist definition of law be displaced by a historical appreciation of the social field in question. This suggests that even debating whether rival orders constitute law is wrong-headed and merely imports centralist notions of law into an approach that has already rejected narrow conceptions. Third, apprehending that fields are composed of multiple forms of ordering leads inevitably to an examination of the cultural and, hence, changeable temporal character of law and legal systems and institutions. Merry encourages us to think of "ordering" and "relationships" as opposed to focusing solely on the particular rules applied in situations of dispute since these rules yield limited, if any, insights into the interconnectedness of those in dispute.[6] In this focus, law ceases to be a series of rules exerting force and becomes a "system of thought by which certain forms of relations come to seem natural and taken for granted, modes of thought that are inscribed in institutions that exercise some coercion in support of their categories and theories of explanation."[7] Fourth, investigating the plurality of legal fields lessens law's focus on resolving disputes by concentrating, instead, on ordering in noncontentious social conditions,[8] an approach premised on the recognition that arguments are atypical conditions in relationships and unreliable indicators of normative orders.[9] Fifth, exploring the collision of normative orders provides a basis for apprehending the give and take involved both in the infiltration of a social group by centralist law and in the resistance to state-issued law.[10] Under legal pluralism, resistance to domination within a group, particularly in the educational context, may also be limited by the ways that this resistance unexpectedly fulfils the domination.[11]

As Merry warns, this is a problematic area for research. Attention to the ideological role of law points to the construction of modes of thinking and of implicit understandings as a central aspect of its power; conversely, however, attention to plural orders examines the limits of the state's authority in areas where it does not penetrate and where alternate forms of ordering persevere.[12] This has resonance for implementation of the *Equity Foundation Statement* and for understanding why law on the books and law in action may differ.

This book illustrates the implications of legal pluralism for our understanding of safe-school management and policies aimed at the achievement of equity and social justice. Formal, state-issued law is one structure that is a factor for sexual-minority youth accessing social justice; patriarchy, race, gender, religion, and family belief-systems, among others, are additional normative social structures that coexist with state-issued law and impact the ability of these students to access social justice. These structures include teacher authority, social conditions of the classroom, belief-systems governing student-teacher relations, gender codes, textbooks, audio-visual aids, arrangements of school space and architecture, dress codes, disciplinary policies, peer pressures, religious expression, parent-teacher relationships, and others. From this perspective, it follows that queer students must rely upon laws, policies, and programs that specifically advocate transformative goals and outcomes that are grounded in social justice and that consider these other social factors and influences rather than merely contemplating responsiveness to specific incidents of physical or verbal harassment. Conventional conceptions of bullying focus on static definitions of power relations, usually understood as limited to and as existing between specific individuals; accordingly, responses have often been restricted to reacting to "incidents." Legal pluralism confirms the need to conceptualize safety in broad terms in order to achieve the kind of cultural transformation sought by so many in this book. This research confirms the argument of scholars such as Gerald Walton that it is important not to regard bullying as a nonspecific form of aggression, as a mere pathological outburst.[13] Doing so disguises the ideological or cultural factors that attend aggression and oppression, such as sexuality, gender, race, class, or other markers. Broadening our conception of safety must include a consideration not only of immediate physical, verbal, relational, or cyber-based threats but also of the heteronormative culture in which queer students experience schooling and heterosexist oppression.

A pluralist approach demonstrates the need for transformational responses. As I pointed out earlier, state-promulgated law may be the most visible, public, and high-profile form of regulation, but it may not be the most significant in terms of its social impact, particularly among students. I do not argue that official law is not up to the task of addressing the oppression of sexual-minority students; in fact, I have come to believe more and more that ultimate, widespread transformational solutions must come from state-issued law. This particular study has focused on an assessment of the effectiveness of current law and policies in the context of the other regulatory influences presently operating at the sites studied.

There are two benefits of understanding that some bullying takes place because the victim is queer, and appreciating that safety means, as Gabriel (Gabe) Picard told me, transforming a culture rather than just responding to individual incidents. First, this knowledge adds refinement to our conception of who must be kept safe (not just some objective, typical student, who, in any event, does not exist). Second, it enlarges the scope of the approach required when deciding how to bring about safe schools, usually by moving the focus from the school setting to the home, not in a quest limited to concerns with psychological-based character flaws or family but in one that argues for approaches and policies that stress the need for education.

With respect to law and policy reform, the proposals that were ultimately preferred by the students captured the key themes that emerged in discussions about bullying, safety, and heteronormativity, with a particular emphasis on changing school culture by educating all students in early grades. Each of the informants stressed, in fact, that they could see only one solution to the power of religion, the anti-snitch code, and the social construction of gender: cultural transformation rooted in early-grade intervention.

Legal pluralism directs us to take this approach. From a positivist perspective, it is assumed that laws have their intended consequences. Legal pluralism directs us to consider, rather than to assume, the effectiveness of state-issued law and policies. A legal-pluralist approach does not demonstrate that state-issued law is not an answer to the oppression of queer students (in fact, it may be the best answer); rather, legal pluralism directs us to consider the reach of legislation and policies as currently written and enacted. In sum, the most effective approach would call for laws, policies, and programs that mandate curriculum and educative responses in order to transform knowledge and knowledge systems throughout all years of the schooling experience for all students. This kind of law and policy reform is currently taking place in Ontario. Bill 13, also known as the *Accepting Schools Act*,[14] which was introduced in the Ontario Legislature on 30 November 2011 to address the issue of bullying in Ontario schools, requires all school boards in Ontario to implement policies that address bullying and to "promote a positive school climate that is inclusive and accepting of all pupils, including pupils of any race, ancestry, place of origin, colour, ethnic origin, citizenship, creed, sex, sexual orientation, gender identity, gender expression, age, marital status, family status or disability."[15] The bill calls for "activities or organizations that promote the awareness and understanding of, and respect for, people of all sexual orientations and gender identities, including organizations with the name gay-straight alliance or another name."[16]

If courage lasts, the *Accepting Schools Act*, laws on human rights and equality, and laws governing the delivery of education in the provinces and territories may be the most hopeful answer for queer students in Canadian schools. History has shown that jurisprudence and legislative responses, including the *Charter*[17] and human rights codes, have transformed the position of sexual minorities in Canada. Although high schools have lagged far behind or been shut out of this legal reconstruction of queer persons in society, it may very well be that it is now their turn in a Canadian society that today sanctions same-sex marriage. The cultural responses to queer suicides may inform this issue. In October 2011 fifteen-year-old Jamie Hubley died by suicide in Ottawa after battling depression and being bullied because he was the only openly gay teenager in his high school.[18] Canadian culture, generally, has taken notice that the culture in schools needs to change.

The *Accepting Schools Act* applies to state-funded public schools and to denominational separate schools – which signals another significant aspect of the need for well-articulated ministerial intervention. The legal construction of safe schools will include a confrontation with competing religion-based rights claims.[19] Elsewhere, I have argued with Bruce MacDougall that the emergence of this competition between religion and sexual-orientation claims cannot be avoided.[20] Students like Azmi Jubran, Gabe Picard, and others in this book who conceptualize the solutions to their harassment and oppression in legal terms seek either access that other students already have or an end to discrimination. Religion-based claims, unlike the assertion of rights based upon sexual orientation, primarily seek to deny inclusion (or services or employment) to those who have legal rights guaranteeing inclusions.[21] Religion-based claims must not be upheld at the expense of the exclusion and oppression of sexual-minority students.

One possible argument against a top-down legislated response that targets school culture is that a mandated nonoppressive climate for sexual-minority students might be resisted because it is being mandated. The argument can be made that unless the cultural transformation being legislated is something that activists and those affected by the laws have struggled for or "won," there will be no real purchase in the law on the ground. My response to this argument is that we are already there. Teachers have been doing this work in the trenches for years. More recently, student-led activism has made a difference. That we have passed this point is underscored by the suicides of so many queer youth: we are indisputably beyond the point of being vulnerable to the charge that we have replaced one hegemony with another. In the year preceding Jamie Hubley's death in Canada, nine teenage boys, referred to as the "September Suicides," died by suicide in the United States during September 2010 in incidents related to queer-based harassment: Tyler Clementi, Seth Walsh, Raymond Chase, Billy Lucas,

Asher Brown, Cody J. Barker, Felix Sacco, Harrison Chase Brown, and Caleb Nolt.[22] As heartbreaking as these and other deaths are, it is important not to limit concerns about a hostile climate to suicide prevention; although, for those troubled about the basis for policy intervention – the justification for replacing an informal and homophobic legal regime with more formal legal management aimed at transforming school culture – these suicides may provide that basis. Widespread legislative action aimed at transforming school culture by addressing the regime of invisibility, silence, and oppression sustained in schools through the routine homophobia, heterosexism, and heteronormativity found there is required and being called for in many diverse quarters.

There are a number of educators whose research on the heteronormativity and heterosexism in schools is well established and significant.[23] They have investigated heteronormative orders in school and theorized about queer education and critical pedagogy as possible approaches to tackling normative gender and sexuality regimes in schools. There is a significant absence of socio-legal work investigating the potential of law to achieve social-justice goals for queer youth and, it must be said, for the benefit of so-called straight students who are also subjected to, and oppressed by, the burdens of normative gender and sexuality regimes. What I have tried to demonstrate is the need to consider the law's potential from a pluralist perspective. Only by appreciating that there is a multiplicity of regulatory regimes at work in youth culture can the totality of the task of resolving the issues of the bullying and oppression of queer students be comprehended and achieved institutionally through official legal responses.

Kevin Kumashiro argues (and the research presented in this book confirms) that inclusive education alone is inadequate and that a more robust regime of "anti-oppressive" education is required.[24] The more broadly based approach of anti-oppressive education, which places culture itself in its sights, including the privileged and the "othered," is required. Cultural transformation is not going to happen ad hoc; it is not going to happen only because teachers have been encouraged in their teacher training to address social-justice concerns in the classroom. Too many teachers do not see the safety concerns of sexual-minority youth as part of their job; too many lack time. Many courageous teachers have led this charge. Many efforts have been undertaken through student-led activism. All of this work is moving and valuable. Emphasizing law makes the issues of bullying, harassment, and oppression institutional concerns that require targeting structures rather than merely relying upon an individual teacher's sense of social justice or a student's bravery. In this approach, bullying and oppression are reconfigured as cultural issues.

The perspectives of those interviewed in this book on the necessity to unite individual rights and school safety can be viewed as expressions of legal consciousness. Legal consciousness can be thought of as the knowledge or awareness possessed by a particular group of people about the law and about its potential not only to settle disputes but also to bring about cultural change.[25] It is clear that the people who speak in this book believe that the climate of schools must be transformed. Given that the curriculum is one component of a larger school culture, changing the curriculum is required, but it is a partial answer, and inclusive education remains a half-done solution. Challenging the marginalizing effects on sexual-minority youth of privileging normative orders requires widespread change – the kind of change that may be brought about by courageous legislative reforms that conceptualize the position of sexual-minority youth as a school-wide issue.

Cultural transformation should not be carried out on the backs of teachers and students, and in fact, it may not be possible. What my research shows is that, at best – although we should be very grateful for it – the work of some great teachers and students creates oases within a much larger, bleaker climate. The curriculum must change to include queer content and to recognize queer families, but the curriculum will not change unless education ministries direct it to change and unless queer youth are reconstructed legally as full citizens within schools. Behind this response lies a wall-to-wall approach that considers the playing fields, the stages, the artwork on display in hallways, the media classes, sports, music, visual arts, friendships, loyalties, clubs, the machine shops, the gyms, and the classrooms in pursuit of a time when the interests of sexual-minority youth will be authorized and valorized so that they may participate in school life and thrive both on and off school property during the years when schools are such a crucial part of their lives. Gabe Picard is right – it *is* all about transforming the culture.

Notes

Chapter 1: Introduction

1 *Equity Foundation Statement and Commitments to Equity Policy Implementation* (Toronto: Toronto District School Board, 1999).

2 Dan Olweus, *Bullying at School: What We Know and What We Can Do* (Cambridge, UK: Blackwell, 1993), 9.

3 Gerald Walton, "Bullying and Homophobia in Canadian Schools: The Politics of Policies, Programs and Educational Leadership," *Journal of Gay and Lesbian Issues in Education* 1, 4 (2003): 23-36.

4 Ibid. See also Donn Short, "Queers, Bullying and Safe Schools: Am I Safe Here?" *Journal of Gay and Lesbian Social Services* 19, 3-4 (2007): 31-46; Donn Short, "Conversations in Equity and Social Justice: Constructing Safe Schools for Queer Youth," *Journal for Critical Education Policy Studies* 8, 2 (2010): 329-57.

5 Gerald Walton, "The Notion of Bullying through the Lens of Foucault and Critical Theory," *Journal of Educational Thought* 39, 1 (2005): 58-59.

6 Ibid., 65-66.

7 Wayne A. MacKay and Lyle (Chip) Sutherland, *Teachers and the Law*, 2nd ed. (Toronto: Edmond Montgomery, 2006); Eric M. Roher, "When Push Comes to Shove: Bullying and Legal Liability in Schools," *Education and Law Journal* 12, 3 (2002): 319-47; Eric M. Roher, *An Educator's Guide to Violence in Schools*, 2nd ed. (Aurora, ON: Canada Law Book, 2010).

8 Peter McLaren, "Critical Pedagogy: A Look at the Major Concepts," in Antonia Darder, Marta P. Baltodano, and Rodolfo D. Torres, eds., *The Critical Pedagogy Reader*, 2nd ed. (New York: Routledge, 2009), 64.

9 Ibid.

10 Bill 81, *An Act to increase respect and responsibility, to set standards for safe learning and safe teaching in schools and to amend the Teaching Profession Act*, 1st Sess., 37th Leg., Ontario, 2000 (assented to 23 June 2000), SO 2000, c. 12 [*Safe Schools Act*].

11 Pamela Maykut and Richard Morehouse, *Beginning Qualitative Research: A Philosophic and Practical Guide* (London: RoutledgeFalmer, 1994), 57.

12 See C.J. Pascoe, *Dude You're a Fag: Masculinity and Sexuality in High School* (Berkeley: University of California Press, 2007); George W. Smith, "The Ideology of 'Fag': The School Experience of Gay Students," ed. Dorothy E. Smith, *Sociological Quarterly* 39, 2 (1998): 309-35; Kevin Davison, "Masculinities, Sexualities and the Student Body: 'Sorting' Gender Identities in School," in Carl E. James, ed., *Experiencing Difference*, 44-52 (Halifax: Fernwood, 2000); Rob Gilbert and Pam Gilbert, *Masculinity Goes to School* (London: Routledge, 1998).

13 Egale Canada (previously Equality for Gays and Lesbians Everywhere) is an advocacy organization that promotes equality for Canadian gay, lesbian, bisexual, transgender, and queer (GLBTQ) people in Canada.

14 C. Taylor and T. Peter, with T.L. McMinn et al., *Every Class in Every School: The First National Climate Survey on Homophobia, Biphobia, and Transphobia in Canadian Schools: Final Report* (Toronto: Egale Canada Human Rights Trust, 2011). The researchers surveyed approximately 3,700 students throughout Canada via individual online participation and in-school sessions conducted with twenty school boards.

15 Sexual and Gender Diversity: Vulnerability and Resilience (SVR) is a research team funded by the Canadian Institutes of Health Research (CIHR).

16 *Picard v. Lakehead District School Board*, Thunder Bay SBHE-5YJRJL (OHRC), "Complaint of the Complainant," para. g.

17 Kath M. Melia, "Producing 'Plausible Stories': Interviewing Student Nurses," in Gale Miller and Robert Dingwall, eds., *Context and Method in Qualitative Research* (London: Sage, 2002), 27.

18 *Canadian Charter of Rights and Freedoms*, Part 1 of the *Constitution Act, 1982*, being Schedule B to the *Canada Act 1982* (UK), 1982, c. 11.

19 *Human Rights Code*, RSO 1990, c. H.9.

20 *Safe Schools Foundation Statement* (Toronto: Toronto District School Board, 1999).

Chapter 2: Safe Schools

1 See most recently Dan Olweus, "Peer Harassment: A Critical Analysis and Some Important Issues," in Jaana Juvonen and Sandra Graham, eds., *Peer Harassment in School: The Plight of the Vulnerable and Victimized*, 3-20 (New York: Guilford, 2001).

2 Dan Olweus, *Aggression in the Schools: Bullies and Whipping Boys* (Washington, DC: Hemisphere, 1978).

3 Dan Olweus, *Bullying at School: What We Know and What We Can Do* (Cambridge, UK: Blackwell, 1993), 9.

4 Ibid.

5 Debra J. Pepler and Wendy M. Craig, *Making a Difference in Bullying: Report No. 60* (Toronto: LaMarsh Centre for Research on Violence and Conflict Resolution, 2000).

This aspect of Olweus's definition, adopted by researchers such as Pepler and Craig, poses particular problems for sexual-minority students, who often feel their safety is jeopardized by "negative actions" or factors that other students might not consider threatening. In this report, the researchers emphasize a "whole school" approach; however, this approach is too narrowly focused, conceptualizing the dynamics of bullying within a child-child, adult-child, child-adult prism. The "whole school" approach they advocate continues the generic Olweus formulation of bullying and insufficiently takes into account children (and adults) manoeuvring within a larger cultural framework that promotes privilege, rewards "normal," and encourages and valorizes homophobic bullying – among other specific forms of harassment founded on the status of "other."

6 Ibid., 4.

7 Dan Olweus, "Annotation: Bullying at School: Basic Facts and Effects of a School Based Intervention Program," *Journal of Child Psychology and Psychiatry* 35, 7 (1994): 1173.

8 Wendy M. Craig, Debra Pepler, and Julie Blais, "Responding to Bullying: What Works?" *School Psychology International* 28, 4 (2007): 466. Cyber-bullying, with its unique implications for out-of-school bullying, merits its own study but is not a major focus of this book.

9 Olweus, "Annotation," 1173.

10 Mona E. Solberg, Dan Olweus, and Inger M. Endreson, "Bullies and Victims at School: Are They the Same Pupils?" *British Journal of Educational Psychology* 77, 2 (2007): 449.

11 Wendy M. Craig, Ray Dev Peters, and Roman Konarski, for Human Resources Development Canada, Applied Research Branch, *Bullying and Victimization among Canadian School Children* (Ottawa: Human Resources Development Canada, 1998), 24.

12 See, for example, Eric Rofes, *A Radical Rethinking of Sexuality and Schooling: Status Quo or Status Queer?* (Lanham, MD: Rowman and Littlefield, 2005); Kevin K. Kumashiro, "'Posts' Perspectives on Anti-Oppressive Education in Social Studies, English, Mathematics, and Science Classrooms," *Educational Researcher* 30, 3 (2001): 3-12; and Debbie Epstein and Richard Johnson, "On the Straight and Narrow: The Heterosexual Presumption, Homophobias and Schools," in Debbie Epstein, ed., *Challenging Lesbian and Gay Inequalities in Education,* 197-230 (Buckingham, UK: Open University Press, 1994).

13 Olweus, "Annotation."

14 Pepler and Craig, *Making a Difference.*

15 Michael J. Boulton and Kerry Underwood, "Bully/Victim Problems among Middle School Children," *British Journal of Educational Psychology* 62, 1 (1992): 73-87.

16 Yoshio Murakami, "Bullies in the Classroom," *Japan Quarterly* 32, 4 (1985): 407-11. In Japan bullying – known as *ijime* – is taken quite seriously as an important cultural phenomenon. In the mid-1990s the issue of *ijime* was the subject of a headline story in Japanese newspapers and on newscasts for over a year following the suicide of thirteen-year-old high school student Kiyoteru Okochi. Okochi's suicide note indicated that he had killed himself to escape the torment of bullies at school. Okochi

had been forced to submerge his face in a polluted river and to deliver cash to his tormentors on a daily basis. The amount of money he had handed over to his victimizers totalled approximately US$10,000.

17 See Jacqueline Noel Treml, "Bullying as a Social Malady in Contemporary Japan," *International Social Work* 44, 1 (2001): 107-17; and Takashi Naito and Uwe P. Gielen, "Bullying and *Ijime* in Japanese Schools," in Florence Denmark et al., eds., *Violence in Schools: Cross-National and Cross-Cultural Perspectives,* 169-90 (New York: Springer Science and Business Media, 2005).

18 Professor Peter Smith of Goldsmith's College in London published research as part of an international program of study assessing the extent of bullying in selected countries and was funded by the Japanese Ministry of Education and the United Nations Educational, Scientific, and Cultural Organization (UNESCO). See Peter K. Smith and Shu Shu, "What Good Schools Can Do about Bullying: Findings from a Survey in English Schools after a Decade of Research and Action," *Childhood* 7, 2 (2000): 193-212.

19 Olweus, "Annotation," 1171-72.

20 Boulton and Underwood, "Bully/Victim Problems."

21 Interestingly, the "Beat Bullying" blue-wristband campaign in the United Kingdom has been declared a failure, not because of lack of popular support but because of the unintended consequences of the campaign as it played out "on the ground" in schools. The campaign was launched by Radio 1/BBC, and the wristbands were made available during Anti-Bullying Week in November 2004. Unfortunately, students who wore the bright blue and intentionally noticeable wristbands to pledge their very visible support for the government-sponsored anti-bullying campaign found that they became targets of bullies. Having been discontinued, the wristbands became a much sought-after item and were being sold in bags of twenty-five on eBay for over £20.

22 Tonya R. Nansel et al., "Bullying Behaviors among US Youth: Prevalence and Association with Psychosocial Adjustment," *Journal of the American Medical Association* 285, 16 (2001): 2096.

23 Olweus, *Bullying at School,* 48.

24 Gerald Walton, "Bullying and Homophobia in Canadian Schools: The Politics of Policies, Programs and Educational Leadership," *Journal of Gay and Lesbian Issues in Education* 1, 4 (2003): 29.

25 Ibid.

26 Wendy M. Craig and Yossi Harel, "Bullying, Physical Fighting and Victimization," in Candace Currie et al., eds., *Young People's Health in Context: Health Behaviour in School-Aged Children (HBSC) Study: International Report from the 2001/2002 Survey* (Copenhagen: World Health Organization, 2004), 133, cited in Craig, Pepler, and Blais, "Responding to Bullying," 466.

27 Pepler and Craig, *Making a Difference.*

28 Ibid.

29 Rona S. Atlas and Debra J. Pepler, "Observations of Bullying in the Classroom," *Journal of Educational Research* 92, 2 (1998): 95.

30 Ibid. (emphasis added).
31 Ibid. (citations omitted).
32 Ibid. (citations omitted).
33 Gerald Walton, "The Notion of Bullying through the Lens of Foucault and Critical Theory," *Journal of Educational Thought* 39, 1 (2005): 59-60.
34 Ibid., 65 (emphasis in original).
35 Gerald Walton, "'Bullying Widespread': A Critical Analysis of Research and Public Discourse on Bullying," *Journal of School Violence* 4, 1 (2005): 91-117. See also Walton, "Notion of Bullying."
36 Walton, "Notion of Bullying."
37 Rofes, *Radical Rethinking.*
38 Ibid., 45.
39 Ibid., 44.
40 Walton, "Notion of Bullying," 57.
41 Ibid.
42 Ibid., 70.
43 Human Rights Commissions in some jurisdictions do have the power to undertake systemic investigations and to order systemic remedies, but these powers are rarely used.
44 Eric M. Roher, "When Push Comes to Shove: Bullying and Legal Liability in Schools," *Education and Law Journal* 12, 3 (2002): 319-47; Eric M. Roher, *An Educator's Guide to Violence in Schools,* 2nd ed. (Aurora, ON: Canada Law Book, 2010).
45 *Canadian Charter of Rights and Freedoms,* Part 1 of the *Constitution Act, 1982,* being Schedule B to the *Canada Act 1982* (UK), 1982, c. 11.
46 See Bruce MacDougall, "Silence in the Classroom: Limits on Homosexual Expression and Visibility in Education and the Privileging of Homophobic Religious Ideology," *Saskatchewan Law Review* 61, 1 (1998): 41-86; Bruce MacDougall, *Queer Judgments: Homosexuality, Expression and the Courts in Canada* (Toronto: University of Toronto Press, 2000); Bruce MacDougall, "A Respectful Distance: Appellate Courts Consider Religious Motivation of Public Figures in Homosexual Equality Discourse: The Cases of *Chamberlain* and *Trinity Western University,*" *University of British Columbia Law Review* 35, 2 (2002): 511-38; and Bruce MacDougall, "The Separation of Church and Date: Destabilizing Traditional Religion-Based Legal Norms on Sexuality," *University of British Columbia Law Review* 36, 1 (2003): 1-27.
47 Bruce MacDougall, "The Legally Queer Child," *McGill Law Journal* 49, 4 (2004): 1091.
48 Ibid.
49 This study and some of my other work seek to address this gap in the literature. See Donn Short, "Queers, Bullying and Safe Schools: Am I Safe Here?" *Journal of Gay and Lesbian Social Services* 19, 3-4 (2007): 31-46; Donn Short, "Conversations in Equity and Social Justice: Constructing Safe Schools for Queer Youth," *Journal for Critical Education Policy Studies* 8, 2 (2010): 329-57; and Bruce MacDougall and Donn Short, "Religion-Based Claims for Impinging on Queer Citizenship," *Dalhousie Law Journal* 33, 2 (2010): 133-60. See also George W. Smith, "The Ideology of 'Fag':

The School Experience of Gay Students," ed. Dorothy E. Smith, *Sociological Quarterly* 39, 2 (1998): 309-35.

50 Smith, "Ideology of 'Fag.'"

51 Bill 81, *An Act to increase respect and responsibility, to set standards for safe learning and safe teaching in schools and to amend the Teaching Profession Act,* 1st Sess., 37th Leg., Ontario, 2000 (assented to 23 June 2000), SO 2000, c. 12 [*Safe Schools Act*].

52 *Equity Foundation Statement and Commitments to Equity Policy Implementation* (Toronto: Toronto District School Board, 1999).

53 Gerald Walton, "H-Cubed: A Primer on Bullying and Sexual Diversity for Educators," *Our Schools, Our Selves* 15, 2 (2006): 117-18.

54 Lynne Ainsworth, "Teachers Learning Security Lesson," *Toronto Star,* 18 October 1990, A1.

55 Derek Ferguson, "Ontario Schools Ordered to Report Acts of Violence to Police," *Toronto Star,* 5 October 1993, A10.

56 Dottie O'Neill and Stan Josey, "School Board Poised to Crack Down on Crime: Policy Could Mean Life Expulsion for Some," *Toronto Star,* 28 October 1993, SD4.

57 Jim Hutchison, "Is Your Child Safe at School?" *Reader's Digest Canada,* September 1997, 46.

58 O'Neill and Josey, "School Board Poised," SD4.

59 Stan Josey, "Policy on School Violence Praised: Boards to Focus on Strategies for Intervention and Prevention," *Toronto Star,* 9 December 1993, SD2.

60 Patrick Abtan, "Guns, Knives Bring 'Zero Tolerance' to Schools," *Toronto Star,* 1 December 1993, A27.

61 Gerri Gershon, "Lessons in Resisting Violence," *Toronto Star,* 31 May 2007, AA6.

62 O'Neill and Josey, "School Board Poised," SD4.

63 Ibid.

64 Ontario Progressive Conservative Party, *Blueprint: Mike Harris' Plan to Keep Ontario on the Right Track* (Toronto: Ontario Progressive Conservative Party, April 1999), 42.

65 *Ontario Code of Conduct* (Toronto: Ministry of Education, 1994).

66 Virginia Galt, "Safe-Schools Policy Would Suspend Bullies: Toronto Board's Proposal Covers Elementary, Secondary Levels and Aims to Provide Principals with a Consistent Set of Rules," *Globe and Mail,* 12 April 2000, A18.

67 *Education Act,* RSO 1990, c. E.2 [*Education Act*].

68 Galt, "Safe-Schools Policy," A18.

69 *Safe Schools Act,* preamble.

70 *Education Act,* s. 23(3).

71 Ken Bhattacharjee, *The Ontario Safe Schools Act: School Discipline and Discrimination* (Toronto: Ontario Human Rights Commission, 2003), 16.

72 Ibid.

73 *Safe Schools Foundation Statement* (Toronto: Toronto District School Board, 1999); *Police-School Board Protocol* (Toronto: Toronto District School Board, 2000); *Safe Arrival for Elementary Schools* (Toronto: Toronto District School Board, 2000).

74 *Education Act,* s. 306(1), as amended by the *Safe Schools Act,* s. 3.

75 *Education Act,* s. 309(1), as amended by the *Safe Schools Act,* s. 3.

76 O'Neill and Josey, "School Board Poised," SD4.
77 *Behaviour, Discipline and Safety of Pupils*, O. Reg. 472/07, s. 2 [*Regulations*].
78 *Safe Schools Foundation Statement*, 1.
79 Ontario, Legislative Assembly, *Official Report of Debates (Hansard)*, 37th Leg., 1st Sess., No. 67B (6 June 2000). After the legislation was introduced, there were significant discussions about a disproportionate impact on black male students, in particular. The Ontario Human Rights Commission and the Ontario Ministry of Education reached a settlement following a July 2005 human rights complaint alleging that the application of the legislation was having a discriminatory impact on racialized students and students with disabilities.
80 Tim McCaskell, *Race to Equity: Disrupting Educational Inequality* (Toronto: Between the Lines, 2005).
81 *City of Toronto Act, 1997 (No. 2)*, SO 1997, c. 26; *Municipality of Metropolitan Toronto Act*, RSO 1990, c. M.62.
82 *Fewer School Boards Act, 1997*, SO 1997, c. 3.
83 Cited in McCaskell, *Race to Equity*, 230-31.
84 Ibid., 230.
85 Ibid., 269.
86 *Equity Foundation Statement*, 2-3.
87 McCaskell, *Race to Equity*, 272.
88 *Jubran v. North Vancouver School District No. 44*, 2002 BCHRT 10 at para. 3, 42 CHRR D/273 [*Jubran* (Tribunal)].
89 *Human Rights Code*, RSBC 1996, c. 210.
90 *Corren v. British Columbia (Ministry of Education) (No. 2)*, 2005 BCHRT 497 at para. 9, 55 CHRR D/26.
91 *Human Rights Code*, RSO 1990, c. H.9.
92 *Picard v. Lakehead District School Board*, Thunder Bay SBHE-5YJRJL (OHRC), paras. a, j.
93 Unfortunately, success on paper did not immediately translate into success on the ground. With the assistance of his mother, a high school teacher at his former high school, Gabe was obliged to bring further complaints before the Human Rights Commission in Ontario in order to compel the school board to comply with its obligations under the settlement agreement.
94 Bill 212, *An Act to amend the Education Act in respect of behaviour, discipline and safety*, 2nd Sess., 38th Leg., Ontario, 2007 (assented to 4 June 2007), SO 2007, c. 14.
95 *Education Act*, s. 306(1), as amended by Bill 212, s. 4.
96 *Policy/Program Memorandum No. 144: Bullying Prevention and Intervention* (Toronto: Ministry of Education, 4 October 2007), 3.
97 Eric Rofes, "Canada: A Videotape Collection Focused on Bullying, Homophobia and Queer Youth," *Journal of Gay and Lesbian Issues in Education* 2, 4 (2005): 94.
98 Susan Talburt, Eric Rofes, and Mary Louise Rasmussen, "Introduction: Transforming Discourses of Queer Youth and Educational Practices Surrounding Gender, Sexuality and Youth," in Mary Louise Rasmussen, Eric Rofes, and Susan Talburt, eds., *Youth and Sexualities: Pleasure, Subversion and Insubordination in and out of Schools* (New York: Palgrave Macmillan, 2004), 2.

Chapter 3: How Schools Conceptualize Safety

1 Bill 81, *An Act to increase respect and responsibility, to set standards for safe learning and safe teaching in schools and to amend the Teaching Profession Act*, 1st Sess., 37th Leg., Ontario, 2000 (assented to 23 June 2000), SO 2000, c. 12 [*Safe Schools Act*].

2 *Safe Schools Foundation Statement* (Toronto: Toronto District School Board, 1999).

3 *Equity Foundation Statement and Commitments to Equity Policy Implementation* (Toronto: Toronto District School Board, 1999).

4 *Safe Schools Foundation Statement*, 1.

5 *Equity Foundation Statement*, 2.

6 Toronto District School Board, "Alternative Schools" (n.d.), http://www.tdsb.on.ca (accessed 12 October 2012).

7 Bruce MacDougall, "The Legally Queer Child," *McGill Law Journal* 49, 4 (2004): 1057-91.

8 *Equity Foundation Statement*, 2.

9 David E. Polkinghorne, *Narrative Knowing and the Human Sciences* (Albany: State University of New York Press, 1988), 13.

10 See Dorothy E. Smith, *The Everyday World as Problematic: A Feminist Sociology* (Toronto: University of Toronto Press, 1987); and Dorothy E. Smith, *Institutional Ethnography: A Sociology for People* (Lanham, MD: AltaMira, 2005).

11 Susan A. Mann and Lori R. Kelley, "Standing at the Crossroads of Modernist Thought: Collins, Smith, and the New Feminist Epistemologies," *Gender and Society* 11, 4 (1997): 391-408.

12 Ken Plummer, *Documents of Life 2: An Invitation to a Critical Humanism* (London: Sage, 2001), ch. 9.

13 *Human Rights Code*, RSO 1990, c. H.9.

14 *Canadian Charter of Rights and Freedoms*, Part 1 of the *Constitution Act, 1982*, being Schedule B to the *Canada Act 1982* (UK), 1982, c. 11.

15 Dan W. Butin, "This Ain't Talk Therapy: Problematizing and Extending Anti-Oppressive Education," *Educational Researcher* 31, 3 (2002): 14. See also Kevin K. Kumashiro, "'Posts' Perspectives on Anti-Oppressive Education in Social Studies, English, Mathematics, and Science Classrooms," *Educational Researcher* 30, 3 (2001): 3-12, more fully discussed in the following chapter.

16 Butin, "This Ain't Talk Therapy," 14, citations omitted.

17 As identified by Kumashiro, these perspectives would include such "posts" as postmodernism, poststructuralism, and postcolonialism. See Kumashiro, "'Posts' Perspectives."

18 Kevin K. Kumashiro, "Three Readings of D. Butin's Commentary," *Educational Researcher* 31, 3 (2002): 18, emphasis in original.

19 Peter McLaren, "Critical Pedagogy: A Look at the Major Concepts," in Antonia Darder, Marta P. Baltodano, and Rodolfo D. Torres, eds., *The Critical Pedagogy Reader*, 2nd ed. (New York: Routledge, 2009), 80, emphasis in original.

20 Henry A. Giroux, *Teachers as Intellectuals: Toward a Critical Pedagogy of Learning* (Westport, CT: Bergin and Garvey, 1988), 212.

21 Ibid.

22 Many schools, presumably, present elements of several or all of these conceptions in varying degrees.

23 Gerald Walton, "Bullying and Homophobia in Canadian Schools: The Politics of Policies, Programs and Educational Leadership," *Journal of Gay and Lesbian Issues in Education* 1, 4 (2003): 7.

24 *Education Act*, RSO 1990, c. E.2.

Chapter 4: Not Keeping a Straight Face

1 *Youth Criminal Justice Act*, SC 2002, c. 1.

2 Dan Olweus, "Annotation: Bullying at School: Basic Facts and Effects of a School Based Intervention Program," *Journal of Child Psychology and Psychiatry* 35, 7 (1994): 1173.

3 Terry Wotherspoon, *The Sociology of Education in Canada: Critical Perspectives*, 2nd ed. (Don Mills, ON: Oxford University Press, 2004), 3.

4 Gerald Walton, "The Notion of Bullying through the Lens of Foucault and Critical Theory," *Journal of Educational Thought* 39, 1 (2005): 55-73.

5 Quoted in Carol Thorbes, "Walton Focuses on Homophobic Bullying," *SFU News*, 2 December 2004, http://www.sfu.ca (accessed 12 October 2012).

6 Walton, "Notion of Bullying," 60.

7 Debra J. Pepler and Wendy M. Craig, *Making a Difference in Bullying: Report No. 60* (Toronto: LaMarsh Centre for Research on Violence and Conflict Resolution, 2000).

8 Ibid., 61.

9 See Nel Noddings, *The Challenge to Care in Schools: An Alternative Approach to Education* (New York: Teachers College Press, 1992); David E. Purpel, *Moral Outrage in Education* (New York: Peter Lang, 1999); and Stephanie Urso Spina, "When the Smoke Clears: Revisualizing Responses to Violence in Schools," in Stephanie Urso Spina, ed., *Smoke and Mirrors: The Hidden Context of Violence in Schools and Society*, 229-59 (Lanham, MD: Rowman and Littlefield, 2000), 229, cited in Gerald Walton, "'No Fags Allowed': An Examination of Bullying as a Problematic and Implications for Educational Policy" (PhD diss., Faculty of Education, Queen's University, 2006).

10 See Andy Hargreaves, Lorna Earl, and Jim Ryan, *Schooling for Change: Reinventing Education for Early Adolescents* (London: Falmer, 1996); David W. Johnson and Roger T. Johnson, *Leading the Cooperative School*, 2nd ed. (Edina, MN: Interaction Book Company, 1994); and Thomas J. Sergiovanni, *Building Community in Schools* (San Francisco, CA: Jossey-Bass, 1994).

11 *Equity Foundation Statement and Commitments to Equity Policy Implementation* (Toronto: Toronto District School Board, 1999).

12 See Jon Young, Benjamin Levin, and Dawn Wallin, *Understanding Canadian Schools: An Introduction to Educational Administration*, 4th ed. (Toronto: Nelson Education, 2008).

13 Blye W. Frank, "Masculinities and Schooling: The Making of Men," in Juanita Ross Epp and Ailsa M. Watkinson, eds., *Systemic Violence: How Schools Hurt Children*, 113-32 (London: Falmer, 1996).

14 Debbie Epstein and Richard Johnson, "On the Straight and Narrow: The Heterosexual Presumption, Homophobias and Schools," in Debbie Epstein, ed., *Challenging Lesbian and Gay Inequalities in Education*, 197-230 (Buckingham, UK: Open University Press, 1994); Gerald Walton, "Bullying and Homophobia in Canadian Schools: The Politics of Policies, Programs and Educational Leadership," *Journal of Gay and Lesbian Issues in Education* 1, 4 (2003): 23-36.

15 Michael Manley-Casimir, "Teaching as a Normative Enterprise," *Education Law Journal* 5 (1995): 1-21.

16 Gad Horowitz, *Repression: Basic and Surplus Repression in Psychoanalytic Theory: Freud, Reich, and Marcuse* (Toronto: University of Toronto Press, 1977).

17 Manley-Casimir, "Teaching as a Normative Enterprise," 3-4.

18 Ibid., 4, citations omitted.

19 Philip W. Jackson, *Life in Classrooms* (New York: Holt, Rinehart and Winston, 1968); Paulo Freire, *Pedagogy of the Oppressed*, trans. Myra Bergman Ramos (New York: Herder and Herder, 1970); Paul Willis, *Learning to Labor: How Working Class Kids Get Working Class Jobs* (New York: Columbia University Press, 1981); W. Gordon West, "Schooling: Discipline and Surveillance in Inculcating Legal Subjectivity," in *Young Offenders and the State: A Canadian Perspective on Delinquency*, 145-70 (Toronto: Butterworths, 1984); Madiha Didi Khayatt, "Surviving School as a Lesbian Student," *Gender and Education* 6, 1 (1994): 47-62; Frank, "Masculinities and Schooling"; Michael W. Apple, *Ideology and Curriculum*, 3rd ed. (New York: RoutledgeFalmer, 2004); Peter McLaren, *Life in Schools: An Introduction to Critical Pedagogy in the Foundations of Education*, 2nd ed. (New York: Longman, 1994); James T. Sears, ed., *Sexuality and the Curriculum: The Politics and Practices of Sexuality Education* (New York: Teachers College, 1992).

20 John R. Gillis, *Youth and History: Tradition and Change in European Age Relations, 1770-Present* (New York: Academic Press, 1974).

21 Ibid.

22 West, "Schooling," 169.

23 R. Dale, "Education in the Crisis and the Crisis in Education," unpublished text (1978), cited in ibid., 166.

24 See Michael Mann, "The Social Cohesion of Liberal Democracy," *American Sociological Review* 35, 3 (1970): 423-39; and Freire, *Pedagogy of the Oppressed*.

25 See Martin Carnoy and Henry M. Levin, *Schooling and Work in the Democratic State* (Stanford, CA: Stanford University Press, 1985); Michael W. Apple, *Teachers and Texts: A Political Economy of Class and Gender Relations in Education* (London: Routledge and Kegan Paul, 1986); and Michael W. Apple, *Education and Power*, 2nd ed. (New York: Routledge, 1995).

26 See Eric Rofes, *A Radical Rethinking of Sexuality and Schooling: Status Quo or Status Queer?* (Lanham, MD: Rowman and Littlefield, 2005); Debbie Epstein and Richard Johnson, *Schooling Sexualities* (Bristol, UK: Open University Press, 1998); Epstein and Johnson, "On the Straight and Narrow"; Debbie Epstein and James T. Sears, eds., *A Dangerous Knowing: Sexuality, Pedagogy and Popular Culture* (London: Cassell, 1999); Madiha Didi Khayatt, "Proper Schooling for Teenage Lesbians in Canada," in Aart Hendriks, Rob Tielman, and Evert van der Veen, eds., *The Third Pink Book: A*

Global View of Lesbian and Gay Liberation and Oppression, 123-39 (Buffalo, NY: Prometheus, 1993).

27 Wotherspoon, *Sociology of Education,* 94.

28 Ibid.

29 Jackson, *Life in Classrooms.* See also Philip W. Jackson, Robert E. Boostrom, and David T. Hansen, *The Moral Life of Schools* (San Francisco, CA: Jossey-Bass, 1993).

30 David Head, "Letter to an Educational Quisling," in David Head, ed., *Free Way to Learning: Educational Alternatives in Action* (Harmondsworth, UK: Penguin Education, 1974), 24, cited in Roland Meighan, *A Sociology of Educating* (London: Holt, Rinehart and Winston, 1981), 52.

31 Michael Haralambos, *Sociology: Themes and Perspectives* (London: Collins, 1991), 1.

32 Samuel Bowles and Herbert Gintis, *Schooling in Capitalist America: Educational Reform and the Contradictions of Economic Life* (New York: Basic Books, 1976); Samuel Bowles and Herbert Gintis, "*Schooling in Capitalist America* Revisited," *Sociology of Education* 75, 1 (2002): 1-18.

33 Wotherspoon, *Sociology of Education,* 97.

34 David Gordon, "The Aesthetic Attitude and the Hidden Curriculum," *Journal of Aesthetic Education* 15, 2 (1981): 56.

35 Benjamin S. Bloom, "Innocence in Education," *School Review* 80, 3 (1972): 343.

36 Gordon, "Aesthetic Attitude."

37 Emile Durkheim, *Moral Education: A Study in the Theory and Application of the Sociology of Education,* trans. Everett K. Wilson and Herman Schnurer (New York/ Toronto: Free Press/Collier-Macmillan, 1973); Emile Durkheim, *Education and Sociology,* trans. Sherwood D. Fox (Glencoe, IL: Free Press, 1956).

38 Talcott Parsons, *The Social System* (London: Routledge and Kegan Paul, 1951).

39 Michael W. Apple and Lois Weis, "Ideology and Practice in Schooling: A Political and Conceptual Introduction," in Michael W. Apple and Lois Weis, eds., *Ideology and Practice in Schooling,* 3-33 (Philadelphia, PA: Temple University Press, 1983); Apple, *Ideology and Curriculum,* 5.

40 Madeleine Arnot, *Reproducing Gender? Essays on Educational Theory and Feminist Politics* (London: RoutledgeFalmer, 2002); Madeleine Arnot and Mairtin Mac an Ghaill, "(Re)Contextualising Gender Studies in Education: Schooling in Late Modernity," in Madeleine Arnot and Mairtin Mac an Ghaill, eds., *The RoutledgeFalmer Reader in Gender and Education,* 1-14 (New York: Routledge, 2006).

41 See Pierre Bourdieu and Jean-Claude Passeron, *Reproduction in Education, Society and Culture,* trans. Richard Nice (London: Sage, 1977); Pierre Bourdieu, *Outline of a Theory of Practice,* trans. Richard Nice (Cambridge, UK: Cambridge University Press, 1977); Henry A. Giroux, *Theory and Resistance in Education: A Pedagogy for the Opposition* (New York: Bergin and Garvey, 1983); and McLaren, *Life in Schools.*

42 Bourdieu, *Outline of a Theory.*

43 Melinda S. Miceli, "Gay, Lesbian and Bisexual Youth," in Diane Richardson and Steven Seidman, eds., *Handbook of Gay and Lesbian Studies* (London: Sage, 2002), 206, citations omitted.

44 William M. Stanley, *Curriculum for Utopia: Social Reconstructionism and Critical Pedagogy in the Postmodern Era* (Albany: State University of New York Press, 1992), cited in Miceli, "Gay, Lesbian and Bisexual Youth," 206.

45 Miceli, "Gay, Lesbian and Bisexual Youth," 206.
46 Tuula Gordon, Janet Holland, and Elina Lahelma, "From Pupil to Citizen: A Gendered Route," in Madeleine Arnot and Jo-Anne Dillabough, eds., *Challenging Democracy: International Perspectives on Gender, Education and Citizenship*, 187-202 (London: RoutledgeFalmer, 2000).
47 Sears, ed., *Sexuality and the Curriculum*.
48 Debbie Epstein, Sarah O'Flynn, and David Telford, "Silenced Sexualities or the Love(s) That Won't Shut Up," in *Silenced Sexualities in Schools and Universities*, 1-14 (Stoke on Trent, UK: Trentham, 2003).
49 Kevin K. Kumashiro, "'Posts' Perspectives on Anti-Oppressive Education in Social Studies, English, Mathematics, and Science Classrooms," *Educational Researcher* 30, 3 (2001): 3-12.
50 Miceli, "Gay, Lesbian and Bisexual Youth."
51 Jacqueline Mikulsky, "Investigating the Relationship between 'School Climate,' School-Related Outcomes and Academic Self-Concept for Australian, Secondary School–Aged Same-Sex-Attracted Youth (SSAY)" (PhD diss., University of Sydney, 2005).
52 Debbie Epstein, Sarah O'Flynn, and David Telford, "Innocence and Experience Paradoxes in Sexuality and Education," in Diane Richardson and Steven Seidman, eds., *Handbook of Gay and Lesbian Studies* (London: Sage, 2002), 273.
53 Ibid.
54 Ibid., 281.
55 Miceli, "Gay, Lesbian and Bisexual Youth," 207.
56 Ibid.
57 Ken Plummer, "Lesbian and Gay Youth in England," in Gilbert Herdt, ed., *Gay and Lesbian Youth*, 195-223 (Binghamton, NY: Haworth, 1989).
58 Ibid.
59 Epstein, O'Flynn, and Telford, "Silenced Sexualities."
60 Victoria Clarke and Elizabeth Peel, "Introducing *Out in Psychology*," in Victoria Clarke and Elizabeth Peel, eds., *Out in Psychology: Lesbian, Gay, Bisexual, Trans and Queer Perspectives*, 1-10 (Chichester, UK: John Wiley and Sons, 2007).
61 Khayatt, "Proper Schooling," 131.
62 Anthony R. D'Augelli, "Teaching Lesbian/Gay Development: From Oppression to Exceptionality," in Karen M. Harbeck, ed., *Coming Out of the Classroom Closet: Gay and Lesbian Students, Teachers, and Curricula* (Binghamton, NY: Haworth, 1992), 214.
63 Miceli, "Gay, Lesbian and Bisexual Youth," 207.
64 Debbie Epstein and James T. Sears, "Introduction: Knowing Dangerously," in Debbie Epstein and James T. Sears, eds., *A Dangerous Knowing: Sexuality, Pedagogy and Popular Culture* (London: Cassell, 1999), 1, citations omitted.
65 Ibid.
66 Epstein, O'Flynn, and Telford, "Silenced Sexualities."
67 Ibid., 9.
68 Miceli, "Gay, Lesbian and Bisexual Youth," 207.

69 Bruce MacDougall, "Silence in the Classroom: Limits on Homosexual Expression and Visibility in Education and the Privileging of Homophobic Religious Ideology," *Saskatchewan Law Review* 61, 1 (1998): 41.

70 Epstein and Johnson, "On the Straight and Narrow," 223-24.

71 Kumashiro, "'Posts' Perspectives."

72 Ibid., 3.

73 Gust A. Yep, "Heteronormativity," in James T. Sears, ed., *Youth, Education and Sexualities: An International Encyclopedia* (Westport, CT: Greenwood, 2005), vol. 1, 395.

74 Jackson, *Life in Classrooms;* Jackson, Boostrom, and Hansen, *Moral Life of Schools.*

75 Kevin K. Kumashiro, "Toward a Theory of Anti-Oppressive Education," *Review of Educational Research* 70, 1 (2000): 32, citations omitted.

76 Steve Fifield and Howard (Lee) Swain, "Heteronormativity and Common Sense in Science (Teacher) Education," in Rita M. Kissen, ed., *Getting Ready for Benjamin: Preparing Teachers for Sexual Diversity in the Classroom,* 177-89 (Lanham, MD: Rowman and Littlefield, 2002).

77 Madeleine Arnot, *Reproducing Gender? Essays on Educational Theory and Feminist Politics* (London: RoutledgeFalmer, 2002), 105. See also Debbie Epstein, "'Boyz' Own Stories: Masculinities and Sexualities in Schools," in Wayne Martino and Bob Meyenn, eds., *What about the Boys? Issues of Masculinity in Schools,* 96-109 (Buckingham, UK: Open University Press, 2001); and Wayne Martino, "'Powerful People Aren't Usually Real Kind, Friendly, Open People!': Boys Interrogating Masculinities at School," in Wayne Martino and Bob Meyenn, eds., *What about the Boys? Issues of Masculinity in Schools,* 82-95 (Buckingham, UK: Open University Press, 2001).

78 Yep, "Heteronormativity," 395-96.

79 Khayatt, "Proper Schooling," 138n17.

80 Ibid.

81 Ibid.

82 Ibid.

83 Ibid.

84 Kumashiro, "Toward a Theory," 27; Signithia Fordham, *Blacked Out: Dilemmas of Race, Identity and Success at Capital High* (Chicago, IL: University of Chicago Press, 1996); Willis, *Learning to Labor;* Stanford T. Goto, "Nerds, Normal People, and Homeboys: Accommodation and Resistance among Chinese American Students," *Anthropology and Education Quarterly* 28, 1 (1997): 70-84.

85 See Gabriele Lakomski, "Witches, Weather Gods, and Phlogiston: The Demise of the Hidden Curriculum," *Curriculum Inquiry* 18, 4 (1988): 451-63.

86 David Gordon, "Hidden Curriculum," in Torsten Husen and T. Neville Postlethwaite, eds., *The International Encyclopaedia of Education,* 2nd ed. (Oxford: Elsevier Science, 1994), vol. 5, 2588.

87 Margaret A. Gibson, *Assimilation without Accommodation: Sikh Immigrants in an American High School* (Ithaca, NY: Cornell University Press, 1988), cited in Kumashiro, "Toward a Theory," 27.

88 Antonio Gramsci, *Further Selections from the Prison Notebooks,* trans. Derek Boothman (London: Lawrence and Wishart, 1995), cited in Epstein, O'Flynn, and Telford, "Innocence and Experience," 276.
89 Michel Foucault, *History of Sexuality,* vol. 1, *An Introduction,* trans. Robert Hurley (New York: Vintage, 1990), 95, cited in Epstein, O'Flynn, and Telford, "Innocence and Experience," 276.
90 Epstein, O'Flynn, and Telford, "Innocence and Experience," 276.
91 Kumashiro, "Toward a Theory," 27.
92 Kevin K. Kumashiro, "Three Readings of D. Butin's Commentary," *Educational Researcher* 31, 3 (2002): 17.
93 Mary Louise Rasmussen, "Safety and Subversion: The Production of Sexualities and Genders in School Spaces," in Mary Louise Rasmussen, Eric Rofes, and Susan Talburt, eds., *Youth and Sexualities: Pleasure, Subversion and Insubordination in and out of Schools,* (New York: Palgrave Macmillan, 2004), 131.
94 Ibid., 134.
95 Willis, *Learning to Labor.*
96 Ibid.
97 See Ari Assor and David Gordon, "The Implicit Learning Theory of Hidden Curriculum Research," *Journal of Curriculum Studies* 19, 4 (1987): 329-39; and Sandra Faimin-Silva, "Students and a 'Culture of Resistance' in Provincetown's Schools," *Anthropology and Education Quarterly* 33, 2 (2002): 189-212.
98 Gordon, "Hidden Curriculum," 2588.
99 Miceli, "Gay, Lesbian and Bisexual Youth," 206.
100 Ibid.
101 See Walton, "Bullying and Homophobia"; Rasmussen, "Safety and Subversion"; Wendy M. Craig, Debra Pepler, and Julie Blais, "Responding to Bullying: What Works?" *School Psychology International* 28, 4 (2007): 465-77; and Beth Reis, *The Safe Schools Resource Guide: Will You Be There for Every Child?* (Seattle: Safe Schools Coalition of Washington, 1997).
102 *Education Act,* RSO 1990, c. E.2.

Chapter 5: Obstacles to the Implementation of Equity Policies

1 *Equity Foundation Statement and Commitments to Equity Policy Implementation* (Toronto: Toronto District School Board, 1999).
2 Kevin K. Kumashiro, "Toward a Theory of Anti-Oppressive Education," *Review of Educational Research* 70, 1 (2000): 25-53.
3 Ibid., 27.
4 Madiha Didi Khayatt, *Lesbian Teachers: An Invisible Presence* (Albany: State University of New York Press, 1992).
5 George W. Smith, "The Ideology of 'Fag': The School Experience of Gay Students," ed. Dorothy E. Smith, *Sociological Quarterly* 39, 2 (1998): 327.
6 Ibid.
7 Lori MacIntosh, "Does Anybody Have a Band-Aid? Anti-Homophobia Discourses and Pedagogical Impossibilities," *Educational Studies: Journal of the American Educational Studies Association* 41, 1 (2007): 35.

8 Ibid., 35-36.
9 Jeffrey White, Anthony Grandy, and Adrienne Magidsohn, "Mission" (n.d.), http://schools.tdsb.on.ca/triangle/mission.html (accessed 12 October 2012).
10 I first encountered the expression "heteronormative citizenship" in the work of Carol Johnson. She uses the term in a different context, namely, in her investigation of the politics of "passing." See Carol Johnson, "Heteronormative Citizenship and the Politics of Passing," *Sexualities* 5, 3 (2002): 317-36.
11 *Jubran v. North Vancouver School District No. 44*, 2002 BCHRT 10 at para. 3, 42 CHRR D/273 [*Jubran* (Tribunal)].
12 *School District No. 44 (North Vancouver) v. Jubran*, 2003 BCSC 6, [2003] 3 WWR 288.
13 *School District No. 44 (North Vancouver) v. Jubran*, 2005 BCCA 201, 253 DLR (4th) 294 [*Jubran* (CA)].
14 *Robichaud v. Canada (Treasury Board)*, [1987] 2 SCR 84, 40 DLR (4th) 577 [*Robichaud*].
15 *Human Rights Code*, RSBC 1996, c. 210, s. 8.
16 *Robichaud*, 89, cited in *Jubran* (CA), para. 30.
17 *Québec (Commission des droits de la personne et des droits de la jeunesse) v. Montréal (City)*, 2000 SCC 27 at para. 30, [2000] 1 SCR 665 [*Montréal*], cited in *Jubran* (CA), para. 31.
18 *Ontario Human Rights Commission and O'Malley v. Simpsons-Sears Ltd.*, [1985] 2 SCR 536, 23 DLR (4th) 321 [*O'Malley*], cited in *Jubran* (Tribunal), para. 97, cited in *Jubran* (CA), para. 22.
19 *Ross v. New Brunswick School District No. 15*, [1996] 1 SCR 825 (*sub nom Attis v. Board of Education of School District No. 15 et al.*), 171 NBR (2d) 321 [*Ross*].
20 Ibid., cited in *Jubran* (Tribunal), para. 116, cited in *Jubran* (CA), para. 65.
21 Ibid., para. 42, cited in *Jubran* (Tribunal), para. 109, cited in *Jubran* (CA), para. 81.
22 *Jubran* (Tribunal), para. 115, cited in *Jubran* (CA), para. 87.
23 Ibid., para. 160, cited in *Jubran* (CA), para. 89.
24 John Allen, "Power," in John Agnew, Katharyne Mitchell, and Gerard Toal, eds., *A Companion to Political Geography* (Malden, MA: Blackwell, 2003), 95.
25 Ibid.
26 Bill 81, *An Act to increase respect and responsibility, to set standards for safe learning and safe teaching in schools and to amend the Teaching Profession Act*, 1st Sess., 37th Leg., Ontario, 2000 (assented to 23 June 2000), SO 2000, c. 12 [*Safe Schools Act*].
27 Kumashiro, "Toward a Theory," 25.
28 Michael Warner, "Introduction," in Michael Warner, ed., *Fear of a Queer Planet: Queer Politics and Social Theory* (Minneapolis: University of Minnesota Press, 1993), xxi.
29 Kumashiro, "Toward a Theory," 26-27.
30 Ibid., 28.
31 Ibid., 31-32.
32 Susanne Luhmann, "Queering/Querying Pedagogy? Or, Pedagogy Is a Pretty Queer Thing," in W.F. Pinar, ed., *Queer Theory in Education*, 141-55 (Mahwah, NJ: Lawrence Erlbaum Associates).

33 Deborah P. Britzman, "Is There a Queer Pedagogy? Or, Stop Reading Straight," *Educational Theory* 45, 2 (1995): 151-65.
34 Gerald Walton, "The Notion of Bullying through the Lens of Foucault and Critical Theory," *Journal of Educational Thought* 39, 1 (2005): 67.
35 Kumashiro, "Toward a Theory," 35-39.
36 Jean Anyon, "Workers, Labor and Economic History, and Textbook Content," in Michael W. Apple and Lois Weis, eds., *Ideology and Practice in Schooling* (Philadelphia, PA: Temple University Press, 1983), 49.
37 Kumashiro, "Toward a Theory," 35-36.
38 Kevin K. Kumashiro, "Theories and Practices of Antioppressive Education," in *Troubling Education: Queer Activism and Antioppressive Pedagogy* (New York: RoutledgeFalmer, 2002), 50.

Chapter 6: The Long Arm of the Law?

 1 Sally Engle Merry, "Legal Pluralism," *Law and Society Review* 22, 5 (1988): 869-96. See also Harry W. Arthurs, *"Without the Law": Administrative Justice and Legal Pluralism in Nineteenth-Century England* (Toronto: University of Toronto Press, 1985); and Martha-Marie Kleinhans and Roderick A. Macdonald, "What Is a *Critical* Legal Pluralism?" *Canadian Journal of Law and Society* 12, 2 (1997): 25-46.
 2 Merry, "Legal Pluralism," 869-70.
 3 Ibid.
 4 H.W.O. Okoth-Ogendo, "The Imposition of Property Law in Kenya," in Sandra B. Burman and Barbara E. Harrell-Bond, eds., *The Imposition of Law* (New York: Academic Press, 1979), 160; Omoniyi Adewoye "Legal Practice in Ibadan, 1904-1960," *Journal of Legal Pluralism* 24 (1986): 60; Kwamena Bentsi-Enchill, "The Colonial Heritage of Legal Pluralism," *Zambia Law Journal* 1 (1969): 1-30, cited in Merry, "Legal Pluralism," 870.
 5 Merry, "Legal Pluralism," 872.
 6 Ibid.
 7 Ibid., 870; Kleinhans and Macdonald, "What Is a *Critical* Legal Pluralism?"; John Griffiths, "What Is Legal Pluralism?" *Journal of Legal Pluralism* 24 (1986): 2; Leopold Pospisil, *Anthropology of Law: A Comparative Theory* (New York: Harper and Row, 1971).
 8 Merry, "Legal Pluralism."
 9 Ibid., 874.
10 Ibid. See also Arthurs, *"Without the Law"*; Stuart Henry, *Private Justice: Towards Integrated Theorising in the Sociology of Law* (London: Routledge and Kegan Paul, 1983); and Stewart Macaulay, "Private Government," in Leon Lipson and Stanton Wheeler, eds., *Law and the Social Sciences*, 445-518 (New York: Russell Sage Foundation, 1986).
11 Merry, "Legal Pluralism," 889.
12 Brian Z. Tamanaha, "Understanding Legal Pluralism: Past to Present, Local to Global," *Sydney Law Review* 30, 3 (2008): 375.
13 Boaventura de Sousa Santos, "Legal Plurality and the Time-Spaces of Law: The Local, the National and the Global," in *Toward a New Legal Common Sense: Law, Globalization, and Emancipation*, 2nd ed. (London: Butterworths, 2002), 91.

14 Emmanuel Melissaris, "The More the Merrier? A New Take on Legal Pluralism," *Social and Legal Studies* 13, 1 (2004): 76, emphasis added.

15 *Canadian Charter of Rights and Freedoms*, Part 1 of the *Constitution Act, 1982*, being Schedule B to the *Canada Act 1982* (UK), 1982, c. 11.

16 *Constitution Act, 1867* (UK), 30 & 31 Vict., c. 3, ss. 91-92, reprinted in RSC 1985, App. II, No. 5.

17 Arthurs, *"Without the Law,"* 1-2. See also Marc Galanter, "Justice in Many Rooms: Courts, Private Ordering and Indigenous Law," *Journal of Legal Pluralism* 19 (1981): 1-47.

18 Ibid.

19 Ibid.

20 Ibid.

21 Leslie Green, "Legal Obligation and Authority," in Edward N. Zalta, ed., *Stanford Encyclopedia of Philosophy* (Stanford, CA: Metaphysics Research Lab, Center for the Study of Language and Information, 2007), 4.3, http://plato.stanford.edu (accessed 12 October 2012).

22 Ibid.

23 Harry W. Arthurs, "Labour Law without the State," *University of Toronto Law Journal* 46, 1 (1996): 1-45.

24 Arthurs, *"Without the Law,"* 3.

25 Ibid.

26 Galanter, "Justice in Many Rooms," cited in ibid., 2.

27 Arthurs, *"Without the Law."*

28 Ibid.

29 Ibid.

30 Ibid.

31 Ibid.

32 Harry W. Arthurs, "Poor Canadian Legal Education: So Near to Wall Street, So Far from God," *Osgoode Hall Law Journal* 38, 3 (2000): 401.

33 Ibid.

34 Ibid., citations omitted. On the results of a project dealing with spousal battery in Hawaii, see Sally Engle Merry, "Global Human Rights and Local Social Movements in a Legally Plural World," *Canadian Journal of Law and Society* 12, 2 (1997): 247-71.

35 William M. Evan, "Public and Private Legal Systems," in William M. Evan, ed., *Law and Sociology: Exploratory Essays* (New York: Free Press of Glencoe, 1962), 166, cited in Arthurs, *"Without the Law,"* 2-3.

36 Julia Black, "Critical Reflections on Regulation," *Australian Journal of Legal Philosophy* 27 (2002): 4-6, citations omitted.

37 Sally Falk Moore, "Law and Social Change: The Semi-Autonomous Social Field as an Appropriate Subject of Study," *Law and Society Review* 7, 4 (1973): 720.

38 *Equity Foundation Statement and Commitments to Equity Policy Implementation* (Toronto: Toronto District School Board, 1999).

39 Moore, "Law and Social Change," 723.

40 Ibid., cited in Merry, "Legal Pluralism," 878.

41 Kleinhans and Macdonald, "What Is a *Critical* Legal Pluralism?" 38, emphasis in original, citations omitted.
42 Peter McLaren, "Critical Pedagogy: A Look at the Major Concepts," in Antonia Darder, Marta P. Baltodano, and Rodolfo D. Torres, eds., *The Critical Pedagogy Reader*, 2nd ed. (New York: Routledge, 2009), 61.
43 Merry, "Legal Pluralism," 889. In fact, Merry suggests five ways that the socio-legal approach known as legal pluralism can expand the research framework.
44 Ibid.
45 *Education Act*, RSO 1990, c. E.2.
46 *Behaviour, Discipline and Safety of Pupils*, O. Reg. 472/07, s. 2 [*Regulations*].
47 *Safe Schools Foundation Statement* (Toronto: Toronto District School Board, 1999).
48 Rebecca Raby, "Growing Up Governed" (PhD diss., Department of Sociology, York University, 2002).
49 A cautionary word about the expression "youth culture" is in order. Researchers must not come to rely upon or be distracted by – sloppily in my view – the term "youth culture." The concept is, in many important ways, unsatisfactory. Much violence that occurs in schools happens because of ideology and the sway of culture. In the same way that generic conceptions of bullying lead researchers and policy makers away from the social dynamics that give rise to bullying, so too can a pervasive reliance on the concept of youth culture distract us from the constituent parts of youth culture and the factors at play within it – the social construction of masculinities but also of femininities, sexualities, and so on. I use the term "youth culture" here not to suggest a monolithic, unified group but to capture, summarily, the various constituent parts of a diverse culture that numerous normative orders seek or claim to influence.
50 Kevin K. Kumashiro, "'Posts' Perspectives on Anti-Oppressive Education in Social Studies, English, Mathematics, and Science Classrooms," *Educational Researcher* 30, 3 (2001): 3.

Chapter 7: Barriers to the Effectiveness of State Law

1 Obie Trice, featuring Akon, "Snitch," *Second Round's on Me*, audio CD (New York: Shady Records, 2006).
2 Jackson Katz, "8 Reasons Eminem's Popularity Is a Disaster for Women" (2002), http://www.jacksonkatz.com/eminem2.html (accessed 12 October 2012).
3 *Equity Foundation Statement and Commitments to Equity Policy Implementation* (Toronto: Toronto District School Board, 1999).
4 Katz, "8 Reasons."
5 *Jubran v. North Vancouver School District No. 44*, 2002 BCHRT 10, 42 CHRR D/273, "Appendix B: Chronology of Events," 11 [*Jubran* (Tribunal)].
6 Ibid., "Proceedings," 32-46.
7 Christian Richardson, "'Teenagers' Harsh Lessons Range from School Bullies to Suicide," letter to editor, *Vancouver Sun*, 19 September 2000, A15.
8 *Jubran* (Tribunal), "Proceedings," 156-59.
9 Ibid., "Proceedings," 11.

10 Derek Kai and Brian Higgins, "School Bullies Dominate with Words," letter to editor, *Vancouver Sun*, 15 September 2000, A18.

11 Benjamin Levin and Jon Young, "Making Sense of Public Schooling," in Judy M. Iseke-Barnes and Njoki Nathani Wane, eds., *Equity in Schools and Society* (Toronto: Canadian Scholars' Press, 2000), 49.

12 For a discussion of internalized disciplinary power in the context of prisons, see Michel Foucault, *Discipline and Punish: The Birth of the Prison*, trans. Alan Sheridan (New York: Vintage, 1995), 201. See also Michel Foucault, "Space, Knowledge, and Power," interview by Paul Rabinow, trans. Christian Hubert, in Paul Rabinow, ed., *The Foucault Reader*, 239-56 (New York: Pantheon Books, 1984).

13 Bill 81, *An Act to increase respect and responsibility, to set standards for safe learning and safe teaching in schools and to amend the Teaching Profession Act*, 1st Sess., 37th Leg., Ontario, 2000 (assented to 23 June 2000), SO 2000, c. 12 [*Safe Schools Act*].

14 *Education Act*, RSO 1990, c. E.2.

15 Toronto District Muslim Education Assembly, "Indoctrination and the Promotion of Homosexual Lifestyle and Moral Corruption in Our Public Schools" (n.d.), http://tdmea.tripod.com/alertflyer.htm (accessed 14 October 2012).

16 *Canadian Charter of Rights and Freedoms*, Part 1 of the *Constitution Act, 1982*, being Schedule B to the *Canada Act 1982* (UK), 1982, c. 11.

17 *Human Rights Code*, RSO 1990, c. H.9.

18 Gareth Kirby, "The Suicide Note," *Xtra*, 22 February 2001, http://archives.xtra.ca/Story.aspx?s=1426766 (accessed 14 October 2012).

19 Cited in Tom Yeung, "Using His Death? Mother Wants BC Teachers Fired," *Xtra*, 29 June 2000.

20 Cited in David Walberg, "Help Gay Kids Escape Parents before They're Totally Brainwashed," *Xtra*, 20 April 2000.

21 Cited in Yeung, "Using His Death?"

22 Eric Rofes, "Bound and Gagged: Sexual Silences, Gender Conformity and the Gay Male Teacher," *Sexualities* 3, 4 (2000): 449.

23 Cited in Debbie Epstein and Emma Renold, "Gender, Power and Difference," *Gender and Education* 18, 3 (2006): 229.

24 Rofes, "Bound and Gagged," 448.

25 Liz Frost, "Doing Bodies Differently? Gender, Youth, Appearance and Damage," *Journal of Youth Studies* 6, 1 (2003): 55.

26 David Plummer, "The Quest for Modern Manhood: Masculine Stereotypes, Peer Culture and the Social Significance of Homophobia," *Journal of Adolescence* 24, 1 (2001): 21.

27 Ibid., 22.

28 Ibid., 17.

29 Ibid., 21.

30 Gad Horowitz, *Repression: Basic and Surplus Repression in Psychoanalytic Theory: Freud, Reich, and Marcuse* (Toronto: University of Toronto Press, 1977).

31 Ibid.

32 Rob Pattman, Stephen Frosh, and Ann Phoenix, "Constructing and Experiencing Boyhoods in Research in London," *Gender and Education* 17, 5 (2005): 555-61.

33 Ibid.
34 I have tried this exercise with adult students, both undergraduates and law students, and have gotten the same results. In some classes, 100 percent of the students will answer "fag" or "gay" in relation to boys and "slut" (by far the most popular choice), "bitch," or "cunt" in relation to girls. "Dyke" or "lesbian" is rarely suggested.
35 See Steve Fifield and Howard (Lee) Swain, "Heteronormativity and Common Sense in Science (Teacher) Education," in Rita M. Kissen, ed., *Getting Ready for Benjamin: Preparing Teachers for Sexual Diversity in the Classroom*, 177-89 (Lanham, MD: Rowman and Littlefield, 2002).
36 Madeleine Arnot, *Reproducing Gender? Essays on Educational Theory and Feminist Politics* (London: RoutledgeFalmer, 2002). See also Debbie Epstein, "Boyz' Own Stories: Masculinities and Sexualities in Schools," in Wayne Martino and Bob Meyenn, eds., *What about the Boys? Issues of Masculinity in Schools*, 96-109 (Buckingham, UK: Open University Press, 2001); and Wayne Martino, "'Powerful People Aren't Usually Real Kind, Friendly, Open People!' Boys Interrogating Masculinities at School," in Wayne Martino and Bob Meyenn, eds., *What about the Boys? Issues of Masculinity in Schools*, 82-95 (Buckingham, UK: Open University Press, 2001).

Chapter 8: Conclusion

1 *Equity Foundation Statement and Commitments to Equity Policy Implementation* (Toronto: Toronto District School Board, 1999).
2 Bill 81, *An Act to increase respect and responsibility, to set standards for safe learning and safe teaching in schools and to amend the Teaching Profession Act*, 1st Sess., 37th Leg., Ontario, 2000 (assented to 23 June 2000), SO 2000, c. 12 [*Safe Schools Act*].
3 *Education Act*, RSO 1990, c. E.2.
4 Sally Engle Merry, "Legal Pluralism," *Law and Society Review* 22, 5 (1988): 889.
5 Ibid.
6 Ibid.
7 Ibid.
8 Ibid.
9 Ibid., 889-90.
10 Ibid., 890.
11 Ibid.
12 Ibid.
13 Gerald Walton, "The Notion of Bullying through the Lens of Foucault and Critical Theory," *Journal of Educational Thought* 39, 1 (2005): 66.
14 Bill 13, *An Act to amend the Education Act with respect to bullying and other matters*, 1st Sess., 40th Leg., Ontario, 2011 [*Accepting Schools Act*].
15 Ibid., s. 3(1).
16 Ibid., s. 12.
17 *Canadian Charter of Rights and Freedoms*, Part 1 of the *Constitution Act, 1982*, being Schedule B to the *Canada Act 1982* (UK), 1982, c. 11.
18 Matthew Pearson, "Suicide of Gay Teen Jamie Hubley Puts Scrutiny on Educators over Bullying," *National Post*, 18 October 2011, http://news.nationalpost.com/2011/

10/18/jamie-hubley-educators-urge-more-work-to-end-bullying-following-suicide (accessed 14 October 2012).

19 See *Chiang v. Vancouver Board of Education*, 2009 BCHRT 319, [2009] BCHRTD No. 319; *Hall (Litigation guardian of) v. Powers* (2002), 59 OR (3d) 423, 213 DLR (4th) 308 (Sup. Ct. J.).

20 Bruce MacDougall and Donn Short, "Religion-Based Claims for Impinging on Queer Citizenship," *Dalhousie Law Journal* 33, 2 (2010): 133-60.

21 Ibid.

22 David Badash, "September's Anti-Gay Bullying Suicides – There Were a Lot More Than 5," *The New Civil Rights Movement*, 1 October 2010, http://thenewcivilrights-movement.com/septembers-anti-gay-bullying-suicides-there-were-a-lot-more-than-5/discrimination/2010/10/01/13297 (accessed 12 October 2012).

23 See, for example, Eric Rofes, *A Radical Rethinking of Sexuality and Schooling: Status Quo or Status Queer?* (Lanham, MD: Rowman and Littlefield, 2005); Kevin Kumashiro, "Toward a Theory of Anti-Oppressive Education," *Review of Educational Research* 70, 1 (2000): 25-53; Debbie Epstein and James T. Sears, eds., *A Dangerous Knowing: Sexuality, Pedagogy and Popular Culture* (London: Cassell, 1999).

24 Kumashiro, "Toward a Theory," 26-34.

25 Lesley A. Jacobs, "Differentiated Corporate Legal Consciousness in International Human Rights Disputes: Security and Transnational Oil Companies in Sudan," *APDR Research Notes* 1, 3 (2008): 41.

Bibliography

Primary Sources

Legislation

Behaviour, Discipline and Safety of Pupils, O. Reg. 472/07 [*Regulations*].

Bill 13, *An Act to amend the Education Act with respect to bullying and other matters,* 1st Sess., 40th Leg., Ontario, 2011 [*Accepting Schools Act*].

Bill 81, *An Act to increase respect and responsibility, to set standards for safe learning and safe teaching in schools and to amend the Teaching Profession Act,* 1st Sess., 37th Leg., Ontario, 2000 (assented to 23 June 2000), SO 2000, c. 12 [*Safe Schools Act*].

Bill 212, *An Act to amend the Education Act in respect of behaviour, discipline and safety,* 2nd Sess., 38th Leg., Ontario, 2007 (assented to 4 June 2007), SO 2007, c. 14.

Canadian Charter of Rights and Freedoms, Part 1 of the *Constitution Act, 1982,* being Schedule B to the *Canada Act 1982* (UK), 1982, c. 11.

City of Toronto Act, 1997 (No. 2), SO 1997, c. 26.

Constitution Act, 1867 (UK), 30 & 31 Vict., c. 3, ss. 91-92, reprinted in RSC 1985, App. II, No. 5.

Education Act, RSO 1990, c. E.2.

Fewer School Boards Act, 1997, SO 1997, c. 3.

Human Rights Code, RSBC 1996, c. 210.

Human Rights Code, RSO 1990, c. H.9.

Municipality of Metropolitan Toronto Act, RSO 1990, c. M.62.

Youth Criminal Justice Act, SC 2002, c. 1.

Jurisprudence

Chiang v. Vancouver Board of Education, 2009 BCHRT 319, [2009] BCHRTD No. 319.

Corren v. British Columbia (Ministry of Education) (No. 2), 2005 BCHRT 497, 55 CHRR D/26.

Hall (Litigation guardian of) v. Powers (2002), 59 OR (3d) 423, 213 DLR (4th) 308 (Sup. Ct. J.).

Jubran v. North Vancouver School District No. 44, 2002 BCHRT 10, 42 CHRR D/273 [*Jubran* (Tribunal)].

North Vancouver School District No. 44 v. Jubran, [2005] SCCA No. 260 (QL).

Ontario Human Rights Commission and O'Malley v. Simpsons-Sears Ltd., [1985] 2 SCR 536, 23 DLR (4th) 321 [*O'Malley*].

Picard v. Lakehead District School Board, Thunder Bay SBHE-5YJRJL (OHRC).

Québec (Commission des droits de la personne et des droits de la jeunesse) v. Montréal (City), 2000 SCC 27, [2000] 1 SCR 665 [*Montréal*].

Robichaud v. Canada (Treasury Board), [1987] 2 SCR 84, 40 DLR (4th) 577.

Ross v. New Brunswick School District No. 15, [1996] 1 SCR 825 (*sub nom Attis v. Board of Education of School District No. 15* et al.), 171 NBR (2d) 321 [*Ross*].

School District No. 44 (North Vancouver) v. Jubran, 2003 BCSC 6, [2003] 3 WWR 288.

School District No. 44 (North Vancouver) v. Jubran, 2005 BCCA 201, 253 DLR (4th) 294 [*Jubran* (CA)].

Policies

Equity Foundation Statement and Commitments to Equity Policy Implementation. Toronto: Toronto District School Board, 1999.

Ontario Code of Conduct. Toronto: Ministry of Education, 1994.

Police-School Board Protocol. Toronto: Toronto District School Board, 2000.

Policy/Program Memorandum No. 144: Bullying Prevention and Intervention. Toronto: Ministry of Education, 4 October 2007.

Safe Arrival for Elementary Schools. Toronto: Toronto District School Board, 2000.

Safe Schools Foundation Statement. Toronto: Toronto District School Board, 1999.

Violence-Free Schools Policy. Toronto: Ontario Ministry of Education and Training, 1994.

Reports

Bhattacharjee, Ken. *The Ontario Safe Schools Act: School Discipline and Discrimination.* Toronto: Ontario Human Rights Commission, 2003.

Craig, Wendy M., Ray Dev Peters, and Roman Konarski, for Human Resources Development Canada, Applied Research Branch. *Bullying and Victimization among Canadian School Children.* Ottawa: Human Resources Development Canada, 1998.

Craig, Wendy M., and Yossi Harel. "Bullying, Physical Fighting and Victimization." In Candace Currie et al., eds., *Young People's Health in Context: Health Behaviour in School-Aged Children (HBSC) Study: International Report from the 2001/2002 Survey,* 133-44. Copenhagen: World Health Organization, 2004.

Ontario, Legislative Assembly. *Official Report of Debates (Hansard),* 37th Leg., 1st Sess., No. 67B (6 June 2000).

Pepler, Debra J., and Wendy M. Craig. *Making a Difference in Bullying: Report No. 60.* Toronto: LaMarsh Centre for Research on Violence and Conflict Resolution, 2000.

Taylor, C., and T. Peter, with T.L. McMinn et al. *Every Class in Every School: The First National Climate Survey on Homophobia, Biphobia, and Transphobia in Canadian Schools: Final Report.* Toronto: Egale Canada Human Rights Trust, 2011.

Ziegler, Suzanne, and Merle Rosenstein-Manner. *Bullying at School: Toronto in an International Context.* Toronto: Research Services, Toronto Board of Education, 1991.

Secondary Sources

Abtan, Patrick. "Guns, Knives Bring 'Zero Tolerance' to Schools." *Toronto Star,* 1 December 1993, A27.

Adewoye, Omoniyi. "Legal Practice in Ibadan, 1904-1960." *Journal of Legal Pluralism* 24 (1986): 57-76.

Ainsworth, Lynne. "Teachers Learning Security Lesson." *Toronto Star,* 18 October 1990, A1.

Allen, John. "Power." In John Agnew, Katharyne Mitchell, and Gerard Toal, eds., *A Companion to Political Geography,* 95-108. Malden, MA: Blackwell, 2003.

Anyon, Jean. "Workers, Labor and Economic History, and Textbook Content." In Michael W. Apple and Lois Weis, eds., *Ideology and Practice in Schooling,* 37-60. Philadelphia, PA: Temple University Press, 1983.

Apple, Michael W. *Education and Power.* 2nd ed. New York: Routledge, 1995.

–. *Ideology and Curriculum.* 3rd ed. New York: RoutledgeFalmer, 2004.

–. *Teachers and Texts: A Political Economy of Class and Gender Relations in Education.* London, UK: Routledge and Kegan Paul, 1986.

Apple, Michael W., and Lois Weis. "Ideology and Practice in Schooling: A Political and Conceptual Introduction." In Michael W. Apple and Lois Weis, eds., *Ideology and Practice in Schooling,* 3-33. Philadelphia, PA: Temple University Press, 1983.

Arnot, Madeleine. *Reproducing Gender? Essays on Educational Theory and Feminist Politics.* London: RoutledgeFalmer, 2002.

Arnot, Madeleine, and Mairtin Mac an Ghaill. "(Re)Contextualising Gender Studies in Education: Schooling in Late Modernity." In Madeleine Arnot and Mairtin Mac an Ghaill, eds., *The RoutledgeFalmer Reader in Gender and Education,* 1-14. New York: Routledge, 2006.

Arthurs, Harry W. "Labour Law without the State." *University of Toronto Law Journal* 46, 1 (1996): 1-45.

–. "Poor Canadian Legal Education: So Near to Wall Street, So Far from God." *Osgoode Hall Law Journal* 38, 3 (2000): 381-480.

–. *"Without the Law"*: *Administrative Justice and Legal Pluralism in Nineteenth-Century England.* Toronto: University of Toronto Press, 1985.

Assor, Ari, and David Gordon. "The Implicit Learning Theory of Hidden Curriculum Research." *Journal of Curriculum Studies* 19, 4 (1987): 329-39.

Atlas, Rona S., and Debra J. Pepler. "Observations of Bullying in the Classroom." *Journal of Educational Research* 92, 2 (1998): 86-99.

Badash, David. "September's Anti-Gay Bullying Suicides – There Were a Lot More Than 5." *The New Civil Rights Movement,* 1 October 2010. http://thenewcivilrightsmovement.com/septembers-anti-gay-bullying-suicides-there-were-a-lot-more-than-5/discrimination/2010/10/01/13297 (accessed 12 October 2012).

Bala, Nicholas. "The Young Offenders Act: A Legal Framework." In Joe Hudson, Joseph P. Hornick, and Barbara A. Burrows, eds., *Justice and the Young Offender in Canada,* 11-35. Toronto: Wall and Thompson, 1988.

Bell, Lee Anne. "Theoretical Foundations for Social Justice Education." In Maurianne Adams, Lee Anne Bell, and Pat Griffin, eds., *Teaching for Diversity and Social Justice: A Sourcebook,* 3-15. New York: Routledge, 1997.

Bentsi-Enchill, Kwamena. "The Colonial Heritage of Legal Pluralism." *Zambia Law Journal* 1 (1969): 1-30.

Berger, Peter L., and Thomas Luckman. *The Social Construction of Reality: A Treatise in the Sociology of Knowledge.* Garden City, NY: Doubleday and Company, 1966.

Black, Julia. "Critical Reflections on Regulation." *Australian Journal of Legal Philosophy* 27 (2002): 1-35.

Black, William. "Grading Human Rights in the Schoolyard: *Jubran v. Board of Trustees.*" *University of British Columbia Law Review* 36, 1 (2003): 45-55.

Bloom, Benjamin S. "Innocence in Education." *School Review* 80, 3 (1972): 333-52.

Boulton, Michael J., and Kerry Underwood. "Bully/Victim Problems among Middle School Children." *British Journal of Educational Psychology* 62, 1 (1992): 73-87.

Bourdieu, Pierre. *Outline of a Theory of Practice.* Trans. Richard Nice. Cambridge, UK: Cambridge University Press, 1977.

Bourdieu, Pierre, and Jean-Claude Passeron. *Reproduction in Education, Society and Culture.* Trans. Richard Nice. London: Sage, 1977.

Bowles, Samuel, and Herbert Gintis. *Schooling in Capitalist America: Educational Reform and the Contradictions of Economic Life.* New York: Basic Books, 1976.

–. *"Schooling in Capitalist America* Revisited." *Sociology of Education* 75, 1 (2002): 1-18.

Britzman, Deborah P. "Is There a Queer Pedagogy? Or, Stop Reading Straight." *Educational Theory* 45, 2 (1995): 151-65.

Butin, Dan W. "This Ain't Talk Therapy: Problematizing and Extending Anti-Oppressive Education." *Educational Researcher* 31, 3 (2002): 14-16.

Campbell, Marie, and Francis Gregor. *Mapping Social Relations: A Primer on Doing Institutional Ethnography.* Aurora, ON: Garamond, 2002.

Carnoy, Martin, and Henry M. Levin. *Schooling and Work in the Democratic State.* Stanford, CA: Stanford University Press, 1985.

Charmaz, Kathy. "Grounded Theory: Objectivist and Constructivist Methods." In Norman K. Denzin and Yvonna S. Lincoln, eds., *Handbook of Qualitative Research*, 2nd ed., 509-35. Thousand Oaks, CA: Sage, 2000.

Clarke, Victoria, and Elizabeth Peel. "Introducing *Out in Psychology*." In Victoria Clarke and Elizabeth Peel, eds., *Out in Psychology: Lesbian, Gay, Bisexual, Trans and Queer Perspectives*, 1-10. Chichester, UK: John Wiley and Sons, 2007.

Cooper, Harris M. *The Integrative Research Review: A Systematic Approach*. Beverly Hills, CA: Sage, 1984.

Craig, Wendy M., Debra Pepler, and Julie Blais. "Responding to Bullying: What Works?" *School Psychology International* 28, 4 (2007): 465-77.

Creswell, John W. *Educational Research: Planning, Conducting, and Evaluating Quantitative and Qualitative Research*. 2nd ed. Upper Saddle River, NJ: Merrill, 2005.

Dale, R. "Education in the Crisis and the Crisis in Education." Unpublished text. 1978.

D'Augelli, Anthony R. "Teaching Lesbian/Gay Development: From Oppression to Exceptionality." In Karen M. Harbeck, ed., *Coming Out of the Classroom Closet: Gay and Lesbian Students, Teachers, and Curricula*, 213-28. Binghamton, NY: Haworth, 1992.

Davison, Kevin. "Masculinities, Sexualities and the Student Body: 'Sorting' Gender Identities in School." In Carl E. James, ed., *Experiencing Difference*, 44-52. Halifax: Fernwood, 2000.

Denborough, David. "Power and Partnership? Challenging the Sexual Construction of Schooling." In Louise Laskey and Catherine Beavis, eds., *Schooling and Sexualities: Teaching for a Positive Sexuality*, 1-10. Geelong, Australia: Deakin Centre for Education and Change, 1996.

de Sousa Santos, Boaventura. "Legal Plurality and the Time-Spaces of Law: The Local, the National and the Global." In *Toward a New Legal Common Sense: Law, Globalization, and Emancipation*, 2nd ed., 85-98. London: Butterworths, 2002.

Diduck, Alison. "*Carignan v Carignan*: When Is a Father Not a Father? Another Historical Perspective." *Manitoba Law Journal* 19, 3 (1990): 580.

Dillabough, Jo-Anne. "Gender Theory and Research in Education: Modernist Traditions and Emerging Contemporary Themes." In Madeleine Arnot and Mairtin Mac an Ghaill, eds., *The RoutledgeFalmer Reader in Gender and Education*, 17-32. New York: Routledge, 2006.

Durkheim, Emile. *Education and Sociology*. Trans. Sherwood D. Fox. Glencoe, IL: Free Press, 1956.

–. *Moral Education: A Study in the Theory and Application of the Sociology of Education*. Trans. Everett K. Wilson and Herman Schnurer. New York/Toronto: Free Press/Collier-Macmillan, 1973.

Epstein, Debbie. "Boyz' Own Stories: Masculinities and Sexualities in Schools." In Wayne Martino and Bob Meyenn, eds., *What about the Boys? Issues of Masculinity in Schools*, 96-109. Buckingham, UK: Open University Press, 2001.

Epstein, Debbie, and Emma Renold. "Gender, Power and Difference." *Gender and Education* 18, 3 (2006): 229-31.

Epstein, Debbie, and James T. Sears. "Introduction: Knowing Dangerously." In Debbie Epstein and James T. Sears, eds., *A Dangerous Knowing: Sexuality, Pedagogy and Popular Culture*, 1-7. London: Cassell, 1999.

-, eds. *A Dangerous Knowing: Sexuality, Pedagogy and Popular Culture*. London: Cassell, 1999.

Epstein, Debbie, and Richard Johnson. "On the Straight and Narrow: The Heterosexual Presumption, Homophobias and Schools." In Debbie Epstein, ed., *Challenging Lesbian and Gay Inequities in Education*, 197-230. Buckingham, UK: Open University Press, 1994.

-. *Schooling Sexualities*. Bristol, UK: Open University Press, 1998.

Epstein, Debbie, Sarah O'Flynn, and David Telford. "Innocence and Experience Paradoxes in Sexuality and Education." In Diane Richardson and Steven Seidman, eds., *Handbook of Lesbian and Gay Studies*, 271-90. New York: Sage, 2002.

-. "Silenced Sexualities or the Love(s) That Won't Shut Up." In *Silenced Sexualities in Schools and Universities*, 1-14. Stoke on Trent, UK: Trentham, 2003.

Evan, William M. "Public and Private Legal Systems." In William M. Evan, ed., *Law and Sociology: Exploratory Essays*, 165-84. New York: Free Press of Glencoe, 1962.

Faimin-Silva, Sandra. "Students and a 'Culture of Resistance' in Provincetown's Schools." *Anthropology and Education Quarterly* 33, 2 (2002): 189-212.

Ferguson, Derek. "Ontario Schools Ordered to Report Acts of Violence to Police." *Toronto Star*, 5 October 1993, A10.

Fifield, Steve, and Howard (Lee) Swain. "Heteronormativity and Common Sense in Science (Teacher) Education." In Rita M. Kissen, ed., *Getting Ready for Benjamin: Preparing Teachers for Sexual Diversity in the Classroom*, 177-89. Lanham, MD: Rowman and Littlefield, 2002.

Fordham, Signithia. *Blacked Out: Dilemmas of Race, Identity and Success at Capital High*. Chicago, IL: University of Chicago Press, 1996.

Foucault, Michel. *Discipline and Punish: The Birth of the Prison*. Trans. Alan Sheridan. New York: Vintage, 1995.

-. *History of Sexuality*. Vol. 1, *An Introduction*. Trans. Robert Hurley. New York: Vintage, 1990.

-. "Space, Knowledge, and Power." Interview by Paul Rabinow. Trans. Christian Hubert. In Paul Rabinow, ed., *The Foucault Reader*, 239-56. New York: Pantheon, 1984.

Frank, Blye W. "Masculinities and Schooling: The Making of Men." In Juanita Ross Epp and Ailsa M. Watkinson, eds., *Systemic Violence: How Schools Hurt Children*, 113-32. London: Falmer, 1996.

Freire, Paulo. *Pedagogy of the Oppressed*. Trans. Myra Bergman Ramos. New York: Herder and Herder, 1970.

Frost, Liz. "Doing Bodies Differently? Gender, Youth, Appearance and Damage." *Journal of Youth Studies* 6, 1 (2003): 53-70.

Galanter, Marc. "Justice in Many Rooms: Courts, Private Ordering and Indigenous Law." *Journal of Legal Pluralism* 19 (1981): 1-47.

Galt, Virginia. "Safe-Schools Policy Would Suspend Bullies: Toronto Board's Proposal Covers Elementary, Secondary Levels and Aims to Provide Principals with
a Consistent Set of Rules." *Globe and Mail,* 12 April 2000, A18.

Gershon, Gerri. "Lessons in Resisting Violence." *Toronto Star,* 31 May 2007, AA6.

Gibson, Margaret A. *Assimilation without Accommodation: Sikh Immigrants in an
American High School.* Ithaca, NY: Cornell University Press, 1988.

Gilbert, Rob, and Pam Gilbert. *Masculinity Goes to School.* London: Routledge,
1998.

Gillis, John R. *Youth and History: Tradition and Change in European Age Relations,
1770-Present.* New York: Academic Press, 1974.

Giroux, Henry. *Ideology, Culture and the Process of Schooling.* London: Falmer, 1981.

–. *Teachers as Intellectuals: Toward a Critical Pedagogy of Learning.* Westport, CT:
Bergin and Garvey, 1988.

–. *Theory and Resistance in Education: A Pedagogy for the Opposition.* New York:
Bergin and Garvey, 1983.

Glaser, Barney G., and Anselm L. Strauss. *The Discovery of Grounded Theory:
Strategies for Qualitative Research.* New York: Aldine de Gruyter, 1967.

Gordon, David. "The Aesthetic Attitude and the Hidden Curriculum." *Journal of
Aesthetic Education* 15, 2 (1981): 51-63.

–. "Hidden Curriculum." In Torsten Husen and T. Neville Postlethwaite, eds., *The
International Encyclopaedia of Education,* 2nd ed., vol. 5, 2586-89. Oxford:
Elsevier Science, 1994.

Gordon, Tuula, Janet Holland, and Elina Lahelma. "Ethnographic Research in
Educational Settings." In Paul Atkinson et al., eds., *Handbook of Ethnography,*
188-203. London: Sage, 2001.

–. "From Pupil to Citizen: A Gendered Route." In Madeleine Arnot and Jo-Anne
Dillabough, eds., *Challenging Democracy: International Perspectives on Gender,
Education and Citizenship,* 187-202. London: RoutledgeFalmer, 2000.

Goto, Stanford T. "Nerds, Normal People, and Homeboys: Accommodation and
Resistance among Chinese American Students." *Anthropology and Education
Quarterly* 28, 1 (1997): 70-84.

Grace, André P. "Writing the Queer Self: Using Autobiography to Mediate Inclusive
Teacher Education in Canada." *Teaching and Teacher Education* 22, 7 (2006):
826-34.

Grace, André P., and Fiona J. Benson. "Using Autobiographical Queer Life Narratives
of Teachers to Connect Personal, Political and Pedagogical Spaces." *International
Journal of Inclusive Education* 4, 2 (2000): 89-109.

Grace, André P., and Kristopher Wells. "Gay and Bisexual Male Youth as Educator
Activists and Cultural Workers: The Queer Critical Praxis of Three Canadian
High-School Students." *International Journal of Inclusive Education* 13, 1 (2009):
23-44.

Gramsci, Antonio. *Further Selections from the Prison Notebooks.* Trans. Derek
Boothman. London: Lawrence and Wishart, 1995.

Green, Leslie. "Legal Obligation and Authority." In Edward N. Zalta, ed., *Stanford
Encyclopedia of Philosophy.* Stanford, CA: Metaphysics Research Lab, Center for

the Study of Language and Information, 2007. http://plato.stanford.edu (accessed 12 October 2012).

Griffiths, John. "What Is Legal Pluralism?" *Journal of Legal Pluralism* 24 (1986): 1-55.

Haralambos, Michael. *Sociology: Themes and Perspectives.* London: Collins, 1991.

Hargreaves, Andy, Lorna Earl, and Jim Ryan. *Schooling for Change: Reinventing Education for Early Adolescents.* London: Falmer, 1996.

Head, David. "Letter to an Educational Quisling." In David Head, ed., *Free Way to Learning: Educational Alternatives in Action,* 7-35. Harmondsworth, UK: Penguin Education, 1974.

Henry, Stuart. *Private Justice: Towards Integrated Theorising in the Sociology of Law.* London: Routledge and Kegan Paul, 1983.

Herdt, Gilbert, and Andrew Boxer. *Children of Horizons: How Gay and Lesbian Teens Are Leading a New Way out of the Closet.* Boston, MA: Beacon, 1993.

Herr, Kathryn. "Learning Lessons from School: Homophobia, Heterosexism, and the Construction of Failure." In Mary B. Harris, ed., *School Experiences of Gay and Lesbian Youth: The Invisible Minority,* 51-64. Binghamton, NY: Haworth, 1997.

Horowitz, Gad. *Repression: Basic and Surplus Repression in Psychoanalytic Theory: Freud, Reich, and Marcuse.* Toronto: University of Toronto Press, 1977.

Hutchison, Jim. "Is Your Child Safe at School?" *Reader's Digest Canada,* September 1997, 46.

Jackson, Philip W. *Life in Classrooms.* New York: Holt, Rinehart and Winston, 1968.

Jackson, Philip W., Robert E. Boostrom, and David T. Hansen. *The Moral Life of Schools.* San Francisco, CA: Jossey-Bass, 1993.

Jacobs, Lesley A. "Differentiated Corporate Legal Consciousness in International Human Rights Disputes: Security and Transnational Oil Companies in Sudan." *APDR Research Notes* 1, 3 (2008): 37-49.

Johnson, Carol. "Heteronormative Citizenship and the Politics of Passing." *Sexualities* 5, 3 (2002): 317-36.

Johnson, David W., and Roger T. Johnson. *Leading the Cooperative School.* 2nd ed. Edina, MN: Interaction Book Company, 1994.

Josey, Stan. "Policy on School Violence Praised: Boards to Focus on Strategies for Intervention and Prevention." *Toronto Star,* 9 December 1993, SD2.

–. "Tough Policy May Ban Students for Life." *Toronto Star,* 2 November 1993, A1.

Jung, Patricia Beattie, and Ralph F. Smith. *Heterosexism: An Ethical Challenge.* Albany: State University of New York Press, 1993.

Kai, Derek, and Brian Higgins. "School Bullies Dominate with Words." Letter to editor. *Vancouver Sun,* 15 September 2000, A18.

Katz, Jackson. "8 Reasons Eminem's Popularity Is a Disaster for Women." 2002. http://www.jacksonkatz.com/eminem2.html (accessed 12 October 2012).

Kehily, Mary Jane. "Producing Heterosexualities: The School as a Site of Discursive Practices." In *Sexuality, Gender and Schooling: Shifting Agendas in Social Learning,* 52-72. London: RoutledgeFalmer, 2002.

Khayatt, Madiha Didi. *Lesbian Teachers: An Invisible Presence.* Albany: State University of New York Press, 1992.

–. "Proper Schooling for Teenage Lesbians in Canada." In Aart Hendriks, Rob Tielman, and Evert van der Veen, eds., *The Third Pink Book: A Global View of Lesbian and Gay Liberation and Oppression*, 123-39. Buffalo, NY: Prometheus, 1993.

–. "Surviving School as a Lesbian Student." *Gender and Education* 6, 1 (1994): 47-62.

–. "What's to Fear: Calling Homophobia into Question." *McGill Journal of Education* 41, 2 (2006): 133-44.

Kirby, Gareth. "The Suicide Note." *Xtra*, 22 February 2001. http://archives.xtra.ca/ Story.aspx?s=1426766 (accessed 14 October 2012).

Kirk, Jerome, and Marc L. Miller. *Reliability and Validity in Qualitative Research.* Newbury Park, CA: Sage, 1986.

Kleinhans, Martha-Marie, and Roderick A. Macdonald. "What Is a *Critical* Legal Pluralism?" *Canadian Journal of Law and Society* 12, 2 (1997): 25-46.

Kumashiro, Kevin K. "'Posts' Perspectives on Anti-Oppressive Education in Social Sciences, English, Mathematics, and Science Classrooms." *Educational Researcher* 30, 3 (2001): 3-12.

–. "Theories and Practices of Antioppressive Education." In *Troubling Education: Queer Activism and Antioppressive Pedagogy*, 31-71. New York: RoutledgeFalmer, 2002.

–. "Three Readings of D. Butin's Commentary." *Educational Researcher* 31, 3 (2002): 17-18.

–. "Toward a Theory of Anti-Oppressive Education." *Review of Educational Research* 70, 1 (2000): 25-53.

Kumashiro, Kevin K., and Bic Ngo. Introduction. In Kevin K. Kumashiro and Bic Ngo, eds., *Six Lenses for Anti-Oppressive Education: Partial Stories, Improbable Conversations*, xvii-xxi. New York: Peter Lang, 2007.

Lakomski, Gabriele. "Witches, Weather Gods, and Phlogiston: The Demise of the Hidden Curriculum." *Curriculum Inquiry* 18, 4 (1988): 451-63.

Levin, Benjamin, and Jon Young. "Making Sense of Public Schooling." In Judy M. Iseke-Barnes and Njoki Nathani Wane, eds., *Equity in Schools and Society*, 45-58. Toronto: Canadian Scholars' Press, 2000.

Livingstone, David W. "Searching for Missing Links: Neo-Marxist Theories of Education." *British Journal of Sociology of Education* 16, 1 (1995): 53-73.

Luhmann, Susanne. "Queering/Querying Pedagogy? Or, Pedagogy Is a Pretty Queer Thing." In W.F. Pinar, ed., *Queer Theory in Education*, 141-55. Mahwah, NJ: Lawrence Erlbaum Associates.

Mac an Ghaill, Mairtin. "Teacher Ideologies, Representations and Practices." In *The Making of Men: Masculinities, Sexualities and Schooling*, 15-50. Buckingham, UK: Open University Press, 1994.

Macaulay, Stewart. "Private Government." In Leon Lipson and Stanton Wheeler, eds., *Law and the Social Sciences*, 445-518. New York: Russell Sage Foundation, 1986.

MacDougall, Bruce. "The Legally Queer Child." *McGill Law Journal* 49, 4 (2004): 1057-91.

–. *Queer Judgments: Homosexuality, Expression and the Courts in Canada.* Toronto: University of Toronto Press, 2000.

–. "A Respectful Distance: Appellate Courts Consider Religious Motivation of Public Figures in Homosexual Equality Discourse: The Cases of *Chamberlain* and *Trinity Western University." University of British Columbia Law Review* 35, 2 (2002): 511-38.

–. "The Separation of Church and Date: Destabilizing Traditional Religion-Based Legal Norms on Sexuality." *University of British Columbia Law Review* 36, 1 (2003): 1-27.

–. "Silence in the Classroom: Limits on Homosexual Expression and Visibility in Education and the Privileging of Homophobic Religious Ideology." *Saskatchewan Law Review* 61, 1 (1998): 41-86.

MacDougall, Bruce, and Donn Short. "Religion-Based Claims for Impinging on Queer Citizenship." *Dalhousie Law Journal* 33, 2 (2010): 133-60.

MacIntosh, Lori. "Does Anybody Have a Band-Aid? Anti-Homophobia Discourses and Pedagogical Impossibilities." *Educational Studies: Journal of the American Educational Studies Association* 41, 1 (2007): 33-43.

MacKay, Wayne A., and Lyle (Chip) Sutherland. *Teachers and the Law.* 2nd ed. Toronto: Emond Montgomery, 2006.

Manley-Casimir, Michael. "Teaching as a Normative Enterprise." *Education and Law Journal* 5 (1995): 1-21.

Mann, Michael. "The Social Cohesion of Liberal Democracy." *American Sociological Review* 35, 3 (1970): 423-39.

Mann, Susan A., and Lori R. Kelley. "Standing at the Crossroads of Modernist Thought: Collins, Smith, and the New Feminist Epistemologies." *Gender and Society* 11, 4 (1997): 391-408.

Martino, Wayne. "'Powerful People Aren't Usually Real Kind, Friendly, Open People!' Boys Interrogating Masculinities at School." In Wayne Martino and Bob Meyenn, eds., *What about the Boys? Issues of Masculinity in Schools,* 82-95. Buckingham, UK: Open University Press, 2001.

Martino, Wayne, and Maria Pallotta-Chiarolli. *Being Normal Is the Only Way to Be: Adolescent Perspectives on Gender and School.* Sydney, Australia: University of New South Wales Press, 2005.

Maykut, Pamela, and Richard Morehouse. *Beginning Qualitative Research: A Philosophic and Practical Guide.* London: RoutledgeFalmer, 1994.

McCaskell, Tim. "Homophobic Violence in Schools." *Orbit* 29, 4 (1999): 20-21.

–. *Race to Equity: Disrupting Educational Inequality.* Toronto: Between the Lines, 2005.

McCaskell, Tim, and Vanessa Russell. "Anti-Homophobia Initiatives at the Former Toronto Board of Education." In Tara Goldstein and David Selby, eds., *Weaving Connections: Educating for Peace, Social and Environmental Justice,* 27-56. Toronto: Sumach, 2000.

McLaren, Peter. "Critical Pedagogy: A Look at the Major Concepts." In Antonia Darder, Marta P. Baltodano, and Rodolfo D. Torres, eds., *The Critical Pedagogy Reader,* 2nd ed., 61-83. New York: Routledge, 2009.

–. *Life in Schools: An Introduction to Critical Pedagogy in the Foundations of Education*. 2nd ed. New York: Longman, 1994.

McLean, Chris. "Men, Masculinity and Heterosexuality." In Louise Laskey and Catherine Beavis, eds., *Schooling and Sexualities: Teaching for a Positive Sexuality*, 25-35. Geelong, Australia: Deakin Centre for Education and Change, 1996.

Meighan, Roland. *A Sociology of Educating*. London: Holt, Rinehart and Winston, 1981.

Melia, Kath M. "Producing 'Plausible Stories': Interviewing Student Nurses." In Gale Miller and Robert Dingwall, eds., *Context and Method in Qualitative Research*, 26-36. London: Sage, 2002.

Melissaris, Emmanuel. "The More the Merrier? A New Take on Legal Pluralism." *Sociology and Legal Studies* 13, 1 (2004): 57-79.

Merry, Sally Engle. "Global Human Rights and Local Social Movements in a Legally Plural World." *Canadian Journal of Law and Society* 12, 2 (1997): 247-71.

–. "Legal Pluralism." *Law and Society Review* 22, 5 (1988): 869-96.

Miceli, Melinda S. "Gay, Lesbian and Bisexual Youth." In Diane Richardson and Steven Seidman, eds., *Handbook of Gay and Lesbian Studies*, 199-214. London: Sage, 2002.

Mikulsky, Jacqueline. "Investigating the Relationship between 'School Climate,' School-Related Outcomes and Academic Self-Concept for Australian, Secondary School–Aged, Same-Sex-Attracted Youth (SSAY)." PhD diss., University of Sydney, 2005.

Mishna, Faye, et al. "Teachers' Understanding of Bullying." *Canadian Journal of Education* 28, 4 (2005): 718-38.

Moore, Sally Falk. "Law and Social Change: The Semi-Autonomous Social Field as an Appropriate Subject of Study." *Law and Society Review* 7, 4 (1973): 719-46.

Murakami, Yoshio. "Bullies in the Classroom." *Japan Quarterly* 32, 4 (1985): 407-11.

Naito, Takashi, and Uwe P. Gielen. "Bullying and *Ijime* in Japanese Schools." In Florence Denmark et al., eds., *Violence in Schools: Cross-National and Cross-Cultural Perspectives*, 169-90. New York: Springer Science and Business Media, 2005.

Nanda, Serena. *Neither Man nor Woman: The Hijras of India*. Belmont, CA: Wadsworth, 1990.

Nansel, Tonya R., et al. "Bullying Behaviors among US Youth: Prevalence and Association with Psychosocial Adjustment." *Journal of the American Medical Association* 285, 16 (2001): 2094-100.

Noddings, Nel. *The Challenge to Care in Schools: An Alternative Approach to Education*. New York: Teachers College Press, 1992.

Okoth-Ogendo, H.W.O. "The Imposition of Property Law in Kenya." In Sandra B. Burman and Barbara E. Harrell-Bond, eds., *The Imposition of Law*, 147-66. New York: Academic Press, 1979.

Olweus, Dan. *Aggression in the Schools: Bullies and Whipping Boys*. Washington, DC: Hemisphere, 1978.

–. "Annotation: Bullying at School: Basic Facts and Effects of a School Based Intervention Program." *Journal of Child Psychology and Psychiatry* 35, 7 (1994): 1171-90.

–. *Bullying at School: What We Know and What We Can Do*. Cambridge, UK: Blackwell, 1993.

–. "Peer Harassment: A Critical Analysis and Some Important Issues." In Jaana Juvonen and Sandra Graham, eds., *Peer Harassment in School: The Plight of the Vulnerable and Victimized*, 3-20. New York: Guilford, 2001.

O'Neill, Dottie, and Stan Josey. "School Board Poised to Crack Down on Crime: Policy Could Mean Life Expulsion for Some." *Toronto Star*, 28 October 1993, SD4.

Ontario Progressive Conservative Party. *Blueprint: Mike Harris' Plan to Keep Ontario on the Right Track*. Toronto: Ontario Progressive Conservative Party, April 1999.

Owens, Robert E., Jr. *Queer Kids: The Challenges and Promise for Lesbian, Gay and Bisexual Youth*. New York: Harrington Park, 1998.

Paechter, Carrie. "Power, Bodies and Identity: How Different Forms of Physical Education Construct Varying Masculinities and Femininities in Secondary Schools." *Sex Education* 3, 1 (2003): 47-59.

Parsons, Talcott. *The Social System*. London: Routledge and Kegan Paul, 1951.

Pascoe, C.J. *Dude You're a Fag: Masculinity and Sexuality in High School*. Berkeley: University of California Press, 2007.

Pattman, Rob, Stephen Frosh, and Ann Phoenix. "Constructing and Experiencing Boyhoods in Research in London." *Gender and Education* 17, 5 (2005): 555-61.

Patton, Michael Quinn. *Qualitative Research and Evaluation Methods*. 3rd ed. Thousand Oaks, CA: Sage, 2002.

Pearson, Matthew. "Suicide of Gay Teen Jamie Hubley Puts Scrutiny on Educators over Bullying." *National Post*, 18 October 2011. http://news.nationalpost. com/2011/10/18/jamie-hubley-educators-urge-more-work-to-end-bullying -following-suicide (accessed 14 October 2012).

Pepler, Debra, Peter K. Smith, and Ken Rigby. "Looking Back and Looking Forward: Implications for Making Interventions Work Effectively." In Peter K. Smith, Debra Pepler, and Ken Rigby, eds., *Bullying in Schools: How Successful Can Interventions Be?* 307-24. New York: Cambridge University Press, 2004.

Pepler, Debra, and Wendy Craig. *Binoculars on Bullying: A New Solution to Protect and Connect Children*. Toronto: PREVNet, 2007.

Pharr, Suzanne. *Homophobia: A Weapon of Sexism*. Berkeley, CA: Chardon, 1997.

Platt, Anthony. "The Rise of the Child Saving Movement: A Study in Social Policy and Correctional Reform." *Annals of the American Academy of Political and Social Science* 381, 1 (1969): 21-38.

Plummer, David. "The Quest for Modern Manhood: Masculine Stereotypes, Peer Culture and the Social Significance of Homophobia." *Journal of Adolescence* 24, 1 (2001): 15-23.

Plummer, Ken. *Documents of Life 2: An Invitation to a Critical Humanism*. London: Sage, 2001.

–. "Lesbian and Gay Youth in England." In Gilbert Herdt, ed., *Gay and Lesbian Youth*, 195-223. Binghamton, NY: Haworth, 1989.

Polkinghorne, David E. *Narrative Knowing and the Human Sciences*. Albany: State University of New York Press, 1988.

Porter, Paige. "The State-Family-Workplace Intersection: Hegemony, Contra-diction and Counter-Hegemony in Education." In David Dawkins, ed., *Power and Politics in Education,* 9-52. London: Falmer, 1991.

Pospisil, Leopold. *Anthropology of Law: A Comparative Theory.* New York: Harper and Row, 1971.

Purpel, David E. *Moral Outrage in Education.* New York: Peter Lang, 1999.

Raby, Rebecca. "Growing Up Governed." PhD diss., Department of Sociology, York University, 2002.

Rasmussen, Mary Louise. "Safety and Subversion: The Production of Sexualities and Genders in School Spaces." In Mary Louise Rasmussen, Eric Rofes, and Susan Talburt, eds., *Youth and Sexualities: Pleasure, Subversion and Insubordination in and out of Schools,* 131-52. New York: Palgrave Macmillan, 2004.

Reis, Beth. *The Safe Schools Resource Guide: Will You Be There for Every Child?* Seattle: Safe Schools Coalition of Washington, 1997.

Richardson, Christian. "Teenagers' Harsh Lessons Range from School Bullies to Suicide." Letter to editor. *Vancouver Sun,* 19 September 2000, A15.

Rofes, Eric. "Bound and Gagged: Sexual Silences, Gender Conformity and the Gay Male Teacher." *Sexualities* 3, 4 (2000): 439-62.

–. "Canada: A Videotape Collection Focused on Bullying, Homophobia and Queer Youth." *Journal of Gay and Lesbian Issues in Education* 2, 4 (2005): 93-97.

–. *A Radical Rethinking of Sexuality and Schooling: Status Quo or Status Queer?* Lanham, MD: Rowman and Littlefield, 2005.

Roher, Eric M. *An Educator's Guide to Violence in Schools.* 2nd ed. Aurora, ON: Canada Law Book, 2010.

–. "When Push Comes to Shove: Bullying and Legal Liability in Schools." *Education and Law Journal* 12, 3 (2002): 319-47.

–. "Will the New Safe Schools Legislation Make Ontario Schools Safer?" *Education and Law Journal* 17, 2 (2007): 203-21.

Sanders, Cheryl E. "What Is Bullying?" In Cheryl E. Sanders and Gary D. Phye, eds., *Bullying: Implications for the Classroom,* 1-18. San Diego, CA: Elsevier, 2004.

Sears, James T., ed. *Sexuality and the Curriculum: The Politics and Practices of Sexuality Education.* New York: Teachers College Press, 1992.

Sergiovanni, Thomas J. *Building Community in Schools.* San Francisco, CA: Jossey-Bass, 1994.

Short, Donn. "Conversations in Equity and Social Justice: Constructing Safe Schools for Queer Youth." *Journal for Critical Education Policy Studies* 8, 2 (2010): 329-57.

–. "Full Frontal Diva." *Prism International* 41, 3 (2003): 46-63.

–. "The Informal Regulation of Gender: Fear and Loathing in the Locker Room." *Journal of Gender Studies* 16, 2 (2007): 183-86.

–. "Queers, Bullying and Safe Schools: Am I Safe Here?" *Journal of Gay and Lesbian Social Services* 19, 3-4 (2007): 31-46.

Skopec, Eric William. *Situational Interviewing.* New York: Harper and Row, 1986.

Smith, Dorothy E. *The Everyday World as Problematic: A Feminist Sociology.* Toronto: University of Toronto Press, 1987.

–. *Institutional Ethnography: A Sociology for People*. Lanham, MD: AltaMira, 2005.

–. *Writing the Social: Critique, Theory, and Investigations*. Toronto: University of Toronto Press, 1999.

Smith, George W. "The Ideology of 'Fag.'" Ed. Dorothy E. Smith. *Sociological Quarterly* 39, 2 (1998): 309-35.

Smith, Peter K., and Shu Shu. "What Good Schools Can Do about Bullying: Findings from a Survey in English Schools after a Decade of Research and Action." *Childhood* 7, 2 (2000): 193-212.

Solberg, Mona E., Dan Olweus, and Inger M. Endreson. "Bullies and Victims at School: Are They the Same Pupils?" *British Journal of Educational Psychology* 77, 2 (2007): 441-64.

Spindler, George, and Louise Spindler. "Roger Harkes and Schonhausen: From the Familiar to the Strange and Back." In George Spindler, ed., *Doing the Ethnography of Schooling: Educational Anthropology in Action*, 20-47. New York: Holt, Rinehart and Winston, 1982.

Stanley, William M. *Curriculum for Utopia: Social Reconstructionism and Critical Pedagogy in the Postmodern Era*. Albany: State University of New York Press, 1992.

Sumara, Dennis, and Brent Davis. "Interrupting Heteronormativity: Toward a Queer Curriculum Theory." *Curriculum Inquiry* 29, 2 (1999): 191-208.

Talburt, Susan, Eric Rofes, and Mary Louise Rasmussen. "Introduction: Transforming Discourses of Queer Youth and Educational Practices Surrounding Gender, Sexuality and Youth." In Mary Louise Rasmussen, Eric Rofes, and Susan Talburt, eds., *Youth and Sexualities: Pleasure, Subversion and Insubordination in and out of Schools*, 1-13. New York: Palgrave Macmillan, 2004.

Tamanaha, Brian Z. "Understanding Legal Pluralism: Past to Present, Local to Global." *Sydney Law Review* 30, 3 (2008): 375-411.

Tanenbaum, Leora. "'Not One of Us': The Outsider." In *Slut! Growing Up Female with a Bad Reputation*, 157-202. New York: Perennial, 1999.

Taylor, Gerald D. "Sociological Interpretations of Schooling: The Functional Perspective." In Lorna Erwin and David MacLennan, eds., *Sociology of Education in Canada: Critical Perspectives on Theory, Research and Practice*, 32-54. Toronto: Copp Clark Longman, 1994.

Thorbes, Carol. "Walton Focuses on Homophobic Bullying." *SFU News*, 2 December 2004. http://www.sfu.ca (accessed 12 October 2012).

Toronto District Muslim Education Assembly. "Indoctrination and the Promotion of Homosexual Lifestyle and Moral Corruption in Our Public Schools." n.d. http://tdmea.tripod.com/alertflyer.htm (accessed 14 October 2012).

Toronto District School Board. "Alternative Schools." n.d. http://www.tdsb.on.ca (accessed 12 October 2012).

Treml, Jacqueline Noel. "Bullying as a Social Malady in Contemporary Japan." *International Social Work* 44, 1 (2001): 107-17.

Trice, Obie, featuring Akon. "Snitch." *Second Round's on Me*. Audio CD. New York: Shady Records, 2006.

Unks, Gerald. *The Gay Teen: Educational Practice and Theory for Lesbian, Gay and Bisexual Adolescents*. New York: Routledge, 1995.

Urso Spina, Stephanie. "When the Smoke Clears: Revisualizing Responses to Violence in Schools." In Stephanie Urso Spina, ed., *Smoke and Mirrors: The Hidden Context of Violence in Schools and Society,* 229-59. Lanham, MD: Rowman and Littlefield, 2000.

Walberg, David. "Help Gay Kids Escape Parents before They're Totally Brainwashed." *Xtra,* 20 April 2000.

Walton, Gerald. "Bullying and Homophobia in Canadian Schools: The Politics of Policies, Programs and Educational Leadership." *Journal of Gay and Lesbian Issues in Education* 1, 4 (2003): 23-36.

–. "'Bullying Widespread': A Critical Analysis of Research and Public Discourse on Bullying." *Journal of School Violence* 4, 1 (2005): 91-117.

–. "H-Cubed: A Primer on Bullying and Sexual Diversity for Educators." *Our Schools, Our Selves* 15, 2 (2006): 117-26.

–. "'No Fags Allowed': An Examination of Bullying as a Problematic and Implications for Educational Policy." PhD diss., Faculty of Education, Queen's University, 2006.

–. "The Notion of Bullying through the Lens of Foucault and Critical Theory." *Journal of Educational Thought* 39, 1 (2005): 55-73.

Warner, Michael. Introduction. In Michael Warner, ed., *Fear of a Queer Planet: Queer Politics and Social Theory,* vii-xxxi. Minneapolis: University of Minnesota Press, 1993.

Weeks, Jeffrey. *Against Nature: Essays on History, Sexuality and Identity.* London: Rivers Oram, 1991.

West, W. Gordon. "Schooling: Discipline and Surveillance in Inculcating Legal Subjectivity." In *Young Offenders and the State: A Canadian Perspective on Delinquency,* 145-70. Toronto: Butterworths, 1984.

White, Jeffrey, Anthony Grandy, and Adrienne Magidsohn. "Mission." n.d. http://schools.tdsb.on.ca/triangle/mission.html (accessed 12 October 2012).

Whitson, James A. (Tony). "Post-Structuralist Pedagogy as Counter-Hegemonic Praxis (Can We Find the Baby in the Bathwater?)." In Peter McLaren, ed., *Postmodernism, Postcolonialism and Pedagogy,* 121-44. Albert Park, Australia: James Nicholas, 1995.

Williams, Walter L. "Multicultural Perspectives on Reducing Heterosexism: Looking for Strategies That Work." In James T. Sears and Walter L. Williams, eds., *Overcoming Heterosexism and Homophobia: Strategies That Work,* 76-87. New York: Columbia University Press, 1997.

–. "The Relationship between Male-Male Friendship and Male-Female Marriage: American Indian and Asian Examples." In Peter M. Nardi, ed., *Men's Friendships,* 186-200. Newbury Park, CA: Sage, 1992.

–. *The Spirit and the Flesh: Sexual Diversity in American Indian Culture.* Boston, MA: Beacon, 1986.

Willis, Paul. *Learning to Labor: How Working Class Kids Get Working Class Jobs.* New York: Columbia University Press, 1977.

Wink, Joan. *Critical Pedagogy: Notes from the Real World.* 3rd ed. Boston, MA: Pearson, 2005.

Wotherspoon, Terry. *The Sociology of Education in Canada: Critical Perspectives.* 2nd ed. Don Mills, ON: Oxford University Press, 2004.

Yep, Gust A. "Heteronormativity." In James T. Sears, ed., *Youth, Education and Sexualities: An International Encyclopedia,* vol. 1, 395-98. Westport, CT: Greenwood, 2005.

Yeung, Tom. "Using His Death? Mother Wants BC Teachers Fired." *Xtra,* 29 June 2000.

Youdell, Deborah. "Sex-Gender-Sexuality: How Sex, Gender and Sexuality Constellations Are Constituted in Secondary Schools." *Gender and Education* 17, 3 (2005): 249-70.

Young, Jon, Benjamin Levin, and Dawn Wallin. *Understanding Canadian Schools: An Introduction to Educational Administration.* 4th ed. Toronto: Nelson Education, 2008.

Index

hegemonic masculinity: costs of, 118-19, 224; Coyt students on, 92; monitoring associated with, 225
hegemony: norms, and root of homophobic bullying, 179; pedagogy and, 97-100; privilege, and root of bullying, 104; role of education system in maintaining, 110
heteronormative citizenship, 141, 251*n*10
heteronormative space. *See* school space as gendered or heteronormative
heteronormativity: costs of, 118-19; Jeffrey White on, 135; need for curriculum to address, 160-61, 202-3; power of, 116, 130; as root of bullying of queer students, 19; in schools, 103, 107-11, 113-16, 129, 224; in society, 117, 121; spatial practices and maintenance of, 162; students on, 127, 131, 132, 145, 149; as threatening to queer students, 228
heterosexism: and counter-resistance to GSAs, 136-40; as root of bullying of queer students, 19; roots of, 128; students' lack of awareness of, 115; students on, 127, 130-31, 132, 157, 201; at Sylvia Avenue, 18; vs homophobia, 116-17
heterosexual students: power of, 149-50. *See also* curriculum, need for implication of heterosexual students in
heterosexuality and power differential, 119
hidden curriculum: criticalists on, 120; defined, 111-12, 115; and formal curriculum, 114; functionalist vs criticalist perspective on, 112-13; and hegemonies of gender and sexuality, 118; legal pluralism, and normative orders, 173; as normalizing oppositions of gender, 216; schooling, and education, 201; students' alertness to, 121

hidden-curriculum theory, limitations of, 165-66
hip hop culture and students' clothing, 70
hip hop music, 182
homophobia: associated with transgressions of gender and sexuality, 215-16; assumptions about, 130; and Coyt, 83, 85; as developed in school system, 201-3; in music lyrics, 182; North Vancouver School Board's failure to address, 143-44; as obstacle to implementing equity policies, 156, 164; rap music, anti-snitch culture, and, 181-82, 185; religion and, 185 (*see also* religion, as obstacle to effectiveness of equity policies); Rofes on approaches to combat, 26-27; as root of bullying of queer students, 19; roots of, 128; students on, 127, 131, 132, 141, 147, 149, 152, 201; at Sylvia Avenue, 18; Toronto schools' unacceptable level of, 56; vs heterosexism, 116-17
homophobic bullying: benefits of understanding, 232-33; as most prevalent form of bullying, 197; roots of, 179; and school culture, 4; suggestions for dealing with, 12-13; used to affirm male gender norms, 224-25
homophobic language: and anti-snitch culture, 194; Coyt's response to, 87, 94; at Handsworth, 193; students' experience with, 1, 53, 54, 61, 71-72, 146, 150, 157, 185, 190, 226; at Sylvia Avenue, 61, 102-3, 167-68, 221; as threat to queer students' safety, 20, 62, 101; used by students and teachers, 18-19; used to declare heterosexuality, 141, 186, 208, 221, 223; used to police gender rebels, 215-16
homosexuality as threat to hegemonic masculinity, 119
Howard, Trevor, 186-88

Melissa Munn and Chris Bruckert
On the Outside: From Lengthy Imprisonment to Lasting Freedom (2013)

Emmett Macfarlane
Governing from the Bench: The Supreme Court of Canada and the Judicial Role (2013)

Ron Ellis
Unjust by Design: The Administrative Justice System in Canada (2013)

David R. Boyd
The Right to a Healthy Environment: Revitalizing Canada's Constitution (2012)

David Milward
Aboriginal Justice and the Charter: Realizing a Culturally Sensitive Interpretation of Legal Rights (2012)

Shelley A.M. Gavigan
Hunger, Horses, and Government Men: Criminal Law on the Aboriginal Plains, 1870-1905 (2012)

Steven Bittle
Still Dying for a Living: Corporate Criminal Liability after the Westray Mine Disaster (2012)

Jacqueline D. Krikorian
International Trade Law and Domestic Policy: Canada, the United States, and the WTO (2012)

Michael Boudreau
City of Order: Crime and Society in Halifax, 1918-35 (2012)

Lesley Erickson
Westward Bound: Sex, Violence, the Law, and the Making of a Settler Society (2011)

David R. Boyd
The Environmental Rights Revolution: A Global Study of Constitutions, Human Rights, and the Environment (2011)

Elaine Craig
Troubling Sex: Towards a Legal Theory of Sexual Integrity (2011)

Laura DeVries
Conflict in Caledonia: Aboriginal Land Rights and the Rule of Law (2011)

Jocelyn Downie and Jennifer J. Llewellyn (eds.)
Being Relational: Reflections on Relational Theory and Health Law (2011)

Grace Li Xiu Woo
Ghost Dancing with Colonialism: Decolonization and Indigenous Rights at the Supreme Court of Canada (2011)

Fiona Kelly
Transforming Law's Family: The Legal Recognition of Planned Lesbian Motherhood (2011)

Colleen Bell
The Freedom of Security: Governing Canada in the Age of Counter-Terrorism (2011)

Andrew S. Thompson
In Defence of Principles: NGOs and Human Rights in Canada (2010)

Aaron Doyle and Dawn Moore (eds.)
Critical Criminology in Canada: New Voices, New Directions (2010)

Joanna R. Quinn
The Politics of Acknowledgement: Truth Commissions in Uganda and Haiti (2010)

Patrick James
Constitutional Politics in Canada after the Charter: Liberalism, Communitarianism, and Systemism (2010)

Louis A. Knafla and Haijo Westra (eds.)
Aboriginal Title and Indigenous Peoples: Canada, Australia, and New Zealand (2010)

Janet Mosher and Joan Brockman (eds.)
Constructing Crime: Contemporary Processes of Criminalization (2010)

Stephen Clarkson and Stepan Wood
A Perilous Imbalance: The Globalization of Canadian Law and Governance (2009)

Amanda Glasbeek
Feminized Justice: The Toronto Women's Court, 1913-34 (2009)

Kim Brooks (ed.)
Justice Bertha Wilson: One Woman's Difference (2009)

Wayne V. McIntosh and Cynthia L. Cates
Multi-Party Litigation: The Strategic Context (2009)

Renisa Mawani
Colonial Proximities: Crossracial Encounters and Juridical Truths in British Columbia, 1871-1921 (2009)

James B. Kelly and Christopher P. Manfredi (eds.)
Contested Constitutionalism: Reflections on the Canadian Charter of Rights and Freedoms (2009)

Catherine Bell and Robert K. Paterson (eds.)
Protection of First Nations Cultural Heritage: Laws, Policy, and Reform (2008)

Hamar Foster, Benjamin L. Berger, and A.R. Buck (eds.)
The Grand Experiment: Law and Legal Culture in British Settler Societies (2008)

Richard J. Moon (ed.)
Law and Religious Pluralism in Canada (2008)

Catherine Bell and Val Napoleon (eds.)
First Nations Cultural Heritage and Law: Case Studies, Voices, and Perspectives (2008)

Douglas C. Harris
Landing Native Fisheries: Indian Reserves and Fishing Rights in British Columbia, 1849-1925 (2008)

Peggy J. Blair
Lament for a First Nation: The Williams Treaties of Southern Ontario (2008)

Lori G. Beaman
Defining Harm: Religious Freedom and the Limits of the Law (2007)

Stephen Tierney (ed.)
Multiculturalism and the Canadian Constitution (2007)

Julie Macfarlane
The New Lawyer: How Settlement Is Transforming the Practice of Law (2007)

Kimberley White
Negotiating Responsibility: Law, Murder, and States of Mind (2007)

Dawn Moore
Criminal Artefacts: Governing Drugs and Users (2007)

Hamar Foster, Heather Raven, and Jeremy Webber (eds.)
Let Right Be Done: Aboriginal Title, the Calder Case, and the Future of Indigenous Rights (2007)

Dorothy E. Chunn, Susan B. Boyd, and Hester Lessard (eds.)
Reaction and Resistance: Feminism, Law, and Social Change (2007)

Margot Young, Susan B. Boyd, Gwen Brodsky, and Shelagh Day (eds.)
Poverty: Rights, Social Citizenship, and Legal Activism (2007)

Rosanna L. Langer
Defining Rights and Wrongs: Bureaucracy, Human Rights, and Public Accountability (2007)

C.L. Ostberg and Matthew E. Wetstein
Attitudinal Decision Making in the Supreme Court of Canada (2007)

Chris Clarkson
Domestic Reforms: Political Visions and Family Regulation in British Columbia, 1862-1940 (2007)

Jean McKenzie Leiper
Bar Codes: Women in the Legal Profession (2006)

Gerald Baier
Courts and Federalism: Judicial Doctrine in the United States, Australia, and Canada (2006)

Avigail Eisenberg (ed.)
Diversity and Equality: The Changing Framework of Freedom in Canada (2006)

Randy K. Lippert
Sanctuary, Sovereignty, Sacrifice: Canadian Sanctuary Incidents, Power, and Law (2005)

James B. Kelly
Governing with the Charter: Legislative and Judicial Activism and Framers' Intent (2005)

Dianne Pothier and Richard Devlin (eds.)
Critical Disability Theory: Essays in Philosophy, Politics, Policy, and Law (2005)

Susan G. Drummond
Mapping Marriage Law in Spanish Gitano Communities (2005)

Louis A. Knafla and Jonathan Swainger (eds.)
Laws and Societies in the Canadian Prairie West, 1670-1940 (2005)

Ikechi Mgbeoji
Global Biopiracy: Patents, Plants, and Indigenous Knowledge (2005)

Florian Sauvageau, David Schneiderman, and David Taras,
with Ruth Klinkhammer and Pierre Trudel
The Last Word: Media Coverage of the Supreme Court of Canada (2005)

Gerald Kernerman
Multicultural Nationalism: Civilizing Difference, Constituting Community (2005)

Pamela A. Jordan
Defending Rights in Russia: Lawyers, the State, and Legal Reform in the Post-Soviet Era (2005)

Anna Pratt
Securing Borders: Detention and Deportation in Canada (2005)

Kirsten Johnson Kramar
Unwilling Mothers, Unwanted Babies: Infanticide in Canada (2005)

W.A. Bogart
Good Government? Good Citizens? Courts, Politics, and Markets in a Changing Canada (2005)

Catherine Dauvergne
Humanitarianism, Identity, and Nation: Migration Laws in Canada and Australia (2005)

Michael Lee Ross
First Nations Sacred Sites in Canada's Courts (2005)

Andrew Woolford
Between Justice and Certainty: Treaty Making in British Columbia (2005)

John McLaren, Andrew Buck, and Nancy Wright (eds.)
Despotic Dominion: Property Rights in British Settler Societies (2004)

Georges Campeau
From UI to EI: Waging War on the Welfare State (2004)

Alvin J. Esau
The Courts and the Colonies: The Litigation of Hutterite Church Disputes (2004)

Christopher N. Kendall
Gay Male Pornography: An Issue of Sex Discrimination (2004)

Roy B. Flemming
Tournament of Appeals: Granting Judicial Review in Canada (2004)

Constance Backhouse and Nancy L. Backhouse
The Heiress vs the Establishment: Mrs. Campbell's Campaign for Legal Justice (2004)

Christopher P. Manfredi
Feminist Activism in the Supreme Court: Legal Mobilization and the Women's Legal Education and Action Fund (2004)

Annalise Acorn
Compulsory Compassion: A Critique of Restorative Justice (2004)

Jonathan Swainger and Constance Backhouse (eds.)
People and Place: Historical Influences on Legal Culture (2003)

Jim Phillips and Rosemary Gartner
Murdering Holiness: The Trials of Franz Creffield and George Mitchell (2003)

David R. Boyd
Unnatural Law: Rethinking Canadian Environmental Law and Policy (2003)

Ikechi Mgbeoji
Collective Insecurity: The Liberian Crisis, Unilateralism, and Global Order (2003)

Rebecca Johnson
Taxing Choices: The Intersection of Class, Gender, Parenthood, and the Law (2002)

John McLaren, Robert Menzies, and Dorothy E. Chunn (eds.)
Regulating Lives: Historical Essays on the State, Society, the Individual, and the Law (2002)

Joan Brockman
Gender in the Legal Profession: Fitting or Breaking the Mould (2001)

Printed and bound in Canada by Friesens

Set in Segoe and Warnock by Artegraphica Design Co. Ltd.

Copy editor: Robert Lewis

Proofreader: Stephanie VanderMeulen

Indexer: Marnie Lamb